Early praise for *Software Estimation Without Guessing*

I hate estimating and I'm all too familiar with the anti-patterns. I was surprised by how much I liked this book. An easy read on why, when, how, and how not to estimate, with pragmatic advice both for the art of estimation itself and for handling the human behaviors that invariably surround it.

➤ **Liz Keogh**
Director, Lunivore Limited

When I first started reading this book, I knew it was providing a good framework for software estimation. I have recommended to my boss that we buy copies for all of our senior developers who are responsible for both creating project estimation and vetting estimations, since it provides a common language for discussing those estimations as well as helping improve our estimations.

➤ **Josef Finsel**
Senior Developer, Mt Mediabox

This book is about different aspects of the estimation process. While it won't teach you how to estimate more accurately, it does the more important stuff: explain how our estimates can be used effectively, and what to do when they aren't.

➤ **Gil Zilberfeld**
Agile Consultant

We all estimate at work. George's book offers helpful advice on when to use which kind of estimation, regardless of the kind of work and the size of the company. Read this book to apply these approaches in your context.

➤ **Johanna Rothman**
  Author and Consultant, Rothman Consulting Group, Inc.

This is not so much a how-to-do-estimates book, but a how-to-think-about-estimation book (though it does have how-to guidance as well).

The book focuses on why people need estimates, and how that affects how one might approach any particular estimate. Context, as always, matters. If you use estimates or are asked to give estimates, this book will be valuable to you.

➤ **Esther Derby**
  President, Esther Derby Associates, Inc.

Software Estimation Without Guessing

Effective Planning in an Imperfect World

George Dinwiddie

The Pragmatic Bookshelf

Raleigh, North Carolina

Our Pragmatic books, screencasts, and audio books can help you and your team create better software and have more fun. Visit us at *https://pragprog.com*.

The team that produced this book includes:

Publisher: Andy Hunt
VP of Operations: Janet Furlow
Executive Editor: Dave Rankin
Development Editor: Adaobi Obi Tulton
Copy Editor: Sean Dennis
Indexing: Potomac Indexing, LLC
Layout: Gilson Graphics

For sales, volume licensing, and support, please contact *support@pragprog.com*.

For international rights, please contact *rights@pragprog.com*.

ISBN-13: 978-1-68050-698-3
Book version: P1.0—December 2019

Contents

Acknowledgements ix

Introduction xi

1. **Starting Something New** 1

   When You're Asked to Estimate Something New   3

   Case: Developing a Fixed-Price Bid   10

   Case: Is This Worth Starting?   13

   Case: Can We Make This Work?   18

   Case: What Should We Budget?   19

   Case: Which of These Should We Choose?   20

   Case: A Mixture of Questions   22

   Stepping Back for a Broader View   25

   Now It's Your Turn   25

2. **Comparison-Based Estimation** 27

   Comparison to Past Experience   28

   Memory vs. Recorded Data   32

   Aspects to Compare   34

   Gestalt Estimation   41

   Decomposition   43

   Estimating the Unknown   43

   Stepping Back for a Broader View   46

   Now It's Your Turn   47

3. **Decomposition for Estimation** 49

   Which Way to Slice?   49

   Decomposing by Phase   50

   Decomposing by Implementation   51

   Decomposing by Functionality   52

   User Stories   53

Decomposition Decisions   56
A Large Number of Small Parts   57
A Small Number of Large Parts   58
Affinity Estimation   58
Ordering the Parts   60
Multi-Level Decomposition   62
Comparing Big Items with Small Ones   63
Decomposition Gotchas   64
Stepping Back for a Broader View   71
Now It's Your Turn   73

4. Checking Progress   75
Getting Things Done   76
Detecting Progress   77
What to Measure   78
Visualizing Progress   83
Showing Value for the Money   84
Efficiency and Effectiveness   87
Optimization   90
Are We Going Fast Enough?   93
Pushing Our Limits   96
Situational Awareness   97
Stepping Back for a Broader View   100
Now It's Your Turn   101

5. Model-Based Estimation   103
Modeling the Size   104
Modeling the Rate   106
Unavoidable Subjectivity   107
The Linear Model Approach   109
Advanced Linear Model Techniques   113
The Parametric Model Approach   119
The Stochastic Model Approach   124
Comparison-Model Hybrid   125
Stepping Back for a Broader View   130
Now It's Your Turn   132

6. Estimating Milestones   133
Deadlines   134
Early Release   136
Coordination with Others   139

Evaluating and Changing Plans   143
Stepping Back for a Broader View   146
Now It's Your Turn   147

7.   **When Estimates and Actuals Differ** **149**
Driving Up Costs   150
Salvaging the Situation   151
Learning from the Situation   153
Stepping Back for a Broader View   160
Now It's Your Turn   161

8.   **Planning for Incorrect Predictions** **163**
Seeking Out Information   164
Setting Traps for Information   167
Avoid Traps for the Unwary   173
Stepping Back for a Broader View   175
Now It's Your Turn   175

9.   **When People Clash** **177**
It Starts So Innocently   178
How It Goes Wrong   179
Understanding Human Behavior   183
Imagine a Better Situation   189
Retraining Ourselves   192
Tools for Better Understanding   196
Stepping Back for a Broader View   201
Now It's Your Turn   201
Conclusion   202

Bibliography **205**
Index **207**

Acknowledgements

I have been blessed with help and encouragement from so many people that there's no way I can mention them all here. If I don't mention your name, it's not an indication that I don't value your influence. It's a matter of time and space and my current attention focus.

First, I want to acknowledge the influence of Jerry (Gerald M.) Weinberg, who introduced me to the work of Virginia Satir. Foolishly, I did not read Satir in college, even though a couple of friends were raving about *Peoplemaking*. Had I done so, I might have learned earlier what I now know, and gone even further by now. I also thank Jerry for his book, *Weinberg on Writing: The Fieldstone Method*, the method I used to start this book. And for pushing me to go further whenever I started to settle into a new comfort zone. Jerry, I wish you were here so that I could show you my book.

I'm also grateful to Esther Derby for her support and encouragement over a great many years, and especially as I wrote this book. Esther has long been my greatest mentor, believing in me when I failed to believe in myself.

Thanks also to Dale Emery, the best question-asker I've ever met, for encouraging me to attend Amplifying Your Effectiveness, where I met Jerry Weinberg and Esther Derby. I also thank Dale for his patient feedback on the story elements. I used as much of that feedback as my writing skill could support.

I am grateful for many conversations, both online and in person, that have helped me formulate and refine my ideas. Some of these conversations were in particular reference to this book as I was writing it. Thanks to Heather Oppenheimer for a delightful conversation on various aspects affecting an estimate. I certainly would have missed some of these on my own. Thanks to David Schmaltz & John Maxwell for discussions on the nature of governance. Thanks to Sharon Marsh Roberts for sharing a long and inspiring tale of accommodating a change in the accounting laws. I ultimately didn't end up using that story in the book, but it inspired some of the stories I did use.

Thanks to Troy Magennis for a sanity check on model-based estimation. And also thanks, Troy, for your inspiring keynote at the Agile 2018 Conference. That keynote reassured me that I was on the right track. Thanks to Chet Hendrickson, Ron Jeffries, and Kent Beck for telling me their memories of the C3 project. Of course, if it wasn't for the mentions of that project getting in my way when I was researching design patterns at the Portland Pattern Repository, I might not have taken the path to my immersion in agile software development at all. But when I looked at Extreme Programming instead of trying to look around it, mostly it just made sense to me.

Thanks to the technical reviewers who took the time to read a draft of this book and send comments back to me and my editor. These include: Keith Braithwaite, Mark Chu-Carroll, John Cutler, Josef Finsel, Liz Keogh, Evan Leybourn, Dave Nicolette, Tim Ottinger, Johanna Rothman, Joshua Smith, James Thomas, and Gil Zilberfeld. Even the comments that annoyed me helped me to improve this book.

Thanks to Jeff Langr for enticing me to work with The Pragmatic Programmers. He made it deceptively easy to take that fateful step.

A great deal of thanks goes to my editor, Adaobi Obi Tulton. When I sent a complete manuscript (which is not the way Pragmatic suggests working) to Adaobi at the beginning of our collaboration, her response was that she liked my material, but we needed to rewrite the Table of Contents. As much as I was dismayed by the prospect of yet another restructuring and rewrite, I knew she was right. She has pushed me gently and firmly, and the book is much better for it. I hope that she is as proud of it as I am. I'm not ready to write another book, but if I ever am, I would work with Adaobi again in a heartbeat.

Thanks to Lucy (the cat) for helping me type. She was always willing to walk on the keyboard when I seemed to be stuck. Thanks to Elliot (the other cat) for helping me find the mouse pointer on the screen. Even with his poor eyesight he could spot it and try to pin it down with his paw.

And most importantly, thanks to my wife, Gail, not only for her support while writing this book, but for her love and partnership for more than half my life. She has led me on adventures I never would have considered. She has taught me to dream big, to focus on value rather than cost, and to try things without knowing how they'll work out. And during the writing of this book, she has endured my preoccupation with the computer and my shouts at Lucy when she steps on the power button to get my attention. Thank you, Love.

Grow old along with me. The best is yet to be.

Introduction

If you've been working professionally in software development for a year or more, I'm sure you've sometimes thought that estimation is a pain in the patootie. It's expensive, contentious, and difficult. Some people consider estimation to be an essential, if distasteful, aspect of software development. Others consider it irrelevant. And I'm sure there are some who estimate out of habit or tradition without giving it much existential consideration. Others argue against estimation to counter such habits.

On the other hand, estimates are all you can know about the future. Within limits, estimates can help you make decisions. You need to be cognizant of the limitations of estimates and the risks of believing they are data. Armed with those precautions, you can use them more freely and discover actual data when reality disagrees with them.

Numbers are not the goal. Successful outcomes are. Those footing the bill would rather have a successful outcome than an excuse to blame the estimator. In exploring better estimation, I'm not looking to protect the estimator or development organization from censure or litigation after a disappointment. Instead, we use estimation to help guide the project to success from the point of view of both those paying for development and those performing it. There's a lot of benefit to be gained—much more than people usually realize.

Benefit of Headlights

There is a reason to burn headlights when driving at night and to slow down when driving in fog. Headlights allow you to anticipate the need for changes in direction earlier and therefore achieve faster flow with no loss in caution. In the fog, you need to slow down precisely because you can't see as far. It's helpful to see the shape of the next bend in the road. It's helpful to know approximately how far it is to our next planned turn or stop. You can benefit from knowing where you might stop for a meal or a night's lodging.

The same is true in software development. You can go faster when you can see further than the work right in front of you. You can strategize ways to incorporate the bigger picture. You can avoid painting yourself into a corner, far from the door you want to go through.

And if you're meeting a hard deadline, you might have better options than developing User Stories in prioritized order until you run out of time. In the case where what you want to build won't fit into the time available, you might do better to add some polish on what you deliver, rather than maximizing functionality. This will give the user an impression of work that's been finished rather than merely stopped. It's the equivalent of turning down a side road to a comfortable hotel instead of spending the night in the backseat of a car on the shoulder of the road.

If a development team can benefit from seeing a few weeks ahead, you can imagine that the larger organization around that team would like to see even further. Some of this desire may be due to artificial but customary rhythms, such as annual budget cycles. Such things are likely hard to change in corporations and likely impossible for government organizations. Even if you can be successful in changing the rhythm, it will take time to do so. And that is time the organization would like you to use in developing systems for use or sale. Beyond that, there are rhythms based on a more substantial basis, such as the amount of time it takes to do related work, the changing of the seasons, or planetary ephemera. And when the CEO asks what's coming up, the CIO would like to have a satisfactory answer.

Beyond Story Points and Planning Poker

If you're unfamiliar with agile software development, the terms "Story Points" and "planning poker" may be completely mysterious to you. If you're new to agile, these terms may have specific meaning to you that aren't universally true. These concepts have a history, and are best understood in the context of that history.

Story Points

In the beginning, there was the Chrysler Comprehensive Compensation or C3 project, the birthplace of Extreme Programming. The short version of the story is that some very smart people tried some things until they got something that worked, and that included breaking up the work to be done into User Stories (c.f., User Stories, on page 53) that could be independently developed and tested. For planning purposes, these were estimated in "ideal days," and later, unitless Story Points.[1] The advantage of Story Points over estimating in absolute time is that it allowed you to calibrate your estimates with what actually happens. We'll take another look at this calibration in Calibrating to Unknown Context, on page 44.

Planning Poker

James Grenning invented Planning Poker[2,3], not to emulate Wide-Band Delphi estimation, but to get a stalled meeting moving again. While he continued to use and teach it, it was when Mike Cohn publicized the technique in *Agile Estimating and Planning [Coh05]* that the practice was widely adopted. Soon many people came to believe that Planning Poker was *THE* agile estimation technique, though James has gone on to use other methods.

Counting Stories

Back in 2008 or 2009, Bob Payne and I were noticing that teams we were coaching spent an awfully long time estimating their stories in Story Points. Even though they spent two or more hours every two weeks doing this, the estimates didn't seem to jibe with reality. Figuring that the primary reason for estimating every two weeks was choosing how much would fit into the two weeks, we did some analysis of the data and determined that a count of the stories had as much predictive power (or a little more) than did these laborious estimates. We presented a session[4] at the Agile 2012 Conference showing our conclusions. We were not, of course, the only ones to discover that counting stories, especially for the short run, was as good as estimating stories—and a lot easier.

Of course, nipping off a bite-sized chunk of work is only one aspect of looking ahead. Another common aspect is figuring out when some major functionality is going to be done. Chet Hendrickson tells me that they started with stories to fill 11 three-week iterations, or about 7-1/2 months. That's a lot of stories to pin down at the start of the project, yet the C3 project had an onsite customer who knew that much about what needed to be done.[5] I've witnessed a lot of customers who don't, whether or not they thought they did. That's made me very wary of starting with A Large Number of Small Parts, on page 57, as that also seems like a waste of effort for the value returned.

---

1. https://ronjeffries.com/articles/019-01ff/story-points/Index.html
2. https://wingman-sw.com/articles/planning-poker
3. https://wingman-sw.com/slides/Beyond-Planning-Poker-v1r1.key.pdf
4. http://idiacomputing.com/pub/Agile2012-What%27s%20the%20Point%20Of%20Story%20Points.pdf
5. http://www.coldewey.com/publikationen/conferences/oopsla2001/agileWorkshop/hendrickson.html

Definitions

In order to communicate more effectively, it will help to build a common understanding of some terms. I see many arguments that seem to revolve around what is, and what is not, an estimate. In the noun forms, a dictionary gives us the following definitions:

Estimate
> an approximate judgment or calculation, as of the value, amount, time, size, or weight of something.

Forecast
> a prediction, especially as to the weather; a conjecture as to something in the future.

Prediction
> something declared or told in advance.

Conjecture
> an opinion or theory without sufficient evidence for proof.

Projection
> calculation of some future thing, usually based on past results.

Guess
> an opinion that one reaches or to which one commits oneself on the basis of probability alone or in the absence of any evidence whatever.

These words are near synonyms, though some people assign specific differences to them in their own use. Estimate, conjecture, and guess are all very general, applying to the past, present, or future. Forecast, prediction, and projection specifically apply to the future. I might estimate how many jellybeans are in a jar, but I might forecast how many will be left tomorrow after a children's party. Some domains prefer a particular word; both weather and company profits are generally foretold as forecasts. Future state is often termed a projection when generated mathematically, and a prediction when it is not.

I'm fond of saying that the abbreviation of "estimate" is "guess." That often gets a chuckle, because the general feeling is that people are pretty bad at estimating and particularly bad at estimating software projects. It seems that grabbing a number out of thin air has as much chance of being helpful as anything.

Beyond that joke, estimates are distinct from guesses. At worst they are "educated guesses," based on slim knowledge or experience thought to be relevant. Sometimes the application of past experience is very "seat-of-the-pants," with insufficient consideration of the details. With a little more attention to what's similar and what's different between now and past experience, estimates can become truly useful.

In conversation, it appears that many people have a more restricted concept of an estimate. They often associate it with whatever type of estimate has been most prevalent in their experience. For software developers, the most prevalent form is usually "when will you be done?" Given that this "when question" is often asked before knowing *what* will be done, it's understandable that the word "estimate" has a bad connotation for many software developers.

Nothing about estimate or forecast states how either is formed, but many people closely associate estimates and forecasts with the technique they most frequently use, or see being used. A weather forecast may be based on the amount of pain felt in the knee, knowledge of last week's weather, or on a complex model of atmospheric humidity and pressure. A software delivery estimate may be based on knowledge of a similar project, on a detailed decomposition into tasks that are independently estimated, or on a model of project attributes.

Who This Book Is For

You may find this book useful no matter what your role in software development. In fact, you might apply these ideas outside of software development, though I haven't specifically addressed that. When writing this book, I've had three broad classes of people involved with software development in mind. They are as follows:

Software Team Members

These are the people who often get asked for estimates they don't care about. These are the people who often get blamed when results aren't the same as the estimates.

Upper Management

These are the people who have business decisions to make and who need forward-looking data to make them. These are the people who aren't close enough to the development work that's going on to directly know how well things are going.

Middle Management

These are the people caught in the middle of the other two groups and catch it from both sides. These are the people with a responsibility to meet the expectations of upper management and keep those expectations reasonable. These are the people with a responsibility to intervene when necessary to help the development effort go well.

All of these people might gain an understanding of some new ways to estimate. They can learn to avoid some of the common pitfalls of relying on estimates with insufficient awareness of their limitations. They can gain some perspective of what needs require what sort of estimates.

All of them might benefit from stepping back to a larger view of the topic, and especially by considering the view from a variety of points of view.

Goal of This Book

The goal of this book is not to make you an expert at estimation. Estimation is a tool rather than a goal in itself. Maintain focus on the real goals: the outputs, the outcomes, and the impact of the system you're building. Estimation is a tool for achieving these goals more reliably in an uncertain, error-prone world. Estimation lets you see into the future and make decisions about the path you're on, before you reach the endpoint. We'll also take note of some other ways that estimation can help us, as an organization working together, achieve common goals and fulfill the responsibilities of our various roles.

Steve McConnell in *Software Estimation: Demystifying the Black Art [McC06]* and Capers Jones in *Estimating Software Costs [Jon07]* approach estimating as getting an answer most close to the eventual actuals. Looking at it another way, they try to estimate a duration and cost that project managers can meet. To do that, they recommend such things as collecting data from past projects and making sure the work being estimated is clearly defined. These preliminaries may be beyond your ability in your current context.

This work is focused on helping you make the most of what you have available. It's about being able to make prudent choices for a successful project rather than winning a prize for coming closest to guessing the number of jellybeans in the jar. It defines a successful project by the desirable outcomes achieved rather than by conformance to prior plans. The view of this book is biased toward iterative projects that are started with the knowledge that information is incomplete and are steered toward desired outcomes as they are developed. Estimates are a valuable tool for learning more as you proceed.

To be honest, plan-driven projects, which "plan the work and then work the plan," tend to start with known incomplete information and are steered toward desired outcomes as they are developed. The difference is that on plan-driven projects, the iterative work is generally hidden from official view. During implementation, design corrections are made. During testing, implementation corrections are made. Throughout, new or clarified requirements affect all stages of work. The plan-driven bookkeeping hides these iterative cycles performed in the "wrong phase" of the life cycle, or it calls them errors. I call them reality.

Approximations

People often expect estimates to give them precise and accurate values that match the future, as if they are a process of calculation rather than estimation. This leads to disappointment in the results, and often induces people to make bad decisions along the way. There is a simpler and healthier path you can take.

Before I got into software development, I worked in electronic repair, and then electronic design. The book that taught me how junction transistors worked was *Transistor Circuit Approximations [Mal68]*. What made this book work so well for me is that it starts with the concepts of an "ideal transistor" (or "ideal diode") for a first approximation of circuit analysis. Sometimes second-order effects are included for a "second approximation." These approximations are good enough to understand how a circuit works. In reality, there is much variation from one transistor to another, so transistor circuits are designed to make the circuit performance almost independent of the transistor characteristics. In Malvino's words, "exact formulas for transistor circuit analysis are of limited value to most of us because the exact characteristics of a transistor are seldom known."

This is an excellent way to think about estimation, too. Ignore the second-order effects until you need them. Most of the time, the first approximation will do most of what you need. This book has no magic for giving you precise and accurate predictions of the future under unknown conditions. Instead, it gives you methods to get "close enough" to understand what's going on. And it gives you tools to calibrate those methods for your own specific context. Along the way, I suggest some ways of working to make your outcomes less sensitive to the vagaries of inaccurate estimates—ways of achieving success despite the uncertainty of the path to get there.

What's in This Book

Ordering the content of this book was difficult for me, and I rearranged it numerous times. Writing it for a broad audience who is facing radically different situations prevented me from imagining a simple story that starts at the beginning and travels an obvious path to its conclusion. In the end, I think I have found a story that most will be able to follow, though there are many cross-references to entice you to read things out of order.

We start with *why* and then proceed with *how*. We repeat this pattern twice, once for anticipating work and once for the situations in the middle of the work. This is followed by how to handle the disappointment of an inaccurate estimate and how to make that not a disappointment, but an opportunity. We end with a look at the people issues surrounding estimation. If you're looking for something in particular, the following chapter descriptions might help you jump right to it.

Starting Something New

We start before the beginning, when we're considering starting something. What questions do we need to consider before we start? There are many different circumstances, and we explore a number of different needs. Likely your need is covered in this chapter, or some of your needs are, though you may have others I've not described.

Comparison-Based Estimation

The basic approach to estimation is comparing something unknown to something known. This is your most likely option when you're starting something new. There are lots of ins and out and wrinkles to this topic, though. This chapter looks at a lot of them.

Decomposition for Estimation

Often it's easier to estimate something if we break it down into smaller pieces. How do you break it down? This chapter explores a number of different ways by several criteria. It offers opinions for the general case, but you must decide what fits your specific case.

Checking Progress

Once we've begun, we start wondering how we're doing. This might be a concern about the finishing date. Or it might be a more general concern if we're on the right track. Sometimes there are concerns about efficiency or speed. This chapter explores ways of checking progress and when it makes sense to do so.

Model-Based Estimation

Direct comparison is the root of estimation, but if we're going to be doing it repeatedly, it's easier if we create a mathematical model of our progress. This lets us recalculate whenever we want, which is important when we're checking our progress. This chapter describes a number of different ways to construct such a model.

Estimating Milestones

The end of the project is not the only date that matters. You'll have interim targets you want to meet, also. There are reasons that these dates might be important for others. This chapter takes a look at these milestones and reasons.

When Estimates and Actuals Differ

Inevitably, what actually happens will differ from your estimate to some degree—sometimes to a large degree. What should you do when that happens? This chapter will give you advice and guidance.

Planning for Incorrect Predictions

Since we're pretty sure that some of our predictions will be incorrect, let's plan for that. Let's figure out how to make use of those incorrect predictions to help us reach our final success. In fact, as this chapter suggests, you might want to create extra predictions just to take advantage of the ones that are inaccurate.

When People Clash

When most people talk about estimation, they talk more about the conflicts between people than about the estimation process itself. This chapter looks at how these conflicts get out of hand, and what you can do to make things better.

Conventions Used

Some of the concepts and lessons around estimation can be noticed in our everyday lives. Where possible, I'll use mundane stories that I hope you will identify with easily. Some of these stories are fictionalized, but they're all based on personal experience.

Other stories are more specific to the business of software development. Since the needs being met via estimates vary greatly with the context of those needs, I'll be using several fictitious companies to represent some of these contexts. These ersatz companies vary in size, focus, and organizational structure. They give us some structure for viewing estimation in the light of concrete details. These examples illustrate the more general principles that govern the needs and practices of estimation. While there are many more possibilities than these three organizations, these examples should help you understand how to apply the principles to your situation.

Empire Enterprises

Empire Enterprises is a large, diversified company with a centralized Information Technology department. The software they create is predominately for internal use. Some of it handles all the corporation's accounting processes. Other systems support the work of the varied business lines which are the focus of other company divisions. It's a continual juggling act to be responsive to the different divisions while keeping a focus on what provides the most benefit to the company as a whole.

Riffle & Sort

Riffle & Sort is a medium-sized business that does data processing for other companies. They started out in the 1980s providing payroll services for small businesses. As the business grew to be successful, they found that calculating payroll for their clients was getting to be more work than they could handle. Fortunately, the president's son-in-law had become interested in personal computers and took on the task to automate some parts of the work. That grew over time, and now the company offers custom software solutions to address other clerical paperwork needs.

TinyToyCo

TinyToyCo has translated their online game, in which the player tries to keep a virtual cat happy with minimal cat treats and scratched hands, into a phone app where the cat clamors for attention at random times while you're doing something else. Now they want to create a physical version: a robotic lap-seeking Fluphy Kitty™ toy.

Now It's Your Turn

Each chapter ends with a challenge to put what you've learned in that chapter into practice. Try the questions as a thought experiment. If they don't quite fit your situation (maybe you're not currently on a project), then modify them to work for you.

There is no answer key in the back of the book. These exercises are for you to stretch yourself. Share them with your colleagues and compare your answers. Return to them sometime in the future and see if you might answer them differently. Return to them and try them out in a different context. Ultimately, the questions are more durable than the answers.

CHAPTER 1

Starting Something New

How do projects get started? Certainly, it varies with the circumstances. Among the most obvious circumstances are the size and life stage of the company. In small companies, a fun idea tossed around in the coffee room can trigger a new project that might triple the size of the company. In large ones, ideas typically need to be described from a financial point of view and passed up the hierarchy for approval.

The Birth of TinyToyCo

It all started when Pat asked Chris why cats didn't have their own computers.

"Why would they need them? My cats play with mine all the time," Chris responded. "Do you remember that program that made a cat run around your desktop chasing your mouse pointer? My real cats do that."

"What would it take to implement that on a website?"

"I guess there's only one way to find out."

The two founders of TinyToyCo worked nights and weekends on their online game as a side project from their regular jobs. At first, it was just a proof of concept to see if they could do it. They could, it turns out. Then they told some friends about it. The friends started asking for features, and Chris and Pat were happy to oblige. Their focus was all on playability of the game, and they were pleased by the acceptance of users. Word got around. More and more people started playing it. Their success made their hosting bills go up. What to do? They added some in-game advertising as a revenue source to pay the bills. The usage dropped a little, but more and more users were still coming to the site. They were surprised when the stream of advertising revenue amounted to a meaningful amount of money.

"What if we created a version for the phone? I bet we'd do even better."

And that's how it started. First as a challenge and then paying attention to what users liked and used.

Notice that no estimates were involved in starting TinyToyCo. Chris and Pat had the time and the skills to do the work, and they had no particular timeline or need to meet. They just worked until they had something, and then tuned it based on customer feedback. They didn't even have a company yet. It was just two programmers with a money-making hobby. It doesn't get much simpler than this.

Now let's look at another end of the scale. What happens in a large company to start an internal project?

Empire Enterprises: The Birth of a Project

Ellis was a purchasing agent for the Motors and Headphones Division of Empire Enterprises. This division designed and manufactured—you guessed it—motors and headphones for private-label customers. One thing that these products had in common is that they often required rare-earth magnets. Different designs, however, used different rare-earth alloys. The end result was that there were hundreds of variations that might be needed and relatively few substitutions that were allowable. It was a nightmare to research the pricing and availability of these magnets in time for a production run.

"If only there was a better way," Ellis muttered, imagining a central magnet clearinghouse that could support trading and procurement of these niche components. "Why can't a computer query the current prices and stocks of all these magnet manufacturers?"

Frankie, the Director of Purchasing, walked in. "Why are we paying so much for these magnets we ordered last month? It's twice what we paid last year for the same thing, and 50% more than I see on the suppliers website today."

"The prices fluctuate quite a bit with supply and demand. I have no way of tracking price and availability over time, so I just look for the best price I can find when the need arises. This particular magnet was in short supply when the requisition came in." Ellis went on to describe the dream system they had in mind.

Frankie listened to the idea, and went to talk with the President of Motors and Headphones. They discussed the value of such a system. Starting with the particular magnet that had attracted attention, they did some back-of-the-envelope estimates of the possible frequency and amount of savings. Such a system would give them a price advantage over competitors. And, once they had it in place, they could use the system to identify historically good opportunities and act as a broker for others. They estimated the potential value of that business.

The President took a proposal to the quarterly planning meeting. There, the CEO agreed it was worth investigating, and the proposal was forwarded to the IT Division. The PMO directed a Vice President to research the costs to build such a system. The VP, in turn, delegated to a Project Manager who delegated to Casey, a Project Technical Lead, for a Rough Order of Magnitude (ROM) estimate of the costs.

In the Empire Enterprises project proposal, there were two estimates prepared. One was of value and the other of cost. These two estimates were done by different people, without direct communication between them. This isolation between value & cost estimation carries the risk that the two estimates will depend on different assumptions. What if the details that make the work particularly valuable are not included in the cost estimate?

There are quite a lot of differences between these two stories, and there are many "getting started" stories we've not mentioned. Yours will be different. I expect they're all unique in some way.

Projects vs. Products

You may notice that the book frequently uses the word "project" for the work at hand. Some people chafe at this word and say that the focus should be on products, not projects.

Let's deconstruct this a bit. Why are projects sometimes considered obsolete or harmful?

One reason is that projects have become associated with endpoints defined by a calendar date. The PMI says a project has a defined beginning and end. I think it's a mistake to assume that the defined end is specified by a date, however. It could be specified by meeting the objective of the project. A project can also be terminated early if it seems doubtful that it can achieve its objectives within an acceptable cost. While this may be considered a failed project, the outcome could be beneficial for the business.

Products are often preferred over projects to reinforce long-term thinking and recognition of durable value. A product has no planned endpoint. We'd be happy to enhance and sell it forever.

In its lifetime, a product is produced and enhanced as a series of projects. Each step along the way has a cohesive intent that clarifies the focus of the moment. Fielding a viable product that people will buy is a project. Enhancing that product to generate greater revenue is a project. If you can state your next product goal in a sentence, then trying to achieve that goal is a project.

This book is not trying to discourage you from thinking in terms of products. Instead, it's trying to help you with each incremental project that contributes to that product.

When You're Asked to Estimate Something New

At Empire Enterprises, estimates were an integral part of the business process to approve new projects. At TinyToyCo, no estimates were needed, and they likely wouldn't have changed the decision if they'd been made. This shows that it's not a given that estimates are always needed. As we saw in Benefit of Headlights, on page xi, though, some level of estimation is usually helpful to most organizations.

Imagine you're the Project Technical Lead at Empire Enterprises who was asked to estimate the rare-earth magnet procurement project. Would you feel nervous? If you would, it's not because of the context at Empire Enterprises, which is a fictional company. It's because you've seen bad behavior in real-life situations during your career.

At first glance, it seems you have two choices. The first is to give a length of time. The immediate fear is that this estimate, given as a rough indication of the effort required, will be misused to create a schedule. Somebody is going to hear this number and take it as your commitment. Or, if they'd like it to be shorter, they may take it as the beginning of a negotiation, and try to talk you into something shorter.

The opposite choice, not giving a length of time, might be worse. It will make you look bad, subject to being labeled as incompetent or "not a team player." Either way, the people asking for the estimate already have a tacit estimate in mind, and they're just as likely to treat their unstated estimate as a commitment as opposed to whatever you give them.

There are never just two choices, though. (See Rule of Three, on page 181 for more details on this.) Let's dig into one possibility.

Uncovering What You Need to Know

You're likely to need more information about what the proposal has in mind. Is this a Cadillac project or a Chevy project? The details can come later, but you'll need a feel for what's intended, even for a rough estimate. For that, you'll need to talk with the originator of the idea. You'll probably also want to talk with everyone between the originator and you, because each of them formed a mental image of what the project is about. It's unlikely to be sufficient if you meet the expectations of Ellis the purchasing agent, but not the tacit expectations of the President of Motors and Headphones. Expect to backtrack along the same path as the request.

You will also want to know the *why* behind the request. Who needs this estimate and exactly why do they need it? This also requires backtracking through the chain that resulted in the request. Bear in mind that you may receive different reasons along that chain. The project manager needs it to satisfy the VP's request. The VP needs it to inform the PMO. The PMO needs it to determine whether or not to the project is a good candidate for implementation based on Return on Investment. (See Return on Investment, on page 13.)

Watch Out for Asking Why

You need to know the "why," but don't ask them why.

Can you imagine what response you'll get if you ask your VP "why do you want this estimate?"

"Because I'm the VP and I need it!"

Why questions tend to trigger defensiveness, as they're easily misunderstood as questioning the actions of another. Your question may be taken as aggression or disdain. Instead, rephrase your *why* questions as *what* questions. That will generally get the type of more specific answer that you want, and is much more likely to result in the data you need.

- What decision depends on this estimate?
- If you have this information, what will that do for you?
- If we don't meet this target date, what will happen?
- If necessary to meet this target date, what can we defer to later?

I think you'll find questions like these to be safer. With "what," you can frame the question to give you the responses that you seek. "Why" is so open-ended it's often interpreted differently than intended.

We'll look more deeply at the human elements in Chapter 9, When People Clash, on page 177.

What Question Are We Answering?

We compound the problems of estimation when we don't explicitly know what we need. Some jump to estimation because of an implicit understanding that managing projects requires estimates. Perhaps that's generally true, but why does this particular project need this particular estimate? Neither projects nor estimates are all the same.

The most critical estimates are those on which a decision depends. If you're not going to change what you're doing or how you work based on this estimate, then why are you creating it? Why does the answer matter? Deciding to start, continue, or cancel a project are examples of this sort of decision.

The next level of importance in estimates are those where you won't make a decision now, but might in the future. As reality unfolds, if it varies from the estimate in important ways, you will make a decision then. Do you cancel this project that's not living up to your expectations? Do you reestimate with your newfound knowledge? Do you examine which assumptions behind your estimate were wrong?

The lowest level of importance in estimates is reassuring yourself that things are OK. These are the ones that are most suspect, also, as you'd like for things to be OK. And when estimates show that things are not OK, and you're not basing a decision on this assessment, then bad behavior toward other people is likely to happen. That's when the blaming usually starts.

A Single Estimate is Not Appropriate for All Needs

The same estimate is not going to be appropriate for all three of these cases. In fact, the same estimate is not going to be appropriate for all cases of the specific question "Is this project worth starting?" Please remember that we're producing estimates, not facts. If we reduce all our information and assumptions down to a single number, it's easy to forget the uncertainty behind that number. A number looks bold and exact. Trustworthy. Immutable. In the case of estimates, a number is none of those. It's still just an estimate.

We'll look at the different cases of "Is this project worth starting?" in a moment. But first, let's consider the way that estimates differ from each other.

Accuracy and Precision

If you don't understand what question you're answering, you won't understand how much accuracy or precision you need.

Accuracy is the "correctness" of the estimate, whether it matches the actuals we achieve. Precision is the extent to which the estimate varies from actuals and can still be considered accurate.

If I say something will take "about a year" and it's completed in 390 calendar days, is that accurate? It depends on the precision that we assume. I would argue that this is an accurate estimate. It's within both "1 year +/- 1 month" and "1 year +/- 10%." If you interpreted my estimate as a commitment of no more than a year, then you would argue that it was an inaccurate estimate, as you assumed a precision of "1 year or less." I've encountered organizations that expected their project managers to estimate within 3% accuracy. That

---

means that this one-year project would be judged to a precision of "1 year +/- 11 days." This seems unreasonably tight to me.

Assumed precision is affected by how the estimate is expressed. The estimate "365 calendar days" suggests much greater precision than does "1 year." I'm generally wary of any estimate with more than two significant digits in the value.

What constitutes a reasonable amount of precision varies according to the span being estimated. If I say something will be done today, then specifying "around lunchtime" or "by close of business" provides useful precision. That level of precision is just noise when estimating that something will be done in a year or so. There, a precision to the month might be more appropriate. By specifying with too much precision, you may make an estimate unnecessarily inaccurate.

Assume that a certain amount of inaccuracy is inevitable, and even more so when trying to also be precise. Remember that you are creating estimates, not measurements.

Desired Direction of Error

Knowing what question you're answering also helps you understand in which direction would you prefer the error. In some cases, you would like the errors to be random, so they cancel out over time. In other cases, you'd like them to pile up in one direction, so you have a good feeling for the minimum or maximum value of what you're estimating. The way you go about estimating may vary considerably depending on this preference. And if you estimate assuming one preference, but the estimate is interpreted with another, then you're not going to be happy.

In cases where life is on the line, either human or that of the company, you generally want to create estimates that keep you outside of the danger zone—plus a little safety margin for error. You don't mind too much when you're further from danger than need be, as long as you're not stepping into another danger on the other side.

When estimating for a contract bid, you're constrained on both sides. You need to estimate your expenses such that, if you are awarded the contract, you can successfully complete the project at a profit. You want to minimize your error in the other direction, though, to maximize your chances at being awarded the contract. What happens if you've overlooked some aspect and underestimate? You lose money and perhaps jeopardize the company.

Or, you find some reason to alter your bid. In the world of large-project contracting, not knowing something is often labeled as lack of due diligence. But inaccurate or ambiguous requirements specifications are common. These can be used to negotiate for a higher fee to cover errors in estimation and bidding. This is common enough that there's a widely used saying describing this practice at its shadiest, "Underbid and make it up in change orders."

Necessary Confidence Level

Estimates with a strong need for the error to be in one direction are often demanding a very high confidence level in the other direction. In some circumstances, the assumptions of the estimate can be documented, and we may be extremely confident as long as those stated assumptions are valid. Other times, the assumptions are tacit and unstated. If those assumptions prove to be false, then the parties may be able to renegotiate the contract. You're probably familiar with scenarios like this with your car repair garage. We'll take a look at an example of this in Misdiagnosis, on page 12.

Other times, the deadline is nonnegotiable. In such cases, you either meet the deadline or you pay the penalty.

> **Meeting SEC Requirements**
>
> At a client, years back, I worked on a web application that delivered financial documents to customers and prospective customers. For some documents, your identity had to be confirmed as an investor of those securities. For others, you could self-certify that you were a prospective investor. There were a few other cases in between these two situations, also, as well as requirements that people couldn't even see the existence of some documents if they didn't have the right permissions.
>
> Then we got word that, since some of the documents were a matter of public record (e.g., 10-K filings), if we were going to continue delivering those documents, we had to serve them to people who were not logged in at all. That is, we had to serve them to anonymous visitors. And we had to do that by January 1 or face daily fines from the U.S. Securities and Exchange Commission.
>
> The problem was that the application required a login before doing anything else. It was built around knowing the identity of the user. And here we had less than two months to make it work, in some cases, without knowing the identity of the user. The project manager urged me to make quick patches where needed, because of the short timeframe.
>
> This worried me. At the very least, that would make the code harder to understand and harder to read. Since the user's identity was globally accessible in the session, it was already hard to know every place it was used. Understanding how far the change had progressed, and therefore how much longer it would take, depended on knowing how much had to change. I didn't know how to judge that given this codebase I didn't know, where such access was written in lots of different ways. I needed more confidence.

Refactoring the code to make the change in a safer manner seemed risky to the project manager. She needed some reassurance that I could complete it in time. At first, my estimate was quite vague. The first week of work, however, clarified what needed to be done and gave some early data on how quickly it was progressing.

In the end, I was able to make the change safely, in plenty of time, by modifying the code so the queries that needed the ID would stand out. This created some breaking changes as I propagated the changes through the layers of code, but those breakages were important for telling me how much had to change. Knowing that, I was able to estimate the work and track the progress of the needed changes toward the goal.

As a bonus, the structure of the code improved in terms of maintainability. I don't know if refactoring the code to make linkages more obvious and reduce duplication was a faster route or not. What I do know is that it was a route that I more easily estimated and tracked. The confidence level was more important than the speed, as long as the deadline could be met.

Slightly lower in the confidence level spectrum is what is often referred to as "a 90% level" estimate. I don't know how we would measure this 90% figure on something as variable as software development. In our field the confidence level is, itself, an estimate. If we were talking about something repeatable, then a 90% confidence level would indicate that 90% of the time the actual would come in within the estimation. Since we don't get to repeat the same software development project in the same circumstances to measure that, we'll just treat that as a colloquial expression meaning "pretty sure." In a high-trust environment, that works pretty well.

Such high confidence estimates aren't always called for, however. For example, when estimating how much work will fit into an iteration, estimating at the 50% confidence level is more appropriate. This means that half the time we overestimate and half the time we underestimate. We can make that work for us over the long haul, especially if we limit the amount of our work in progress. The errors cancel out and don't bother us. If we were to make a high confidence estimate for this, then we would be underestimating most of the time. That would result in either having to replan on a regular basis to pull more work, or allowing the work to expand to fill the time, slowing development.

At the far end of the confidence level scale is the minimum possible estimate. Here we estimate everything at the smallest, shortest value we can imagine. This gives us a rock-bottom estimate as a sanity check. There's no way we can accomplish what we want any faster, and we should not expect anything close to that performance. Our confidence in meeting that estimate is virtually zero, but it's useful information. If that's not fast enough, now is a good time to quit.

Let's take a closer look at some of the many needs to estimate at the start of a project. This review will emphasize that not all estimates are the same. It may also help you empathize with those who need estimates and understand those needs a bit better. We'll look at the following cases:

- Developing a Fixed-Price Bid
- Is This Worth Starting?
- Can We Make This Work?
- What Should We Budget?
- Which of These Should We Choose?

Plus, a situation that's less distinct.

Case: Developing a Fixed-Price Bid

The poster child for estimation is the development of a bid in response to a request for proposals (RFP), so let's look at this situation first. A potential customer waves a requirements document and says, "I want to buy one of these; what will you charge me for it?" A bunch of other people go off between a rock and a hard place to figure out an answer to this question. Each wants to charge as much as the customer is willing to pay, but just low enough that the customer chooses their proposal instead of a competitor's. Most importantly, they don't want to bid so low that they can't make a profit. That's the estimation part of this game in a nutshell, though there's certainly more to this game than estimation.

Big Contract Bids

We're most familiar with this game in the government-contracting space. It's an attempt to keep costs low while maintaining some impartiality in the process. The intentions are good but the results are mixed.

From the point of view of the bidding contractor, it's a big expensive undertaking to respond to such an RFP. This fact, of course, tends to limit the competition to only corporations who have made a business of responding to such RFPs. It's a hard business to break into. The resulting estimate is expected to be both accurate and precise, at a high confidence level. The time and cost for the proposed work is expected to be of the form "no more than" the estimated amount, while still maintaining precision.

To create such an estimate, you need a lot of expertise in the type of system being developed and good data on what it took in the past. If you need this, you probably have a whole department experienced in developing such estimates. Learn from them. *Software Estimation: Demystifying the Black Art*

[McC06] by Steve McConnell and *Estimating Software Costs [Jon07]* by Capers Jones describe such procedures in detail.

The process recommended in these books is to have a large dataset available for comparison to the requirements specified in the RFP. If you don't have that data, start collecting it. And there are programs for modeling the costs based on recorded data from other companies in other situations. We'll later look in more detail at estimating by comparison (see Chapter 2, Comparison-Based Estimation, on page 27) and using mathematical models (see Chapter 5, Model-Based Estimation, on page 103). I suspect that there are other factors in addition to excellent estimation that are required to pull off a successful project under these condition.

Capers Jones, in particular, has a strong preference for automated model-based estimation performed by estimation tools such as the one he sells. We'll take a look at some of the parameters of his model in Chapter 5, Model-Based Estimation, on page 103. Keep in mind that Jones is very concerned with large-scale government contracting and the possibilities of lawsuits arising out of contract disputes. His estimation model is calibrated for such situations. He intends to use estimates as protection in these situations, and therefore takes a conservative "kitchen sink" approach. If you can think of a potential cost, you better put it in the estimate. Capers Jones' estimates include such things as administrative and management personnel and travel costs, which are not specifically called out in this book.

Note that these large-scale contracting situations involve a lot of handoffs and checkpoints between the two parties. As Troy Magennis points out, delays during development will quickly swamp the work itself in terms of time consumed. Therefore, experience with the client and understanding the likely delay durations may be more valuable than understanding the time required for the development work. This experience comes from working on similar large-scale contracts. If you're planning to start your own large contracting corporation, I advise you to work for a successful one first, and take good notes on the experience.

Smaller Bids

For smaller bids, the power dynamic is often reversed from that of large bids. Usually the development company is offering their expertise at building a type of product for clients who want a customized version of that product. The development organization knows a lot more about what's involved than does the customer.

What the development organization may still lack is knowledge about delays the customer may cause. The customer might be slow in collaborating, leaving the development organization waiting for information or decisions. Or the customer may have unusual circumstances that aren't obvious. The customer might also be wanting things that are outside of the ordinary range of difficulty.

Misdiagnosis

"What's that ticking sound coming from the engine of the car? Must be a loose valve. I'll take the car to the mechanic for a valve adjustment."

At the garage, they look up the flat-rate time estimate for a valve adjustment. It's easier to estimate when we've measured the actual time from lots of competent people doing very similar work. They multiply that time estimate by their labor rates, add in some extra for gaskets, shop supplies, and such, and give me a cost estimate.

"It should be ready by 5:00."

I go on my way, knowing I can pick up my car in the evening and how much it's going to cost me. All is right with the world.

But in the late morning, I get a call from the mechanic. "Your car doesn't need a simple adjustment. The pushrod is bent. The reason it got bent is that the threads holding the rocker arm assembly are stripped out of the cylinder head. We're going to need to keep your car another day, and the cost will be about triple the original estimate."

Note that the strength of the promise provided by the quote estimate is under the control of the development company rather than the customer. It's prudent to make some provisions explicit.

- State what is considered usual and ordinary.

- State that delays caused by the customer are not in the estimate and will incur additional time and perhaps additional cost.

- Define allowances for things that may have a wide variability, such as aesthetic design. Specify the amount of work allotted for these things, and state that overages will be additional. There's an example of this in Estimating an Online Storefront, on page 120.

You may not need to be so explicit with some customers, but you won't know which ones until too late if the provisions are not in the contract or quote. For good customer relations, you should try to pin down the largest or scariest uncertainties as early as possible. And as soon as you discover something unforeseen, let the customer know.

Case: Is This Worth Starting?

There are many ways that projects get started, and most of them have some explicit step where a decision is made on some quantifiable criteria. Sure, there are times where the decision is made implicitly, based on some hunch or on the relative power of the person who wants the project. Usually organizations at least want to justify such decisions with some more defensible rationale. And it's in those explicit decision steps where estimates play a part.

Let's look at some of the criteria for these decisions.

Return on Investment

A fundamental question for investment is "Will this provide more value than it costs?" If so, it's quickly followed by "How much more?" and we weigh the benefits and costs. Not all benefits are measured in money. We may need to weigh some intangibles. What is the value of happiness or health? Some benefits, such as brand goodwill, are hard to quantify in dollars. We often think in terms of products, where the value is mostly equated to the revenue it brings in. For IT systems, we might judge the value by the labor saved or the increased volume of work we can handle. In some cases, the value is in new capabilities that the organization didn't have before. These are generally estimated based on assumptions we make about what will change when we have this new system. Sometimes market research or tests with prototypes inform these estimates.

In addition to estimating the return from having the system, we estimate the cost of acquiring it. How many people will have to work for how long in order to build it? How much will that cost us? What equipment will we need to develop it and to run it in production?

Return on Investment at Empire Enterprises

Casey looked at the proposal for a magnet clearinghouse. "How am I to estimate this? It's way too vague." Fortunately, the proposal included the source of the idea, so Casey set up a meeting with Frankie and Ellis to go over the details.

Frankie and Ellis were happy to describe their vision to Casey. They went on and on about all the features they envisioned while Casey took notes. Then Casey went off and estimated the work to produce such a system.

Casey gave the estimate to the Project Manager, who forwarded it to the VP, who reported it to the IT PMO, who gave the report to the CEO. At a regular C-level planning meeting, the senior leadership compared this cost estimate with the benefit estimates. The CFO noted that, if the estimates were accurate, it would take at least 8 years to recover the cost with internal savings. On the other hand, with the projected revenue of offering an external service, it would only take about a year to reach break-even.

"Not so fast," the Product Director interjected. "How can we be sure that this business will be a success? How do you propose to test the interest of potential customers, many of whom are competitors?"

The CEO looked thoughtful. "What are the assumptions about how quickly this business will ramp up when it's launched? And what's the synergy with our existing business lines?" Ultimately, they decided that it wasn't a good strategic decision for Empire Enterprises to enter the magnetics brokerage business.

When Frankie brought the news, Ellis was crushed. It seemed like such a good plan. Frankie thought a minute. "Let's go back and talk to Casey. We got carried away describing the Cadillac of systems. Perhaps we can find a cheaper one that will help you do your job."

And so they did. This smaller system didn't have any of the bells and whistles needed for a commercial offering, but it would still make Ellis' job easier. This time, the analysis showed the internal-only system would pay for its development in one to three years, depending on the volatility of market conditions. The project was given the green light.

In this instance, we see the flip side of separating the estimation of value and the estimation of cost from what we worried about in Empire Enterprises: The Birth of a Project, on page 2. The cost estimate included a lot of extra work that wasn't aligned with the value that made strategic sense for the company. That extra cost torpedoed the project. It was only by reestimating with reduced scope that the project made sense.

Capacity

Before you start something new, you may need to consider if you have the capacity to undertake the endeavor and make everyone reasonably happy. Even when you're not facing a firm deadline, you can't take on an unlimited amount of work. I would expect that your answer might generally be one of "no problem," "no way," or "it's hard to tell." The first two answers give clear signals. The third will require more precise analysis, and takes on more risk if it's wrong.

Riffle & Sort Get an Inquiry from a New Customer
"Let me run some numbers and I'll get right back to you."

Kai hung up the phone and went down the hall to talk with Jesse.

"Jesse, I just got a call from a potential customer. They want what sounds like a fairly simple online presence, but they want it by the end of March. Given that it's mid-October and holiday season is approaching, I thought I'd better check with you about our capacity to take on the job."

"We've got one development team that's currently working on maintenance and improvement items, but the rest of the teams are dedicated to significant projects. The team that has some development bandwidth is intentionally being held in reserve for high-priority work that might come up during tax season, from January 1 to April 15. It's crucial for us to be able to respond immediately to any legal discrepancies or operational problems that show up during that time."

"I guess that effectively gives us about a month to a month and a half of team time before the end of the year. That's not enough to build the site they want."

"Historically, the tax season on-call development team has at least 50% unused capacity during the season."

"That would be enough capacity, I'm pretty sure."

"The worst case I've ever seen was the year they were 80-85% busy with emergency work. I hope we never have that crisis again!"

"Let me call the client back and see how flexible they are. I suspect we could do this job using a third of their capacity from January through March, but that's too close to guarantee. Perhaps we can identify a subset that's valuable, but small enough to guarantee before April, with the rest following on a time-available basis. We should still be able to complete it by the end of May, even with the worst-case tax season. If they've got some flexibility, then I'll do some more rigorous estimates."

These are some of the questions you might consider when doing capacity estimates:

- What are the needed people doing now, and when will they be done with that?
- If you lose some people, how much longer will it take?
- If you do this, what else will you have to give up or defer?
- How long might it delay other desired development?
- When can you move on to the next thing?
- How long will these people, currently allocated elsewhere, be tied up with this project?

You may have plenty of capacity, but also plenty of potential projects. Where should you spend your capacity? What projects should you do? This requires an estimate of the potential projects, of course. A moderate return at low cost may be just the low-hanging fruit you need right now. Or a more expensive project may justify the cost by having a huge potential for return. You must weigh the plusses and minuses and risks and make a decision.

- If you add some people to work on it, will it take less time?
- Either way, will it cost more or less? How much?
- Can you afford the cost of devoting your manpower to this project, or the cost of increasing staffing for it?

If you don't want to redirect your current capacity, how many people should you hire to staff it? Similarly, when you want to provide contracted development for someone else, what will be the demand and how many people will be needed to meet that demand? This requires a much more precise estimate.

It's not easy to ramp up capacity. Finding people who are available and competent and interested in doing this work takes time. Forming them into effective teams takes time. And while things are getting organized, we're spending for potential capacity that isn't yet producing. This is one way that projects start out behind schedule from the very beginning, if the schedule assumes steady-state productivity right from the start.

Cashflow and Break-Even

Cost precedes value; investment precedes return. How far does it precede and at what rate? When will the break-even point be? How soon can we start earning value?

It's popular these days to think that the earlier we deliver a system, the better. Is that always true, though? Certainly, there are times when the value of a new product is greatly enhanced by delaying for a splashy rollout. The iPhone didn't debut with a Minimally Viable Product and incremental improvements. The old advertising saw, "Sell the sizzle, not the steak," still holds true.

On the other hand, trying to achieve feature parity with an old version or a competitor's offering may delay the new system to its detriment. Keep an eye on the market desires.

There are so many variables to consider even if we knew the cost precisely. Yet we can hardly begin to analyze the risks and trade-offs without any cost information. And so we look to estimates. We don't need precision at this point, but we need something reasonably accurate for making decisions.

Funding the TinyToyCo Mobile App

Recall that TinyToyCo founders, Chris and Pat, created an online game in their spare time, and then were able to create a stream of income from advertising in that game. They had a hunch that if they created a mobile app version, they'd do even better.

They felt they were beyond the point of nights and weekends, though. They had been doing that too long. As the web game had increased in popularity, the demands on their time had grown. There were inquiries from users, relationships with advertisers, maintenance of the application, and scaling to meet demand. These things were taking up the time they would otherwise spend in development.

Was it time to quit the day jobs and go full time? Was it time to hire someone? If so, should they hire a developer with more mobile development experience than they had, or hire an administrator to free up more of their time? The next step felt like a big one.

Both Pat and Chris had been good about saving money, and they each had about six months of living expenses in the bank. If they hired someone, that buffer would be cut in about half, as both of them were depending on frugality to stretch their savings to six months. Hiring someone would require paying industry standard wages, or close to it, plus payroll taxes.

There's nothing like being broke to focus your attention on income. Pat and Chris weren't broke, yet, and they didn't intend to be. They were willing to come close if it would catapult TinyToyCo to success. They decided to focus on three specific income milestones and weigh the intangibles and probabilities from that.

Financial Milestones

Out of all the questions popping up in their brains, three rose to the top.

1. How long would it take to start generating net income with a mobile app?
2. How long would it take until the income matched their living expenses?
3. How long would it take to reach the break-even point, where the income had repaid the costs?

The first milestone would be the point where the drain on their savings would start to diminish. That would extend the time they could stay afloat without other jobs. The second milestone would be the point where they quit draining their savings. Once they reached that, they could breathe easier. They'd be able to continue indefinitely, as long as no unexpected expense came up. The third milestone was the turnaround point. At that point, their six months of living expenses would be back in the bank. After that, their work would start returning a profit. That's when they could declare success. But when would that be, and could they make it that far?

It didn't take a detailed estimate to decide that hiring someone was more than they could afford. That seemed entirely too risky given they were starting on a shoestring. Shortening the first milestone seemed like a prudent way to go. As long as they didn't do something that would limit them in the future, the earlier they started earning money, the better.

There's nothing like being broke to focus your attention on expenses, too. Pat and Chris didn't want to be broke. They also didn't want to shift their attention to the legalities of hiring and payroll. And they didn't want to commit to "go for broke" or to have to let someone go in a short time if the finances looked bad. If it was just them working on the project, they could mothball it at any time that seemed prudent, without having to officially cancel it.

Industry Data is Better Than None

Pat called up some friends who had successfully developed mobile apps to ask for advice and information. How long had it taken them to field a working app, and then to monetize it? Chris started searching for publicly available information from strangers to answer the same questions. Together, they started envisioning a few minimal starting points they could build to test customer interest. They estimated how long it would take for each of these. The easiest one seemed as likely a starting point as the others. If it flopped, they could transform some of the same code into other attempts. As a rough guess, they could probably try four or five attempts until they were broke.

As soon as they found a starting point that connected with customers, then they could monetize it with advertising and a paid version without advertising. That would be the first milestone.

They did some calculations based on their research to estimate the second and third milestones based on the experience of others. Of course, these were the survivors. There were many other startups who didn't get that far, and left no data behind. They recalculated at half the growth rate, and at one quarter. The slowest growth rate gave them some pretty grim predictions, but if their first, or maybe second, version resonated with people, then it might be enough.

And they really, *really* wanted to try this. With that burning desire, and estimates that gave them some hope, they decided to go for it. They would go with their eyes wide open, though, and re-evaluate frequently.

Case: Can We Make This Work?

There are times where the primary question isn't financial, but feasibility. We may not know if what we propose is within our capability to accomplish. In such cases, identifying the pieces that we cannot estimate is as important as estimating the pieces we can.

TinyToyCo used lean-start-up techniques to find market fit with an online game and mobile app. Now they want to venture into physical product development.

TinyToyCo and the Robotic Cat

"What if we broke free from the boundaries of the phone?"

Pat looked puzzled. "What do you mean, Chris?"

"What if we created a robotic lap-seeking Fluphy Kitty™ toy?"

"Oh! Wow, that would be great. Do you think we could do that?"

"Let's try to figure it out."

Chris and Pat started listing the behaviors they wanted the robot cat to have. These behaviors already existed in virtual form in the web and phone-app versions. They had the cat-like logic pretty well covered. It was the interface with the physical world that was the puzzle.

"We'll need to detect the presence of humans, so Fluphy Kitty™ can seek them out. Just doing that and getting underfoot would be a good beginning."

"If we can determine whether the person is sitting down, and make the robot cat jump high enough, it could jump in their lap."

It's easy to get carried away planning something. But can you really build it? That's when caution is prudent.

Caution Sets In

"Before designing our own robot, let's buy a robotic cat toy and add some franken-features to it to explore the possibilities. First up is infrared video to detect the human."

"And then jumping. If we can't get jumping to work, then the lap-seeking feature isn't going to work."

"Before jumping, I bet we could do clawing on the leg."

"I think we're going to need some specific robotics expertise. This is a lot more than our experience can handle."

"You're right. But we don't want to go deeply in the hole on this. Our current products are generating income, but not so much that we don't have to watch expenses."

"We'll set a budget on each physical capability. I think we can estimate the costs of integrating the capability and tuning the realism of the behavior based on our experience with the virtual cats."

The principles are simple. Estimate what you can based on past experience. We'll look at that more in Chapter 2, Comparison-Based Estimation, on page 27. For the unknowns, you have to set a budget on how much you're willing to spend to see if it's possible to do what you want. Validate those budgets as early as possible.

If you reach a budget limit on an item, you need to stop and replan. It could be that you feel you're close enough to budget a little more. It could be that you've come in under budget on prior items, so you're willing to spend a little more on this one. Or it could be that you want to rethink your plans altogether. Maybe you need to drop this particular capability, at least for now. Can you still move forward toward your vision without it? A lesser version that you can build is worth more than a grand version that you can't.

And don't overlook the possibility it may be time to quit and cut your losses. (See Sunk Cost Fallacy in Cognitive Biases, on page 72.) Product development is a gamble. Don't gamble more than you can afford to lose. Taking risks can become addictive, and you need to watch out if you want to remain responsible.

Case: What Should We Budget?

For a lot of IT work, there's no real need to allocate money on a project-by-project basis. Did the IT department meet the organization's needs last year? If so, it will probably cost about the same this year, perhaps with a slight increase for inflation. It makes sense to maintain a stable workforce to provide the IT capabilities that the organization generally needs. If you do that, there's no need to worry about every nickel and dime of every project.

Of course, there's still competition for those IT capabilities. We'll look at that shortly, in Case: Which of These Should We Choose?, on page 20. Sometimes, though, the competition is rigged. We may have a project that *has* to be done, or else... and we've got no choice about it. What choice we do have is about what projects it will replace or delay. The people waiting on those projects have a right to know.

Budgeting for a Required Project at Empire Enterprises

"Legal Department says we've got until the end of next June to meet a new federal requirement. There could be big daily fines if we don't. We have to report every dollar we spend that might end up in the hands of one of our clinical investigators of our medical equipment. That includes indirect payments, such as through a university they work for. I need to know how many people to put on this to ensure we get it done in time."

"Who should I talk to in Legal?"

"Darby has the information. You'll need to find someone in Accounts Payable and Clinical Research to find out whom we pay how much for what reason."

"I'm on it."

This is similar to the capacity question. How many people and for how long? It has the added wrinkle of a firm deadline and the impetus of an absolute requirement. You'll want to be careful not to underestimate in such a case.

There will be quite a bit of work involved in figuring out how to capture the input data for this report. Even knowing which data is pertinent will be a research product. If it were me, I'd start with the specific things that the Legal Department mentions and leave an allowance in the plan for discovering new things.

Remember that "how many people" is misleading. Productivity does not go up linearly with the number of programmers. In fact, it can go down in some situations. If you can depend on an existing team with a track record of working together, your job will be so much easier.

Case: Which of These Should We Choose?

No matter how much you budget for IT development projects, you're likely to have more demand than capacity. You'll have different stakeholders within the organization competing for that software development capacity to accomplish their favorite projects. When you can't do them all, how do you know which to choose? Which do you choose to do first? For internal IT projects, while you can generally figure on spending about the same the next year as you did the past, there is still competition for the capability that budget is buying.

Empire Enterprises Chooses between Competing IT Projects

"We've allocated project teams for our strategic initiatives, and it looks like we've got some capacity for the more mundane projects in our queue. One team is finishing up a project this month, and another team will be available in a month or two after that."

"The Sales and Marketing department of the Motors and Headphones Division is complaining that their consumer sales website is too pedestrian to attract much attention. They feel they could sell more product direct to consumers if the website could accept promotional coupon codes. The discounts of the coupons would be less than the wholesale discount to retailers."

"The new Accounting Manager has noticed that the Accounts Payable system pays invoices in the order in which they're entered into the system, rather than according to the due date of the invoice. This means that invoices are paid up to a month before they have to be, and we lose the interest on that money."

"The Contract Management office often feels overwhelmed by the processing and monitoring of bids let out to contracting companies. While they could hire more clerks, they feel that the root problem is that the Bid Monitoring system is clunky, outdated, and hard to use. They suggested streamlining that system to make it easier to avoid errors and oversights. If it were easier, they could avoid increasing the labor costs."

How do you decide which of these projects to take on next? There are lots of different ways you could make the decision.

Criteria for Choosing Which Project

"The Sales group has been very vocal about their needs. They call me every week. They keep emailing my manager."

"The Accounting office can calculate how much money we're losing in interest. Their project has a guaranteed payoff."

"The Contract Management office has had their request in for almost a year now. We can't keep putting them off. They've been waiting longer than anybody."

Which of these arguments is most convincing to you?

One common way of looking at this problem is in economic terms, recognizing the time value of money. If something has high value and can be done quickly with low effort, we certainly would rather do that before something else that has low value and high effort. That's a clear choice. But what about the choice between low-hanging fruit, the low-value, low-effort projects, and the bigger initiatives that have higher value, but also take more effort? How do you choose between those alternatives?

Presuming that cash flow isn't a critical issue (as in Cashflow and Break-Even, on page 16), you might want to use the Cost of Delay, a concept popularized and named by Don Reinertsen, to decide. The value of the project may be in increased revenue or reduced costs. How much is it costing you to delay this project a month? Or the value may be more foundational, in terms of protecting revenue, such as maintaining market share, or avoiding future costs. How much will this cost you over the lifetime of the product if you delay a month, now? Any of these values can be expressed as money per unit of time, even though the latter ones may not accrue the cost for some time.

Using the Cost of Delay to determine priority order of projects involves dividing by the project duration to calculate a weighting factor called CD3, or Cost of Delay Divided by Duration. The highest CD3 is generally scheduled first, an approach called Weighted Shortest Job First (WSJF). This prioritization is often done with relative estimates of cost and duration. Relative estimates are easier to produce, but should be used with caution. Nonlinearities in the relative estimates might juggle the outcomes.

Cost of Delay Is Still an Estimate

 Some people add in a risk assessment to their Cost of Delay estimate. Others presume a product lifecycle revenue shape that may have lower peak profits if the launch is delayed. Some try to quantify the time criticality. Most leave out less-direct costs, such as reputation, though these can result in tangible costs, also. All these different ways of determining Cost of Delay should emphasize the fact that these are estimates, not calculations. Use them with caution, as with any other estimate.

The bottom line is still: go for the biggest bang at the cheapest cost.

Case: A Mixture of Questions

"If only things were that simple. Around here, there's a lot going on at once. Different people have different questions and their questions change constantly without notice. That's why I need to come up with an accurate and precise estimate that will answer all their questions."

Yes, the context of an organization, especially a large one, can be daunting and confusing. And if it's not, you're probably overlooking something. Seeking the mythical Precise and Accurate Estimate, however, is an unlikely solution to deal with it. I'm sure you've tried that before and have many times traded stories with compatriots about how things didn't go well.

Intuitive, Sensing, and Imposed Projects

One thing that helps clarify confusing situations is a mental model that focuses you on certain aspects, making them clear in spite of the noise of all the other aspects. A model can help you sort out what you see and highlight the relationships between things. While a single model can blind you to important aspects that are not represented in the model, no one is trying to limit you to just one. Here are models of different types of projects based on why they're being proposed or undertaken.

Intuitive projects are based on somebody's vision. "It would be fun to build a robotic cat." "Let's start our own HMO to contain our payments as an insurance company." These may be little more than a hunch, otherwise known as the "highest paid person's opinion" or HiPPO. Or they might be based on market research, where a committee has chosen a product definition that will likely be successful. Intuitive products often focus on the solution, and the underlying needs may be less distinct.

Estimating the size or cost of intuitive projects can be a trap. It may seem obvious as to what needs to be done, but the doneness is likely to be determined by how well what's produced matches a vision in someone's head. This is very hard to see from the outside of that head. There are likely to be surprises that were not assumed when initial estimates were made.

The scope of intuitive projects tends to be flexible, and mostly in the direction of bigger. It's easy to expand the expectations with additional thoughts of "useful features." Scope can be negotiable downwards if you can talk to the person whose intuition underlies the project.

Sensing projects are based on a desired outcome. "We need to reduce the payouts we make on health insurance claims." The scope is outcome-based, though it may be bounded by available time and money. "We can afford to spend $1 million to reduce health insurance claim payouts by 10% in the next year." Or they can be more exploratory, done a bit at a time, measuring the outcome that is desired and steered by the success shown. "We have these three ideas for reducing health insurance claim payouts. Let's try some small experiments and see what effect each of these ideas has."

Initial estimates of sensing projects can also be deceptive, as the solution to reach a given goal may not be visible at the start. Such projects are excellent choices for a lean-start-up approach, and budgeting the work done before arriving at a solution worth pursuing. Exhausting that budget is a good indicator that it may be time to switch to a different project.

When you can talk with the source of an intuitive project, you may be able to identify measurable outcomes to track and turn it toward a sensing project. Such a hybrid gives you the potentially bigger wins of bigger ideas with the risk containment of taking smaller steps.

Imposed projects are handed down from someone else. They may also be due to changing circumstances: a new legal requirement, an obsolete dependency (language, framework, operating system, hardware), or keeping parity with a competitor. They may also have started as intuitive projects by someone out of communications range of the development team, such that negotiating scope and clarifying goals is difficult. Sometimes, the barrier of a contracting relationship turns an intuitive project from the client's point of view into an imposed one from the contractor's point of view. These tend to be the least flexible, and give people the most problems with regard to estimation. The conversation shifts from vision or outcomes toward contracts and obligations.

You can likely find aspects of all three in most projects, especially when you consider multiple points of view.

The Need for a New Call Center

Ryan, the Director of Customer Service at Empire Enterprises, frowned at the numbers. "We've got twice the customer service reps that we had three years ago. We're only handling 50% more calls, though. All the reps are busy when I visit any of the call centers. They're working more overtime than ever. This doesn't look sustainable. What's the root of the problem?"

Tracy, Manager of Analytics, replied, "Unfortunately, we don't have the data to know for sure. Our call center software is limited in the metrics it can collect. The average length of call is only slightly longer than it was three years ago. The average time between the first ring and a rep answering the call is also only slightly longer than it was. The biggest clue is that once or twice a week there's a ten-to-fifteen minute gap with no calls at all."

Sidney, the Director of Internal IT Services, spoke up. "We've looked at enhancing the call center software for better metrics, but that system is fragile. It started as a purchased product, and our programmers have enhanced it considerably over the years. For a long time, we put in every feature that was requested. Now, though, it's hard to find good programmers who want to work on an old PHP system. And ever since the attempt last year to update the version of PHP on the system, we've had those intermittent problems where it mysteriously locks up and doesn't deliver the calls. In some of those cases, we have to reboot the server. We've been trying to track down the problem, but it happens so infrequently that no one is watching when it happens, and our logs don't contain enough information to identify why it happens."

"So we can't fix it?" Ryan asked. "What would it take to replace it?"

Sidney gulped. "Can we list the features that the call center really needs?"

"Just use the old system as the requirements. Do what it does now."

"And add better auditing metrics," added Tracy.

Duplicating the existing call center system is an imposed project. It needs to be done because the old system is falling apart. Fortunately, the old system still works, more or less. We'll see that we can lean on that to turn it into more of a sensing project, replacing uses of the old system bit by bit.

Adding better auditing metrics is an intuitive project, based on Tracy's dissatisfaction with the current system. Addressing that dissatisfaction is the current operative definition of "better metrics." With a good working relationship, that can also be turned into a sensing project, iteratively trying things and judging if they're meeting the need.

Stepping Back for a Broader View

As we've seen, there are very many reasons a business will want to look forward to the future. There are a variety of decisions to be made, depending on the situation and the desired outcome. Each of these decisions has its own different needs in terms of accuracy, precision, and the distribution of error. Without knowing the business need, it's not possible to know how to satisfy that need with an appropriate estimate. It's important to find out what those needs are and recognize that they may require different estimates.

It's important to remember that estimates are different from calculations. There's nothing exact about them. Given that error is expected, you'll want to do your best to keep that error from causing damage. Often, accuracy and precision are not very important if you can constrain the error in one direction. Other times, the distribution of error is not important because the need for precision is not great. It's only when the decision is close that you need to worry much about accuracy and precision. When that's the case, you should realize that the risk of noticeable error is greater. That risk may help make the decision. There's little cause to incur a large risk for a small return on investment.

Next, let's look at how to develop an initial estimate to meet these needs.

Now It's Your Turn

1. When you were starting your last project, what questions needed to be answered before the start? Were the produced estimates suitable for answering those questions? Were the people producing the estimates informed of how they would be used?

2. List the different types of needs for estimates that you've encountered at the start of your projects. Consider the accuracy, precision, and probability distribution of error to suit those needs. How many different sorts of estimates have you needed (whether or not that's what you received or provided)? How many times was the desirable accuracy, precision, and error distribution estimate unknown?

CHAPTER 2

Comparison-Based Estimation

It's always a conundrum when you face a new project and want to know how long it will take and how many people are needed to accomplish it. There are so many variables and so little is known with any certainty. It's tempting to throw up our hands and declare, "There's no way of knowing!" As we saw in Chapter 1, Starting Something New, on page 1, there are often good business reasons for estimating a new project.

What's a pragmatic way to meet those business needs? There are two ways to estimate something. One way is to build a computational model to calculate the estimate based on things we know or that we can more easily estimate. We'll look at that method in Chapter 5, Model-Based Estimation, on page 103. The simpler way of estimating, especially when starting something new, is by comparison, i.e., comparing the things we want to know about to the things we already know.

Comparison-based estimation is such an ordinary part of our lives that we often don't notice when we do it.

Everyday Estimation

Let's see. My train is at 1:13 p.m., and the last time I went to the train station, it took about 30 minutes to get there. I think I'll allow for double that. I really don't want to miss that train.

Notice how this estimation process is modeled as a multiplicative factor applied to a known past experience. In this case, the factor is designed to cover any natural variability and give a buffer for safety. See Multiplicative and Additive Adjustments, on page 30) for more discussion of simple multipliers and additions to account for possible variances between the current situation and past experience.

Everyday Estimation—Another Take

Let's see. My train is at 1:13 p.m., and the last time I went to the train station, it took about 30 minutes to get there. I was being dropped off that time and I'm driving myself this time. Maybe

I'd better allow 10 or 15 minutes to park the car and walk down from the parking garage. The last time I took the train, it was midafternoon. Today, it's lunchtime, so traffic might be heavy. Let's make it an hour, in total. I really don't want to miss that train.

Here we've started to build a mental model of what makes up the variances. We've specifically allowed additional time to park the car and walk down to the station. We've cataloged another possible variance, traffic delays, but we haven't quantified them. In the end, we fell back to a comparison-based estimate and allowed for a lump variance. Itemizing the elements of that variance may have helped us choose an appropriate factor, but we didn't build an explicit model.

Magne Jørgensen, in *Expert Estimation of Software Development Work: Learning through Feedback [JS06]*, states, "Several empirical studies report that expert estimation of software development and maintenance effort is the dominant estimation approach. We were not able to find a single study that reported a dominance of model-based effort estimation." I think most people tend to minimize the use of math when they can get away with it. This promotes the use of simple comparisons or comparisons with simple mathematical adjustments. As we'll see in Chapter 5, Model-Based Estimation, on page 103, model-based estimation has a component of comparison, too. It's just quantified so mathematical manipulations can be performed. Clearly, comparison-based and model-based estimation are not completely distinct. It's a matter of where you put the effort. Building a mathematical model you can trust can take considerable effort, so let's start with the easy approach.

Comparison to Past Experience

Let's apply the comparison approach to software development estimation.

What past work was similar to this work?

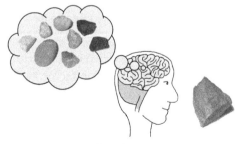

Is this *yet another* custom report for the business? Or a starter website for *yet another* small company? Sometimes our projects are amazingly similar to what we've done in the past.

Other times, they're startlingly different. That's not surprising. If we already had software to do what we wanted, we probably wouldn't be starting a new project. It could be something that *no one* has ever done before, or, at least, no one that we know.

More often it's somewhere in the middle, with both similarities and differences from our past experience. What projects in our experience have the most similarities? You may want to choose more than one, especially if they're similar in different ways or to different parts.

Once we've chosen a piece of work that's comparable to the one we're estimating, we can ask ourselves questions about how it compares.

How does that work compare to this work?

Is this work about the same size, bigger, or smaller? Note that we're saying "about the same size." We're estimating, not calculating. We're not generally concerned if this work might be 2% larger or smaller. We're probably not concerned if this work might be 10% larger or smaller. We're unlikely to have enough accuracy to warrant that precision. If this work is 100% or more larger, we might want to take notice.

How does this work differ from that work?

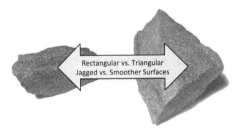

Asking how the work is the same is helpful for sizing, but it may encourage you to overlook some variations that make a difference. Turning the question around helps you spot the uncertainties. You may want to temper your estimate with those uncertainties, or investigate to learn more and reduce the uncertainties.

How many of those bits of work would it take to make up this work?

Don't jump to big numbers. How would you tell that something anticipated seemed 100 times as big as something remembered? How would you tell the difference between that and 1000 times as big? When you feel the need to use orders of magnitude, that's a signal that you can't really judge the size relationship—judging something as eight or 10 times (some parameter) may already be too hard. People, in general, aren't very good at precise comparisons of things widely differing in size. Doing so for something as intangible as software development is even harder.

When you're facing a new software development project, you can use the same familiar skills you use in your everyday life. But it's a little different, of course. Undeveloped software is more abstract, and you likely don't estimate it as frequently. For those reasons, and because you may have important consequences riding on the outcome, be a bit more mindful about how you go about it.

We just talked about comparing size in terms of multiples of our reference. Other times we might find a similarity to our reference, but there's something additional. Or we may find both. And, of course, we might substitute division for multiplication and subtraction for addition, if it seems appropriate to us. Let's look at such adjustments in more detail.

Multiplicative and Additive Adjustments

What's the difference between your previous experience and your current one? Maybe you had a development project last year, but this one seems more complicated. Or that first one used a familiar technology stack but this one is based on new technology that none of us have used before. It's still relevant experience. You'll just have to adjust your expectations to account for the differences.

If this project seems more complicated, how much more is it? Twice as complicated, or 10 times? You can make a rough multiplicative adjustment to your past results to approximate your expected results.

What Can We Tell Them?

Sidney, the Internal IT Director of Empire Enterprises, called his top project manager, Marion, to his office. "I've just come from a meeting with the Customer Service department, and Ryan and Tracy say it looks like we're going to have to bite the bullet and replace the call center software. What do you think that's going to take in time and labor?"

"What do they want?"

"Basically a rewrite of the current system, plus some additional work to add metrics for auditing."

"That's not nearly enough information to start work. I'll need to research the current system, research the current usage, and get some details on the driving force behind the metrics."

"What can we tell them right now?"

"Given the need to research the requirements, I'd say roughly twice what it took to build the old system. And another 25% to add the metrics. I'll have to research what the old system took to build to convert that to numbers. That's a rough order of magnitude. Should I start working on a more refined estimate?"

"I don't know, yet. Let's at least look at the costs of the old system so we can give this in numerical terms."

That's an example of a multiplicative adjustment. Even the additive part for the metrics was expressed as a multiple of the original project. This lets us compare to a project without knowing the numbers, yet. Next we'll need to calibrate to the actual time and effort of that project.

Foreseeable Delays

If you need to learn a new technology, then how long will it take you to come up to speed? That's an additive component to our estimation model. If last year's project took you six months and it'll take you two months to learn the technology, then eight months might be a reasonable estimate for this work. Or, since you'll have much less experience in the new technology, perhaps there's a multiplicative adjustment, also, to account for the friction of working in unfamiliar territory.

Considering the Learning Curve

Marion walked into Sidney's office. "I've got some bad news. I've asked around about who knows anything about the last call center project. No one does. It seems that all those people have left the company, taking all of our call-processing expertise with them. I guess we'll have to hire someone with that experience. That's going to take three to six months, and then longer for them to bring the rest of the team up to speed."

Do you have a different set of people this time around? Will they work together as well as the previous group? How long will it take them to bond well as a group? Will they jell as a team and will their synergy surpass the historical comparison?

The further our reference experience is from the upcoming work, the more you'll have to adjust that model to predict the future. And the more you have to adjust our model, the more likely it is for error to creep in. How do you know how much to adjust? That, too, is an estimate.

You make things harder on yourself when you make unnecessary changes in the way you work. Often people dissolve the team at the end of each project and build a new one for the next project, thinking they can more efficiently include just the skills they need. There are big benefits of keeping durable teams together and bringing the work to the team. One of these is having a track record for the team and how effectively it works together. Another benefit is that the team doesn't have to ramp up new working relationships for each project.

You also benefit from working on one thing at a time. That makes it easier to track how much effort has actually gone into a project. When you multitask—working on a major project but also being pulled off onto unplanned work that pops up—you have a harder time figuring how much of your effort went toward that major project. Rarely do people keep accurate notes on how much they worked on one project versus other tasks. In fact, that's quite hard to do in knowledge work like software development. How do you keep track of what problem you're mulling over from hour to hour? And when you pay more attention to timekeeping, it distracts you and compounds the problem you're working to solve.

So, while estimating future work based on past experience is simple, it's still not always easy. We can make our job easier by changing how we arrange the work (see Ordering the Parts, on page 60) and how we approach it. There's advantage in doing so, not only in easier estimation but in being more productive at accomplishing our projects, too.

Memory vs. Recorded Data

Steve McConnell, in *Software Estimation: Demystifying the Black Art [McC06]*, reports that "individual expert judgment is by far the most common approach used in practice." When we talk about estimation by expert judgment, we're really talking about comparison with past experiences. You can augment memories of those experiences with recorded data, when that's available. There are often files of information about past projects that can be mined for data. How similar were the requirements of this old project to the one we're contemplating? How many people worked on it, in what roles, and for how long?

Inaccurate Memories

Most manuals on estimation warn you that estimating based on remembered data is fraught with inaccuracies. You might remember the estimate for a past project rather than the actual results. Or, due to proximity, you might remember the staffing at the end of the project, rather than the actual staffing throughout it. You might remember the project start from some date other than the actual starting point, perhaps when you joined it or the date that it was announced to a wider audience. You might neglect accounting for rework done after the project was initially delivered.

Recording Data for Future Estimates

Estimation experts will say that you should record significant data for your projects, and use that data to estimate future ones. As Capers Jones advises in *Estimating Software Costs [Jon07]*, "The best defense against having a cost estimate rejected is to have solid historical data from at least a dozen similar projects." That's good advice, but it probably won't help you immediately. You're likely facing the need for an estimate before you can organize your data collection program.

If you do have detailed data from past projects, you're probably working for a company that needs high-precision, high-accuracy data to support pricing fixed-scope, fixed-price bids for large projects. But if you're in that situation, then you probably have a department full of experts at doing that in your business domain, using a standardized process approved by your company. It's the same department collecting and maintaining all that data. They'll help you

For the rest of us, there's still hope of finding recorded data from past projects. There is almost always some data that was recorded contemporaneously, if you can only find and understand it. Asking around for memories may give you a starting point. Look for accounting data for costs charged to past projects. Look for email conversations about those projects.

Inaccurate Recorded Data

Beware, though, of inaccuracies in the data. Even when recorded at the time, the data that was recorded likely does not tell the whole story. There is much that happens "off the record" due to inattention or embarrassment.

It's Worse Than We Thought

Once again Marion strode into Sidney's office. "I've been digging deeper researching the last call center project, and I've got data, this time. Accounting looked up the numbers for me. There were five programmers working on the last call center project code. They billed 40-hour weeks for 15 months. And there were two testers on that charge code for the last five months of the project."

"Fifteen months?" Sidney looked unhappy. "And you think it's going to take longer this time?"

"Yes, our rough order of magnitude was two and a quarter times as long, factoring in requirements gathering and the additional metrics requirements. That would be 34 months. I know that's not what you wanted to hear."

"No, Ryan won't go for that. He'll insist on an off-the-shelf solution, not realizing that customizing such a system is a big project in itself. And I don't like running the risk of not being able to deliver the functionality that's requested. If we hit a wall with a purchased solution, we likely won't have any options."

"It's worse than that." Marion shifted uneasily. "I ran into Blaise who's still friends with the lead programmer of the old call system. It turns out that the project turned into a death march once the testers started looking at it. That's not reflected in the accounting numbers because the development team were all on salary, so their timesheets reflected 40 hours no matter how much more they worked in a week. If we planned the new project assuming those were 40-hour weeks, we'd doom it to failure before we started."

There was a long pause. "Are you sure Ryan needs everything in the current system?"

Collected data often has pernicious errors. Unrecorded overtime is common; programmers are forced to donate extra time to the project. Even when timesheets aren't forced by policy to be inaccurate, the allocation to charge codes may not be correct. People often think that contemporaneous data collection will be accurate. When data collection is extra work, in addition to the work of accomplishing the project itself, it seems like a nuisance to those doing the work. Therefore, they may not spend a lot of effort keeping it accurate. It's easier to duplicate a previous time sheet than to consider precisely how we've split our time among multiple accounting buckets. The more detailed this task is made, the less accurate it's likely to be.

The data collection may have other types of omissions, too. Timesheet records may collect only direct value-adding work, not overhead activities such as meetings. These may be charged to a different category. Your upcoming project, though, is sure to have its share of meetings, also.

Aspects to Compare

There are many aspects you will want to consider when estimating a software development project. Too narrow a view is likely to lead you into trouble. A narrow view increases the chances that significant contributors to the schedule lie in the blind spots you've failed to consider.

When comparing future work to past experience, if you neglect to think about some aspect that is roughly the same in both cases, no harm is done. But if you neglect some aspect that differs in a way that affects the pace of accomplishment, it can have a major impact on the accuracy of your estimate. Let's look at what aspects might differ. This checklist is, of course, not exhaustive, but it will help you consider the matter more thoroughly.

Aspects of the System to Consider

The most obvious consideration when estimating system development is what's known about the intended system itself. That is, after all, what we're building. And it's the building of it that we're estimating. Therefore, looking at those desires, or "requirements" as some call them, is a natural starting point.

Quantitative Aspects of the System

Of course, the scope of the development is a primary concern. Ask yourself how big is the code being developed, and how much functionality is being added. Notice the things that you can count, such as the following examples:

- How many user workflows are needed?
- How many screens will that take?
- How many "logical items" will need to be stored?
- With how many other systems does this one communicate?
- How many interfaces does this system provide to others, and how many functions per interface?

These, of course, might be approximate counts based on a naive implementation model. That's OK. This is an estimate we're making, not a prediction. Such quantitative measures can alert you to differences in size compared to your reference.

Qualitative Aspects of the System

Dig into the qualitative aspects of the system:

- How complex is the functionality being developed?
- Has something like this been implemented before?
- Are there significant interactions between the parts, or are they relatively independent of each other?

These, also, can alert you to differences in size compared to your reference, even though they don't have numbers attached.

Quality Aspects of the System

Consider the quality of implementation:

- How much emphasis should be given to maintainability of the system and to future extensibility?

- For that matter, if you're building on an existing codebase, how much emphasis was given for it?

- And how good is the development team at writing maintainable, extensible code?

People often take such quality issues for granted, but there can be a wide range of interpretations. If the attention to quality in the reference system or of an existing codebase which you'll modify differs from the current expectations for the future work, then that's a significant difference which must be accommodated in your estimate.

Internal code and architectural quality can be quite cheap if you've learned the knack. As Philip Crosby said, "Quality is free." Attention to detail quickly pays for itself, but some people don't recognize how to work that way. Having to come back and try to put in the quality after the fact can be very expensive. And building on a system made without concern for quality will certainly have a lot of unexpected work.

Aspects of the System Context to Consider

The way the system relates to the systems around it can also have a major impact on how much time and effort development takes. The relationship of the system being developed and the people and organization that interact with or otherwise depend on the system has an effect, too.

Constraints of the System Context

Consider the constraints placed on the development:

- Are there decisions that are assumed and can't be changed, such as aspects of the architecture or deployment configuration?

Implicit expectations can easily blow your estimate out of the water. Better to ask these questions now than be surprised by them later.

Non-functional Expectations of the System Context

Consider the "-ilities," the characteristics that cut across the functional requirements:

- What is the need for scalability, or the immediate and long-term needs in terms of users and data?

- What are the expected throughput and service-level agreements?

- How much safety factor should be included beyond expected needs?

- What level of system availability is needed?

- How responsive does it need to be?

- How reliable does the system need to be?

- Is there a need to degrade gracefully in the face of problems outside of its scope, such as other systems being down or communication bottlenecks?

- When something goes wrong, how will people know what went wrong? Can you give them clear and relevant information? Can you store information to be examined later? Can Customer Service deduce what happened when talking with the user over the phone?

The expectations surrounding implementation quality can be widely varied and are often implicitly assumed rather than explicitly discussed. Mismatches in expectations can have major impact on the suitability of your estimates.

Security Expectations of the System Context

Consider the expectations of the system security in its intended environment. Sometimes, these dimensions haven't been fully explored when you're asked for an estimate. That's OK; they can probably be deferred. If you're practicing lean product discovery, you don't want to expend energy on bulletproofing a feature until you've validated that customers will use it. In other situations, you may be surprised by people saying, "of course it needs to be bulletproof."

- How secure does the system need to be, and against what threat models?

- Does the system need to be auditable? To what level of detail?

- Does traceability data need to be stored and, if so, at what detail and for how long?

- Is there personally identifiable information that needs to be protected from disclosure to others?

- Are there privacy laws that govern the system?

Such requirements are often overlooked prior to the approval of a project. There could be a significant amount of functionality that's invisible to the nominal user and will take development time.

Usability Expectations of the System Context

Consider the expectations of user factors. This is another category of expectations that are often not mentioned explicitly until later, when someone outside the project complains.

- How stringent are the usability requirements?

- What are the accessibility requirements?

- Is the system required to conform with Section 508 or other regulations protecting the disabled?

- Does the system need to be internationalized to support multiple languages and cultures?

Such concerns can add a lot to the effort, especially if the development team isn't experienced at meeting such demands. There can be a broad range of potential expectations.

Priority of Expectations of the System Context

Consider when these contextual considerations become important. Early releases may not have the same needs and expectations as others. Perhaps you can validate the core functionality with a limited audience for earlier feedback.

- Do you need to include these at the start?
- Will it be sufficient to patch any issues raised?
- Can you iteratively add these after each function is developed?

Consider how much support needs to be implemented for operations and customer service to detect, identify, and analyze problems during operation. This is another category of often invisible requirements. Neglecting these functions can save a lot of development time, but greatly reduce the long-term satisfaction with the system.

All of these contextual demands are generally under-discussed at the beginning of a project. They are hard to bring up, also, as asking "do we need such-and-such" will often trigger the "kitchen sink" response. "Well, of course we need it. If we can think of it, put it in." Bloating the project with expectations that have not been thought through thoroughly can blow more than your estimate.

Aspects of the Development Context to Consider

The details of the development process have a huge impact on development speed. In my experience, rushing into development without proper preparation is a major cause of systems development taking much longer than anticipated. Setting things up for success is, of course, the prudent plan. If that's not within your power, then being aware of the potential issues is necessary for an understanding of what might slow down the development process. Perhaps that awareness will also aid in improving some of these aspects.

Familiarity of the Development Context

Consider the familiarity of the functionality and proposed implementation:

- How much of the scope is well understood and how much is vague or new?
- Do you have a solid background in the business domain?
- Are you fluent in the implementation technology?
- Do you even know yet who will be doing the implementation?

All forms of novelty impose a learning tax on the development process. Giving the process of learning short shrift will undoubtedly lengthen the amount of time required.

Relationships Surrounding the Development Context

Consider the relationship with the customer or manager requesting the system:

- Are they congenial and easy to please, or nit-picky and opinionated?

- Are they willing to engage throughout the project to clarify the requirements as they are addressed or as new questions come up?

- Are they likely to want "the kitchen sink" when presented with options?

You can easily spend significant time convincing a stakeholder of some essential fact. Or, you may be constrained to doing something the hard way because you can't convince them. On the other hand, a good working relationship with the customer can save a lot of unnecessary work and avoid needless rework.

Building the Customer Relationship

Sidney called Ryan to talk about the Empire Enterprises call center situation. Sidney's first question was "When can I have the new call center?"

"We've got a few people exploring some new-to-us technology to support it. We've got some people examining the current system to figure out what it currently supports. Our rough order of magnitude estimate for a replacement system based on the time it took to build the old system seems way out of whack to me."

"When will the whole thing be ready?"

"We calculated it might take about three years. I think that's too long, but we need a better sense of what the 'whole thing' entails. Reverse-engineering the current system is a slow way to determine the requirements. It's also likely to pull along current errors in implementation, plus create some new ones. We can surely do better than that, but we'll need your help."

Ryan looked at him suspiciously. "What sort of help? Why can't you just build what we need?"

"Building custom software isn't like assembling a known product. You've seen how sometimes you don't get what you expected. Neither one of us likes it when that happens. But if you'll work with us, we can order the work to give you some value earlier, make sure we're on the right track, and take care of any problems as we go, when they're still small problems."

"But I've got a Customer Service department to run. Developing software isn't my expertise or responsibility."

"I know. But handling customer service calls isn't our expertise, either. We don't know your operation like you do. Why don't we meet next week some time. You can bring one or two of your most experienced people and I'll bring a couple of good analysts. Let's spend an hour or two and see what we can come up with. It's a small price to pay that might pay off big."

"Let me check our schedules, and I'll get back to you."

Rewrites don't always have to have all the features of the system they're replacing. Often there are features that are little used, or will be obsolete when other new features are added. Resisting the temptation to provide feature parity offers a potential solution to such rewrites.

As this story shows, business people easily assume that the software development organization will do whatever it is that the business people will later find they want. If you're working from that assumption, then it makes sense to concentrate on your own work and wait for the solution to be delivered to you. As anyone who's been in software development awhile probably realizes, this is a recipe for repeated cycles of building something to have it rejected and rebuilt.

Business: *Bring me a rock.*

Development: *Here is your rock.*

Business: *No, not that rock. Bring me a different rock.*

Even when the relationship isn't as unhelpful as this, the nature of the relationship between those asking for the software and those building it can have a huge impact on the time it takes to successfully complete it. Consider the following aspects:

• Is there one customer voice to be satisfied, or multiple constituencies?

- What is the procedure when there's a difference of opinion on the requirements?

- How clear and unambiguous is "done" for each requirement?

Any fuzziness in understanding the requirements will surely slow things down. In the worst case, gaining an understanding with one constituency may result in work that must be redone when another constituency disagrees. If you find yourself in the middle of a battle between two powers who want different systems, you may never complete it.

Also consider issues that might arise as you try to untangle uncertainties and miscommunication.

- Do you have easy access to determine the answers to questions that will arise in the future?

- Are you dealing directly with the decision-maker, or with a proxy?

- When you ask a question, how quickly can you expect a response?

Duration depends on effort plus waiting. Proceeding without waiting can waste even more effort and leave a lot of work in progress. The open questions will slow you down more than you might imagine.

Effort also depends on duration. It takes effort to get back up to speed after an interruption or delay.

Consider the organizational components to the rate at which work can be done.

- Will there be interruptions in the work?
- What else will be going on at the same time?
- Will there be task switching between projects vying for attention?

Consider all these aspects, and any others that come to mind when comparing the future work to past experience. They are all ways in which that experience could differ and have a significant impact on the time and effort. Are they multiplicative or additive effects? How big? Handle these the same way we saw in Multiplicative and Additive Adjustments, on page 30.

As you consider these aspects, particularly Aspects of the System to Consider, on page 35, you have a choice to think of the system as a single whole thing, or as composed of smaller parts.

Gestalt Estimation

gestalt (noun)
an organized whole that is perceived as more than the sum of its parts.

One way of comparison is to take the project as a whole and compare it with other whole projects. If you've built a number of starter "business card" websites with little or no active code, you can have a pretty good idea about how much work the next one will be. The more you've done some sort of work, the more you're likely to be able to estimate a project that's similar to one you've done before. Or, perhaps, you might estimate relative to a previous one: "This seems bigger than the Foo Project but smaller than Baz."

Dan North makes the point that experienced people in the software development field internalize this sense of comparison and don't have to make explicit comparisons to past projects. He calls this *blink estimation*. He tells a couple of wonderful stories[1] about estimating project staffing and duration. When asked how he did it, he replied, "I got a group of really smart people in a room, with at least 10 years' experience each, and asked them." In effect, he ran one round of Planning Poker (see Planning Poker, on page xiii) on the project as a whole, based on the gut experience of people who had studied the problem and knew the development context. Humans can be quite good at balancing a whole lot of poorly quantified and tentative knowledge in a useful way.

Dan offers a number of cautions about this technique. He emphasizes the need for deep experience, and a diversity of backgrounds and disciplines in the group. He also cautions to be aware of cognitive biases. (See Cognitive Biases, on page 72.) The diversity helps fight groupthink, and everyone displaying their answer simultaneously guards against Anchoring Bias. It's important to keep things loose and in the realm of estimation rather than calculation.

Could it be wrong? Of course it could—it's an estimate! It's a way to get close to an answer. If you're nervous, you can cross-check with a second estimation technique.

One advantage of gestalt estimation is that it saves a lot of time. It also defuses the fractal nature of decomposition estimation. People pay attention to the factors that will materially shift the answer and don't worry about the small perturbations.

A disadvantage of gestalt estimation is that you might not have a good comparison in mind. Or you might not notice some significant differences without looking in more detail. That's why you might prefer comparison of smaller components.

---

1. http://dannorth.net/2013/08/08/blink-estimation/

Decomposition

If you don't have data that's similar enough to the whole project, then perhaps you have data that's similar enough to parts of it. If the project being estimated is really large, then it becomes difficult to compare, anyway. This is generally true in estimation of all sorts. You can judge if two cardboard boxes are approximately the same size, but you might be hard-pressed to tell if two counties are. We lose our perspective when the thing to be estimated is larger than we can view or imagine all at once.

If you break it down into pieces, then there's more likelihood of those pieces being similar to pieces of other projects: "The reporting for this project is similar to the reporting we did last year. And the user interface looks about the same size and complication as the project we just finished."

When I had little experience in software development, I fell back on decomposition as my primary estimation tool. I would take the large chunk of work that I was estimating and imagine doing it as a number of small pieces of work. If these pieces were small enough, I could imagine how long it might take me to accomplish each of them. Then it was a simple matter of adding them up to get my large chunk estimate. This always gave me a number to report, and sometimes that number was useful.

When you consider breaking the work down into smaller pieces to estimate, you open a whole new can of worms. How you break it down depends on who breaks it down. It depends on their understanding of the problem being solved and the possible ways of solving it. Different decompositions can lead us in entirely different directions. And there are many ways in which you can fool yourself. We'll look at the details of this in Chapter 3, Decomposition for Estimation, on page 49.

What do you do when you have no appropriate analogs for the upcoming work, whether or not you decompose it into smaller pieces?

Estimating the Unknown

As you've already seen, there's always the possibility of having items that you don't know how to estimate. Some of these are difficult because they're too large, and you've already looked at decomposition as a means to make them more amenable to estimation.

Sometimes, though, you don't have reasonable historical data for comparison. We can still compare the parts with each other, but that gives us an ungrounded estimate. How do you turn that into something you can share with others?

Calibrating to Unknown Context

Perhaps the work is relatively well-known, but the conditions for doing it are not. You might have a new team that's not used to working with one another. Or a team that's not used to this type of work, or for this client. You can end up with an estimated pile of work, but no way to associate that with calendar time.

That's one of the advantages of using Story Points (see Story Points, on page xii), or, as they were alternatively named, Nebulous Units of Time (NUTS) or Gummi Bears of Complexity. These fanciful titles are a reminder that you can't just add up the numbers and expect a precise and accurate prediction. But you can use them to plan your work and track our progress. If you start working and see how many of these you accomplish in a week, you can guess, using the concept of Yesterday's Weather, that next week you'll do about the same.

This gives a current rate of progress, and you can use that to calibrate your estimates. Be wary here. You don't know the variability in your rate of progress. You don't know the variability in the work. You're putting a lot of faith into a small amount of data if you use this to look very far into the future. The use of Story Points works well for selecting how much work would fit into the next iteration, perhaps looking ahead two weeks, where the consequences for being wrong is very low. If you take on too little work, you can bring in the next prioritized story. If you take on too much, then you won't get it all done this iteration. The wise advice was, and is, to have as few stories in progress as practical, so that it's no big deal if one or two spill over. This avoids having them all "almost done" with no trustworthy indication of progress. This approach also supports projecting approximately how many iterations it will take to implement a particular pile of User Stories. This longer-term estimate is more reliable if the shorter-term errors tend to be wrong roughly equally in both directions.

Calibrating with Industry Data

Another way of estimating the unknown is to purchase the information we need. Sometimes historical information from some other context is available for purchase from a consulting agency, for example. They may be willing to share that information with us if we hire them for their advice. Be wary in such situations. The nature of such a relationship is that they need to make their information look as valuable as possible in order to induce us to buy. It may not be as applicable as we hope. Often their historical information is packaged in a high-priced estimation tool. These tools are created by analyzing a large number of projects and trying to isolate significant factors that affect the time and cost of them. Some mathematical curve-fitting gives an approximation based on that particular sample of projects. Is your project like them? In what ways might it be similar to the central measures of that population, and in what ways might it be an outlier?

Performing a Spike

You can also purchase information by running your own experiments. You may not know how long something might take to do if you don't know whether it can be done at all. When you need some information, consider how you could learn that information. Often there's some small but critical bit of info that you need. Articulate what that critical bit is. Devise the most inexpensive way that might possibly give you that information. How much are you willing to spend on that?

This is often called a *spike solution*, or just *spike*, evoking an image of a very slender solution driven through the heart of the problem. I recommend the following procedure for spikes:

1. Articulate the question to be answered. If it's vague, it's hard to tell whether you've answered it or not.

2. Decide how long you're willing to work on it. Setting a budget is important to prevent a research project that dwarfs the importance of the question.

3. Work on a solution until either the question is answered or the time budget has been expended. If you still don't have your answer, start over and thinking about it again. Is it worth spending a little more? Would it likely be more fruitful to try a different approach? Is there a way to bypass the need for this answer, at least, for now?

A spike is a handy tool for answering many questions:

- Can this library do the job we need?
- Can we develop an algorithm to do the job we need?
- Can we calculate this to the needed precision?
- If we have a data stream that looks like *this*, can we process it to extract *that* information?
- If we offer users a way to do *something*, will they be interested in it?

You can also admit what you don't know, and perhaps can't know, given your current circumstances. It's also worth knowing why you can't know. That also gives you ideas about how you could go about learning what you would need to know. It can also give you credibility over people who are claiming to know the unknowable.[2]

How soon do you need to turn this into numerical information? If it's a small part of the whole, it's not likely to have a big impact. There's enough noise in the process of estimation that this unknown may be unnoticeable. When you get to the point where it matters, perhaps you'll have the information you need to estimate it.

Building a prototype is similar, though typically larger. Sometimes people estimate a prototype like they do a production project. Given the uncertainty that's leading you to explore, I recommend setting a budget and seeing what value you can produce within that budget. You retain the option to explicitly add to that budget if it seems worthwhile.

Stepping Back for a Broader View

Software development estimation routinely depends on comparison to past experience, either your own or someone else's experience that has been documented. Either way, the experience won't be a direct comparison, because no two software development projects are exactly alike. There's no need to produce the exact same system and, if you were to do that, it would be a different experience because it would be informed by having done it before. There are too many variables to expect an exact match, but there is plenty of opportunity for success if you have reasonable expectations about accuracy and precision.

Some questions you might consider as you're making such a comparison include:

- What aspects of this system are the same as the reference experience? What aspects are different?

- How does the context of this system resemble the context of my past experience? How does it differ?

- What is similar to past experience about how we're going to develop this system? What is different?

---

2.   http://dannorth.net/2013/08/08/blink-estimation/

• How sure am I of the details of the past experience that I'm using for reference? What might be missing or misremembered?

Don't forget that these initial estimates are still estimates. They can be used to make decisions, but don't trust them too far. For accuracy, you'll want to track your progress and compare it to your initial estimate. In order to do that, you'll need to decompose the work into smaller chunks, even if you were able to come up with a total estimate without doing so.

There's a number of ways to split up the work, and they have different advantages and disadvantages. In the next chapter, let's look at the alternatives and the potential gotchas when decomposing the work.

Now It's Your Turn

1. Think of your current project. What projects in your past, or your organization's past, seem similar to it? Is this one larger or smaller? How much larger or smaller?

2. Where could you find information about the actual time and effort required for your reference project? In what ways might that information be incomplete or misleading?

3. Look back at Aspects to Compare, on page 34. What aspects of this project are significantly different from the reference you have in mind?

CHAPTER 3

Decomposition for Estimation

As we've seen, most approaches to estimation involve breaking the work down into smaller chunks and estimating the chunks. Not only does this make it easier to get a chunk of work for estimating completely in your head at one time, but it's more flexible when you change plans and want to replace some planned work with something else.

Not all approaches to decomposition are the same, however. Which way should we split it? How small should the pieces be? Should they all be the same size? What do we do if we don't know how to make them the same size? These are some of the issues we'll explore in this chapter. In addition, there are some traps for the unwary, which we'll explore in Decomposition Gotchas, on page 64.

The way you approach decomposition can affect not only your estimates, but also your ability to validate your estimates. Decomposition for estimation can also bleed through to the work itself; it's likely you'll use the same decomposition you used for estimating when planning the work. And if you've put more effort into planning than the current needs warrant, you'll find it more difficult to change those plans when it becomes apparent they're obsolete.

Let's look at some different ways to decompose the anticipated work for estimation. After you've decided how to divide the work, then you can consider how much to do so.

Which Way to Slice?

I've often pondered the different ways chicken is prepared in European recipes versus Chinese ones. European cooks tend to separate the chicken at the joints. This gives us well-defined, identifiable and named pieces of chicken: this is the thigh and this is the leg. In Chinese cuisine, the cooks tend to chop the chicken in the middle of the long bones rather than between them. I used to think this was "wrong," but I now see some advantages to doing it that way. This opens access to the marrow and takes away the temptation to remove connective tissue in the joints. These are two things that can add flavor to stewed chicken. And with a sturdy, sharp knife, chopping the chicken at arbitrary points can be done very rapidly. I've come to the conclusion that both approaches have value and both have advantages and disadvantages. You can choose which way you want to work based on habit or based on how those advantages and disadvantages work for your needs.

The same situation applies to software development. There are ways to divide the work that gives you recognizable pieces that are easy to name. And there are ways that provide a bit more value.

There's More Than One Way to Cut a Chicken
Blaise walked into the project manager's office. "You asked me to look at the code and documentation of the old call center. I've gotten through it at a high level."

Marion replied, "Great, what have you found?"

"There are a couple of major components: an automated call distributor or ACD to forward calls to an appropriate customer service representative, and an Interactive Voice Response system or IVR to let the computer chat with the caller before transferring them to a human. Then there are a handful of interface components to connect to the phone company, the company's PBX internal phone system, the CRM customer relationship database, and the CSR's screen. These can logically be clumped into two efforts, one for the phone systems and one that's customer centric. That and the two major components give us four components to specify and estimate."

"Blaise, those components make sense, but I don't want to implement component by component," Marion replied, "nor estimate by component. I've found it too risky. Let's talk with Ryan and the customer service representatives to find out how they actually use the current system. I'm sure we'll need a part of each component for their first Use Case."

Decomposing by Phase

When working in a linear phased, or waterfall, approach, it is common to decompose into development phases and estimate those.

"We'll spend a month on the *System Requirements* and another month on the *Software Requirements*. Then, we'll hand those to the Solution Analysts who'll have a month for the *Analysis Phase*. They'll give it to the Software Architects who'll have a month for *Program Design*. That's four months, so we'll give the programmers eight months for *Coding* and the Testers two months *Testing*. Just to be on the safe side, we'll add another two months for remediation of any problems the Testers might find."

The advantage of decomposing by phase is that, when you're working according to a phased software development lifecycle, you've already got the phases laid out for you. And they're the same from project to project. You can take the estimation from your previous project and edit it for this one. Most likely you'll keep some phases the same, and multiply others by a factor representing your hunch of relative complexity. You'll quickly check off the box for "Rough Order of Magnitude Estimation Document."

The disadvantage is that it will be a long time before you can test the accuracy of that estimate. The early planning and design phases typically just produce documents, so it can be rather difficult to determine how "done" they are. That makes it temptingly easy to declare them "done" when the estimated time allotment has expired. When programming and testing are treated as separate phases, the same strategy is casually applied, too often, to programming, too. By the end of the coding phase, the program has to look like it works to the programmer and casual observers. This is admittedly harder than producing a document, but are we really sure that it's *done* in the time allotted in the plan?

Only testing, coming at the end of the chain, is sure to exceed its estimated time allotment. That's where the mistakes and holes in the programming phase are discovered. That's where it may be found that the programmers accurately implemented an unsuccessful design. That's where omissions and inaccuracies in the Requirements and Analysis phases are discovered. Testing has to absorb all the rework in planning, design, and programming that has gone unnoticed in the interest of "meeting the estimates."

If a phase has errors and omissions, can it really be said to be *done*, even if we stop working on it after the estimated period of time? It can look like our estimate was accurate, but we can't verify that until later, when we find out whether or not it was satisfactorily completed. Estimates that can't be compared to actuals until the end are a huge risk. If there's no way to be sure that an isolated part of the work is truly done, then there's no way to validate the estimates along the way. We'll explore this ongoing validation in more detail in Chapter 8, Planning for Incorrect Predictions, on page 163.

Decomposing by Implementation

Estimating component by component is another common way of dividing up the work. The architect draws up a diagram showing named components–Billing, Advertising, Catalog, Order Entry, Warehouse Picking, Shipping, and some possible "framework" elements to connect them, such as an Enterprise Service Bus. Or it could be as simple as Front End (user interface), Back End (business logic), and Database (data persistence). Whatever the choices, these are the components that are presumed will result in the desired functionality.

Then, for each of the components, people think about what functionality belongs to that component, and estimate based on that analysis. There are some advantages to this, as the time to build out the database schema is roughly correlated to the number of tables needed. The problem is that this presumed need is not tested by actual use by the client code. What if actual use requires a different schema? That becomes unestimated rework.

Working component by component is also a common way of approaching implementation, assigning a team or even an individual to be expert on each component. Since the developers have a pretty good idea of when a component is done, they have some idea of how accurately the estimates are panning out. Unfortunately, that idea of "done" often does not include integration with other components. There are seams between them where undoneness can lie hidden. This can spring some nasty surprises when integration finally happens.

Correctness can also be hard to judge. If we say the database schema is finished, what does that mean? Does it mean it looks complete now? Does it mean it won't need any changes in the future? How do we tell a database schema is correct until we use it for the intended purpose? The value of a component mostly lies in its use by client components. Until that use happens, we can't be sure that the component is meeting the needs of its clients.

Often the development of components is staged so that a component that depends on another is developed after the dependency. This reduces the apparent need for collaboration. If the client component is developed by a different team at a different time, though, then problems discovered in the earlier developed component require that component's team to revisit it, causing delays in this project and likely in whatever else they were working on. Or, the team developing the client component could possibly create their own workaround, which would be a delay for them *plus* a degradation of the intended architecture.

The risks of major problems with these first two approaches always leads me to prefer the third.

Decomposing by Functionality

Rather than dividing the work by the development activities being performed, or the software architectural components used, you can divide it by the functionality being implemented. This is called a *functional slice* both because it's thin and because it cuts through the different components of the system. It even tends to cut through the different development activities if you're practicing evolutionary design.

What's a functional slice? It's a chunk of work defined by what it does rather than how it's built. "Getting to the train station" indicates functionality. It doesn't mention the "how" of driving a car or any alternate means. It concentrates on the "what" of the desired outcome. You could satisfy "getting to the train station" with a low-budget solution like walking, and then replace that strategy later when higher performance was required.

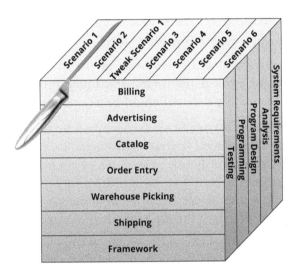

Estimating by functional slices has a lot of advantages. First, these slices are things that those asking for the software can understand. They can verify whether they're done or not by trying out the system. The functionality cuts through the component boundaries, ensuring that they've been integrated. There's still opportunity for unnoticed failures to meet performance or other -ility goals. And if the limits of the functionality are not well understood, it's likely that the scope will grow a bit. Overall, though, working by functional slices has the least risk of all the ways I know to decompose the scope of work.

User Stories

In agile software development, when people think of functional slices, they often think of User Stories. This is a term and technique originating with Extreme Programming. As usage of the term has spread, the understanding of it has become a bit fuzzy.

A User Story is a small slice of functionality that's describable in terms of the user's goals and capabilities. It's so named because it involves an interaction with a system user, either accepting input or providing some observable result, and usually both. In general, a User Story is smaller than a Use Case, which is a more comprehensive set of related interactions. I often think of it as a single path through a Use Case. Each alternate flow would likely make a separate User Story.

Like a Use Case, a User Story describes the system requirements from the point of view of interactions and responses. When the system does all the things you want it to do—in other words, all of the User Stories have been implemented—then the system is ostensibly completely functional. It's either that or the list of User Stories was incomplete.

By using User Stories to define the system by the things it needs to do, you can also estimate the work using them. How much time and effort would it take to add this User Story's increment of functionality to the system?

Some people think that a User Story is described by the Connextra format: "As a <role> I can <capability>, so that <some benefit>." This, however, is just the title of a story, and a wordy title at that. It's worth noting that the originators of this format went back to using short titles very quickly, once they had reminded themselves to consider the benefits to the user. The heart of a User Story is a conversation telling the story about the user's needs.

> "Say that Joe has been handling the Parsnip Industries account, but Joe is going on a two-month cruise with his wife to celebrate their twenty-fifth wedding anniversary. While he's gone, Joe wants to delegate the Parsnip Industries work to his colleague, Sue. With regard to that account, Sue should be able to do everything that Joe can do, enter new orders, expedite existing orders, update orders, and so on. Upon his return, Joe wants to take charge of the Parsnip Industries account again. Everything that Sue had done in his stead should be visible to Joe, and he should be able to perform operations on these items just as if he'd entered them himself."

Notice that there is quite a bit of functionality here. It's not a single interaction with the system. This is not a small story.

Big and Small Stories

Some people call this a feature, as "Delegate an account" might be the name of something you would put in the advertising brochure. Some people call such stories "epics" because of their size, but they're not as grand and poetic as that might suggest. Instead, the term "epic" suggests that the story is intended to be further split before implementation. There's no universal naming convention for big stories, so I often just call them that, *Big Stories*.

While this story is large for implementation, it might be just the right size for estimating in the moderately long term. For implementation, split your stories into slices that can be implemented in two days or less. This will let you see the progress. Larger stories seem to disappear into a black hole, and you can't tell if they're stalled or not.

This story might be split into a number of smaller stories like the following:

- An account can be delegated.
- A delegated account can be undelegated.
- A delegatee can enter orders on an account belonging to the delegator.
- A delegatee can update orders entered by the delegator.
- A returned delegator can update orders entered by the delegatee.
- ...

For each of these story splits, explicit acceptance criteria should indicate when that User Story has been satisfactorily completed. This acceptance criteria should be illustrated with example scenarios that can be verified. Ultimately this can get quite detailed. That's not surprising, given the detailed nature of telling a computer what we want it to do.

Each of the small story splits can be estimated. In fact, that's the level that most people expect to estimate, using Story Points, on page xii and Planning Poker, on page xiii. It's my experience that estimating such small stories generally takes more time and effort than it's worth. For short-term estimates, such as how much work a team can accomplish in the next two weeks, just count the stories. If you've kept track of how many stories the team accomplished in the last two weeks, that's probably a close enough estimate, and requires less work. (See Counting Stories, on page xiii.)

For longer-term estimates, I don't recommend going down to the small story level. That is also a lot of work, and things can change between now and when you go to implement those stories. Plus, it results in A Large Number of Small Parts, on page 57 which has its own challenges.

Completing User Stories

Implemented User Stories can provide value even when the full list of User Stories has not been completed. For the most part, User Stories can be added to the system in any order that makes sense at the time of implementation. Usually this order is determined by priority of value or minimizing risk.

Necessary system support is built as needed by the story. This adds another ordering priority–simplest first. The ability to create usable functionality in an arbitrary order makes User Stories a great building block for incremental and iterative development.

One of the big advantages of tracking progress by User Stories is that, as functional slices, you can test to verify that they're completed. User Stories are determined to be implemented when all of the example scenarios are verified. Given that they're small and rather unambiguous, User Stories are excellent for estimating short-term milestones and tracking progress during development.

Decomposition Decisions

Deciding which way to slice the work for decomposition is only the first step. There are a number of other choices you must make when estimating by decomposition. Again, you can make your choices by habit or by examining how the choices fit your needs.

One of the most obvious choices is how far you go in decomposing the work for estimation. You need to decide how far to slice it. Do you make a detailed list of items or just a few major categories? And how much to slice it now versus how much later.

Finding the Big Picture Functional Requirements

Sage, a senior customer service representative, groused, "I hope this meeting doesn't take too long. I don't want it to affect my performance numbers."

"Don't worry, Sage. I've got you covered. I'll put a special note in the monthly report," Tracy, the Manager of Analytics replied. "Besides, Ryan really wants this done right. If the Director of Customer Service thinks it's important, it won't be held against you."

Marion, the IT project manager jumped in. "We'll try to take as little of your time as possible, but we really need your expertise to do this right. Let's start with the primary needs. Call centers can work in lots of ways, but how do we use our call center at Empire Enterprises? What is your typical day like?"

"Mostly I and the other reps get calls routed through our headsets. We pull up the CRM system data for that customer, so we know what they've got and any history to their issue. We also use that to record the important details of this call. If we can answer their questions, we do that and close the issue. Some issues are more complicated, though."

"How does the system know which rep gets which call?" Blaise asked.

"Mostly by the phone number that was called. We have different customer service phone numbers for different divisions of the company. Most reps are only familiar with one division."

...

After Blaise and Marion got the big-picture view of how the system works from the customer service representative point of view, Sage went back to work and they talked with Tracy about the metrics gathering. They didn't go into great detail, just enough to understand the major needs and a little bit of background on why they were important. The details could come later.

What would happen if they continued digging into those details right now?

A Large Number of Small Parts

If Blaise and Marion continued digging into the details of the requirements they'd discovered, they'd probably end up with a large number of small parts. People have a tendency to want to do the things they're doing completely. That's understandable, but maybe not all at once.

An advantage in estimating small pieces of work is that these pieces are more easily comprehended. Because they are small and easier to comprehend, they are easier to estimate. Being small, they are also more likely to be similar to something we've done before, and that makes them easier to estimate as well.

And, when you add all the estimates up, you'll get a number with higher precision because of the large number of pieces. That may not make it more accurate, but it's generally more impressive. This is often called the Precision Bias or Numeracy Bias, which inclines people to give more trust than they would to round numbers. It "seems scientific." (See Cognitive Biases, on page 72.)

Seriously, round your results when you add up your small estimates. There is no way you're going to have three digits of precision given the nature of the input numbers. That extra numerical precision is just noise. Filter it out.

The approach of breaking everything down to small parts, specifically estimating long-term work decomposed into User Stories (see User Stories, on page 53), is the most familiar to most Scrum teams because it's the approach described in Mike Cohn's *Agile Estimating and Planning [Coh05]*. Mike got this idea from Kent Beck's approach on the original Extreme Programming project, the Chrysler Comprehensive Compensation (C3) project. I asked Kent Beck about this, and he recollected that they started with a backlog of about 18 months' worth of stories, but I didn't think to ask him how big these stories were. He didn't remember, after 20 years, how much churn there was in that backlog. Based on my observations of a number of companies, I would recommend not breaking down that much work to the detailed story level all at once. See Decomposing into an Unmanageable Number of Pieces, on page 66 for more on this.

A Small Number of Large Parts

The other end of the scale is to break the planned work down into a small number of large parts. This reduces the amount of work at the start of the project, especially that time-consuming work of chasing down all the details. It's good to defer as much of the detail until later, when you know more, as you can.

It's quite possible you can get a gut-level feel for how big these large parts might be, especially if you're not too concerned about high precision. If you don't have a comparison of equal size, you might compare with something that seems similar, but smaller. Then you can imagine how many of these smaller items would fit into this one big one.

The Achilles heel of this approach is, of course, that the large parts may be just as hard to estimate as the whole. Large chunks of work are hard to get your head around to get a feel for how large or complicated they are. Large chunks are fuzzier in definition, so it may be difficult to tell with certainty whether something is part of that chunk or belongs elsewhere. This makes it difficult to declare any of these chunks completely done.

It's also harder to find good analogs for the large parts in your past experience. Unless you've been doing very similar projects, as the size of the parts you're comparing goes up, the probability of having similar experience goes down.

It may seem like you're caught between a rock and a hard place with small parts that are too numerous and large parts that are too hard to estimate. If you're stuck on this, be patient. We'll look at a middle ground shortly, in Multi-Level Decomposition, on page 62.

Affinity Estimation

Sometimes it's hard to give an estimate to each of the decomposed parts. Or, if it's not hard, it's tedious. When you've got a large number of parts to estimate, comparing each of them to past data can be a lot of work. You can do this work more efficiently if you first "bucket" them into rough sizes. Often people use what they call T-shirt sizes—small, medium, large, extra-large. Then, you can compare the typical item in each bucket with past experience, and estimate all the items in that bucket to be roughly similar.

Sorting the Big Call Center Stories

Marion and Blaise sat down with their notes from their meeting with Sage and Tracy. Marion put the list of major functional needs they had identified on the table.

- Call Routing
    - Routing based on number the customer dialed
    - Routing based on continuity of an ongoing issue
    - Routing based on representative availability
    - Balancing the workload between reps
- CRM Interface
    - Display customer by service rep search
    - Display customer based on caller ID
    - Display customer based on info collected by IVR
    - Enter new data during call
- Analytics
    - Monitoring the System

        One of the current issues is that "once or twice a week there's a 10–15 minute gap with no calls at all." To debug that, we need to longitudinally monitor each call—when it came in, when it was routed, when an agent picked it up, when they finished with it.

    - Monitoring Customer Satisfaction
        - How quickly are issues resolved? Calendar time, number of calls, call minutes.
        - Time in IVR? Time between IVR and talking with a human.
        - How many reopened issues?
    - Monitoring Agent Performance
        - # of issues resolved
        - # of calls per issue
        - # of issues remaining open

Blaise looked at the list. "There's probably a missing story for reporting on analytics, but most of the analytics items look about the same size. The outlier is 'Monitoring the System.' That cuts across a lot of things. Much of the details will be included in other analytics stories, but the big unknown is how to trace one customer interaction across different components implemented with different third-party frameworks."

They studied the list some more. "Interfacing to the CRM system should be about the same for searching and for updating. Interfacing to the Caller ID and IVR systems add a little, but if we've already built a CRM interface for searching, that should be a wash. I'd call all of these about the same size."

Blaise went on. "Call routing maintaining continuity with a given rep for an ongoing issue is going to have lots of little but important details. I'd say that's bigger than the others in Call Routing."

"What about across the categories?" Marion asked.

"Without including the reporting, the analytics stories seem the smallest. Except for 'Monitoring the System,' of course. I'm not ready to give that a size. The CRM stories and the smaller stories in Call Routing seem roughly the same size, but bigger than the analytics stories. Let's call those 'medium' sized. Then 'routing based on continuity' can be a 'large.' That gives us four piles: 'small,' 'medium,' 'large,' and 'don't know.' That was quick! It was easier than I thought it would be."

How many buckets do you need? And what if you start at the wrong place? If you say "this" is a medium, then you may find that you need more buckets on one side or the other.

Sometimes it's easier to sort things into unnamed buckets and see how many you need. Is this item bigger than the ones in that bucket but smaller than the ones in the next? Let's put a bucket between them. When you're done, let's look at where the gaps in size seem to be. Some gaps between buckets will seem smaller than others. Do the items in this bucket seem only slightly larger than the items in that bucket? Consider combining the contents of both into one bucket.

Grouping in this manner is called *affinity estimation* and is useful for reducing the complexity of the job. Most of the time, people find that the items seem to naturally fall into groups. One of those groups might be labeled "I have no idea." That's OK. There's advice on dealing with the unknown in Estimating the Unknown, on page 43.

Ordering the Parts

When you're estimating how long it takes to drive somewhere, the road constricts what can happen first and what can follow after that. The decomposed parts are almost certainly various stretches of road. Geography limits the order in which you can travel those roads.

When you're estimating software development, you have a wide range of choices about the order in which you do things. The way you decompose the whole into parts is almost entirely up to your own ability to conceptualize it. This freedom comes with a cost. Some orders may be harder and therefore more expensive than others. Other times, there's an initial cost to pay for the first of several similar items, but their order doesn't otherwise matter.

- You can add the additional effort to one of these arbitrarily. This can be misleading if someone doesn't notice the relationship between the items and reorders them.

- You can average the additional effort across all the items. This is misleading as it doesn't represent the reality of the cost being paid with the first item.

- You can split out the scaffolding into a separate item. This is risky, as its relationship to the items might get overlooked. It's not generally valuable, or perhaps testable, on its own. It needs to be paired with one of the User Stories.

All of these require special attention to avoid fooling people, but the consequences are generally low. Any of them can work, with a little care.

The assumed order of the identified parts can have an effect on the riskiness of the estimation. Working by functional slices, as discussed in Which Way to Slice?, on page 49, lets us judge how finished a work item is, reducing the risk of unnoticed incompleteness. There are differences, though, in how people form functional slices. Some people are satisfied if there is some measurable output. Using this definition, being able to test a method in a test harness counts as measurable output. At the other end of the spectrum is output that is being used. If people are using the functionality for their daily work, they are likely to notice most forms of incomplete implementation.

Build what Alistair Cockburn calls a "Walking Skeleton." (*Crystal Clear: A Human-Powered Methodology for Small Teams [Coc04]*)[1] This gives a framework supporting a subset of usage from inputs to outputs. Elaborations can be hung on this framework to expand the range of usage. If there is a hard stop deadline, then prioritization of the most common and most critical use cases can reduce the risks of missing it. You can stop there and adjust the requirements to match what has been built.

This may seem like a cheat, but it's not. It's sometimes true that delivery is more important than being full-featured. Some of the requested features may be speculative to handle situations that have never arisen. Some situations may be so rare that it's more cost effective to handle them manually than to automate them. A design that is grown from a Walking Skeleton should already have the means to detect and enable manually adjustment of situations that cannot yet be handled automatically. These are capabilities worth having in the delivered product.

---

1. Also see https://web.archive.org/web/20171205050356/http://alistair.cockburn.us/Walking+skeleton

Starting Your Walking Skeleton

As a rule of thumb, it's best to start with the output of the system. Even if the system inputs are hardwired and it's only suitable for one situation, you can use it in that situation to get feedback, as well as potential business value, earlier.

If you're replacing a legacy system, whether automated or paper, it's easier to drive the fledgling new system from some point within the flow of the old system than it is the other way around. Then, work your way back toward the inputs. You'll have some flexibility and can decide whether it's better to elaborate the later stages, or continue to replace legacy functionality with the new skeleton.

Multi-Level Decomposition

When the small number of large parts leaves me with parts still too big to estimate, I often take the first (in development order) of those parts and break it down again.

Can you estimate the first item? If not, you can decompose that first item in a similar fashion. Now you've got smaller, more easily estimated items. If it's still too big, you can repeat this strategy.

In extreme cases you might need to go to a third level of detail, but realize that each time you're increasing your uncertainty. That's to be expected. The longer the time horizon, the more uncertain you are. You don't want to forget about that uncertainty, though, lest you fool yourself.

I don't think I've ever gone beyond three levels of doing this—but I could if it helps.

Breaking It down Another Level

"I know what we're missing," Blaise said. "A simple end-to-end Walking Skeleton. Before we route a call based on the number dialed, let's support a single customer service rep and route any call to them. Before we build a CRM customer search screen, let's support only a single customer and pull them up automatically. This will connect the major pieces and make sure they're integrated from the start. Then we can add all the other features to this basic framework."

"What size would that be?" Marion asked.

"I'd say another 'medium.' It's got some minor unknowns about the integration points, but that's the point of it. If it weren't for those, it would be tiny."

"Let's break it down."

"That seems pretty simple. We need to…

• recognize the call,

- forward it to a single CS rep station,

- and display a customer on the CRM system.

I think that's sufficient for now."

Once you get something small enough to estimate, then you can use relative comparisons and affinity grouping to estimate the other large parts that are not broken down in detail. This leaves you with a fairly high level of uncertainty, but does provide ballpark figures. And as you complete the early work, you can recalibrate your estimate with your actuals so far.

You can then extrapolate from that first item, both from its estimate and, later, from its actual. You will have built a really long lever when you do this. A small variation in the initial measurement makes large variations in the expected total. Hold this expectation loosely and check it along the way.

Rule of Thumb: How Many Parts?

 For longer term estimates (e.g., longer than a few months), decompose into a half-dozen to three dozen parts, not hundreds. Less than a half-dozen gives too little help. It requires you to do a major amount of the work before you have any information. Also, the fewer the parts, the less they naturally fall into similar sizes. More than three dozen requires too much detail. Unless you've done something quite similar and kept good notes of that experience, it will be a major effort to develop the list and will become more likely that you've neglected items. It's best if the decomposed parts seem roughly similar in size, less than an order of magnitude difference. If you can't do this, you can't—but trust the results accordingly.

Comparing Big Items with Small Ones

How big is that building? How big is that city? You could estimate both in terms of the number of people they could hold. If you estimated the capacity of all the buildings in the city and added them up, you'll get quite a different answer than your direct estimate for the city. In part, that's because the capacity for cities and buildings have somewhat different meanings, and partly because we think of cities and buildings differently, which is reflected in our estimates.

Frequently, I see people trying to estimate large chunks of vaguely defined functionality, epics or features, using an extension of the same scale they use to estimate small slices of more explicitly defined User Stories. They may use the numbers 1, 2, 3, 5, 8, 13, 20 for the small slices and 100, 200, 300, 500, 800, 1300, 2000 for the large chunks to keep them separate. The temptation is great to perform simple arithmetic to group a number of small slices into one large chunk, or break a large one into a number of small slices. There are even agile project management tools that do this automatically, with no way to override it. This hides the uncertainty in your estimates and story slicing.

Life is not that simple. If you do this, you will surely fool yourself. Estimate stories of different granularity separately. Use different scales so others don't get confused. For large items, you might use T-shirt sizes—small, medium, large, extra-large. Or use something unusual to emphasize the imprecision. I've heard of using animals—rat, cat, dog, pig, cow. The astute reader will notice that, in unusual cases, there are overlaps in the sizes of these animal categories. You're likely to find similar overlap in your story sizes. Certainly no one will assume that two cats equals one dog.

How many explicitly defined slices fit into one dog? That's an estimate. You can decompose the dog-sized chunk of work and count the smaller pieces. Or, if you prefer, you can estimate the smaller pieces and add up those estimates. Either of those is a starting point.

When you implement those smaller pieces, you get a chance to see what you got wrong. Some people like to compare estimates to actuals. If you do that, there's a temptation to relate the small scale to the large scale using these actuals instead of the estimates. Resist that temptation. At the times you need the relation between items on the small scale and items on the large scale, you'll only have estimates available.

You can, however, check the aggregate time for all the smaller pieces to get one data point on how long a dog-sized chunk of work takes. And, if you pay attention as you go, you can count up all the small slices that were discovered while you implemented the functionality. This gives you a feel for how much work is still invisible when you're considering future large chunks of work.

Decomposition Gotchas

The law of large numbers says that random errors tend to cancel each other out. Beware, however, of errors that are not random. If the errors are an integral part about how you're doing the work, they are more likely to reinforce each other than to cancel out. If you're adding up a large number of small estimates and the errors all tend in the same direction, the resulting error will be large. This can catch you by surprise if you don't consider the systematic errors that may exist in your estimation process.

Here are some common causes of accumulating errors. Watch out for them. As the proverbial "they" say, "forewarned is forearmed."

Making Consistent Size Errors

You may consistently imagine the pieces as larger or smaller than they are. When you estimate a lot of small pieces, you don't expect to get each estimate "right." It's perfectly fine that you've estimated two tasks at 3 hours each, but one takes 2 hours and the other 4. The errors cancel out and your overall estimate is useful to you.

If you have a consistent bias in your estimation, though, the errors add up and your overall estimate is likely further off than if you'd estimated the large chunk as a whole. In software development, the empirical evidence is that most developers are optimists. They underestimate much more often than they overestimate. That's rather a shame, because underestimations are less likely to be challenged, and cause us more disappointment down the road, than overestimations.

As described in Calibrating to Unknown Context, on page 44, once we get started, we can easily adjust our expectations by calibrating them with actual results. This might be too late for some people, who might have built a rigid plan on the early uncalibrated estimates. It's good enough for those who are flexible enough to accommodate reality.

Most of the time, you'd like your errors to cancel out, so your result is still accurate even if individual estimates are wrong. Sometimes, however, you're trying to avoid some calamity. If you estimate such that all the errors are intentionally in the direction of that calamity, you should be safe should the result still be in the safe zone. This reduces risk at the cost of reduced accuracy. (See Danger Bearings, on page 167.)

Overlooking the Space between the Pieces

One of the typical ways to consistently underestimate the time required for a piece of work is to focus on the core of the work and neglect the periphery. Software developers think about the programming part. They may not consider the work to get their local environment ready to do the programming, setting aside any partial work and updating with the appropriate source code and libraries. They may neglect the time it takes to read the code to understand the details of the needed change. They may forget the time it takes to verify that the change is correct, and that it hasn't broken existing functionality or introduced any new problems.

> Years ago, I had a project lead who asked me to estimate how long it would take to fix a reported bug in some code written by a colleague who'd since moved to a different project. I looked at the bug report and made a list of the changes I would have to make. Then I estimated how long it would take to edit, compile, and verify each of those changes. I handed this annotated list to the project lead. He took one look at it and said, "You can't do any task in 10 minutes. It will take you longer than that to checkout the code, find the place to change, and check it in again. Never estimate a programming task at under 30 minutes." That's when I realized that I was only estimating part of the required work, the programming part on which I was focused, not the necessary parts that enabled the programming. I was also leaving out the context switching from one item to another.

Overlooking Some of the Small Pieces

When you build the list of pieces of work, you try to include every task that's required to accomplish our goals. That's a hard job, of course. When you're doing the work, as you go to make one change you realize "Oh, that's connected to this; I need to change it, too." The work itself prompts us to notice related tasks. When you're just listing them, those related tasks may be left off the list. This almost certainly leads to underestimation.

I once worked for a company where those estimating the work for bids neglected to consider the work to migrate the data from the customer's old system to the new. This happened for two or three bids in a row before any of the projects got far enough along to realize this omission. Since the price for the work had been heavily dependent on the estimates, this was a major blow to the profitability of those projects.

Of course, you might also add tasks that aren't really necessary, and then overestimate. "We need a method to handle negative input values; oh, I see it already handles those." This happens much less frequently, in my experience.

Decomposing into an Unmanageable Number of Pieces

The whole may be so big that it takes a huge number of small pieces. When you break your work down into a large number of pieces, the decomposition itself is a lot of work. It's also subject to a lot of error, as it's depending on pretty detailed understanding of future work.

How Many Stories Can It Be?

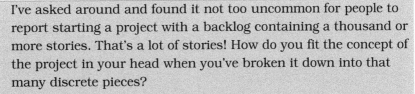

I've asked around and found it not too uncommon for people to report starting a project with a backlog containing a thousand or more stories. That's a lot of stories! How do you fit the concept of the project in your head when you've broken it down into that many discrete pieces?

This is an all-too-typical example of trying to get the requirements complete before starting the project. Sometimes that drive for completeness comes from a vain attempt to calculate a high-precision estimate of how much effort it will take. Striving for certainty, people spend an inordinate effort to capture all the details at the start.

Take, for example, the frequently recommended practice of breaking a planned release into User Stories for estimation. A User Story is a small slice of functionality that adds "one thing" to the system being developed. It has observable completion criteria, so you can tell when it's done. It is a useful tool for getting things done on a development project. Getting one baby step done before going on to the next acts like a ratchet, moving us forward and preventing us from slipping backward. In order to act like a ratchet, the stories need to be pretty small—something we can accomplish in a short period of time before we go to accomplish the next small thing. As a rule of thumb, teams should size User Stories such that they take a day or two of calendar time to accomplish. It doesn't matter how many team members might be working on the story to get it done in that time. And it's alright if the stories are smaller. When I'm working by myself, I generally prefer them smaller.

If a three-month (13 weeks of 5 days) release is broken into User Stories that take two team-days each, then that's about 32 stories. That's a lot of stories, and it's even more if multiple stories are in progress simultaneously, or if some of the stories are smaller. If half the team gets involved in each story, and half of the stories are only one day, then our story count balloons to 96. Imagine the team churning through a list of 96 stories at the start of the project so that they can know what fits into three months, or that they can know how long it will take to do what they want. Sounds like a lot of effort, doesn't it? (And this is for a small project.)

As they expend that effort, they learn a lot of details about those stories. We'll want to record what they learn so they don't have to relearn it later. That will take more effort, especially to record it in a way that won't be misinterpreted later.

How Much Work Could It Be?

How hard is it to create a backlog of a couple thousand "story-sized" and bigger items? In one case, I'm told it took a few dozen people three months to list them all. They were deriving them from a legacy system that was to be retired, as well as asking subject matter experts in the company. Unfortunately, nobody seemed to know why some of the legacy functionality was in the system.

As they learn the details, some of these details build on details they've learned or decided before. But since they've just learned them in a short time, they often forget some. It takes time for learning to "soak in." The prior thoughts are likely to be stronger, asserting themselves in later decisions. So far, in the hypothetical scenario, they've only talked about the system. They haven't actually built anything with which they can interact. That's a clue that some of the details they've "learned" are certainly wrong, but they don't know which ones, yet. As they build the system and interact with it, they'll learn more, and they'll learn more deeply. Do they abandon the early pre-start learning, or do they try to maintain it, fixing it where it's incorrect and incorporating new things they've learned? Either represents extra work.

What Happens to These Stories?

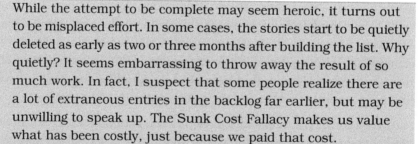

While the attempt to be complete may seem heroic, it turns out to be misplaced effort. In some cases, the stories start to be quietly deleted as early as two or three months after building the list. Why quietly? It seems embarrassing to throw away the result of so much work. In fact, I suspect that some people realize there are a lot of extraneous entries in the backlog far earlier, but may be unwilling to speak up. The Sunk Cost Fallacy makes us value what has been costly, just because we paid that cost.

Adding insult to injury, in all the cases I've heard of people developing a "complete backlog" at the beginning of a project, there was always new information uncovered later. That complete backlog continued to grow over time, in spite of having unneeded items included.

I frequently hear or read about people suggesting the use of User Stories for relatively long-range planning. Sometimes they mean something as short as a release in a few months. Sometimes they're talking about multiple releases over a year or two. In all of these cases, they're talking about breaking down the work to be done into small slices, so that they can better measure it's perceived size for predicting the future. This is a great deal of planning up-front, when people know the least about the work they need to do.

All in all, creating a long product backlog of User Stories is very reminiscent of creating a detailed Work Breakdown Structure at the start of the project. It starts to separate the work into distinct phases that are executed in a linear fashion. The details of User Stories are typically oriented more in functional terms than construction terms, but it's still a difficult and error-prone way of defining the work. It does, of course, let us come up with numerical estimates.

Making the Whole Look Larger

What is the length of the coastline of Great Britain? It depends on the length of your measuring stick. Large measuring sticks skip over the nuances. The smaller the unit of measurement—that is, the closer you look—the larger the length of the coastline. This is known as the *Coastline Paradox*. Before you know it, you're counting the grains of sand on the perimeter.

Estimation is Fractal

"It turns out that *estimation is fractal.* The more fine-grained you break down the requirements, the more 'edges' you will discover. This means that the more detailed your estimate, the more the total will tend towards infinity, simply due to rounding errors and the fear factors that we multiply into fine grained estimates."

– Dan North[2]

Measuring the size of software development follows a similar pattern. The deeper you look at it, the more you discover and the larger the work appears to us. The deeper you look into requirements, the more you discover and the more details you want to specify, making the work demonstrably larger. More features always seems better than fewer when looking at things in isolation where there's no counterbalancing tendency to keep it in check.

Losing Focus

When you decompose your big picture into lots of tiny details, you lose sight of the original intent. It becomes hard to remember which aspects are essential and which are elaboration. It's even harder to communicate the focus to someone else. They see an undifferentiated sea of details, not a clear picture of the important goals.

---

2. https://dannorth.net/2009/07/01/the-perils-of-estimation/

When you change your focus from "delivering what the customer wants" to "delivering these items on your planned backlog," you make it easier for the project to go astray. The end customer doesn't want a collection of stories. They want a system that works coherently to accomplish the work they need.

Imagining Pieces Not Appropriate for the Implementation

I remember a manager handing me a work breakdown list to estimate so he could create a Gantt chart for the executives. As one of the programmers, I was supposed to estimate how long it would take me to do each of the tasks on the list. Unfortunately, I couldn't even recognize what some of the tasks were. Those that I recognized clearly split the system between a user interface and a database without considering the complexity of anything in between. Where was the interaction between different actions and business rules? It was clear to me that the listed development tasks would not result in the system we wanted to build.

Requirements-Based Decomposition

Think back to the example User Story in User Stories, on page 53, where a user can act on behalf of another user. One naive approach would treat this as a new module of code, mostly duplicating the code for acting on your own behalf. Keeping these modules in sync will be nearly impossible. If you notice this duplication, you might instead modify every place where a user action is implemented, modifying it to accommodate acting on your own behalf or acting on another's behalf. This will touch LOTS of places in the code.

The need for "shotgun surgery" will alert you that there is a concept that needs encapsulation. In fact, the old concept of "user" needs splitting into two concepts, "actor" and "beneficiary."

It's unreasonably optimistic to expect this level of analysis before starting implementation, so estimates based on premature decomposition will likely expect such a naive decomposition based on the stated requirements. If this decomposition becomes the implementation plan, then the implementation will be naive and hard to build and maintain.

Even if you're not starting with a bogus list of programming tasks, the initial design is likely to be the most prosaic and naive implementation. Insight comes from working with the system.

When the details are about the way you're going to build the system, that is, components of the system, you're locking in the design of the system from the very start. If you find that some other arrangement of components works better, that invalidates the entire estimate and plan.

A similar problem happens even if you're the one breaking things down into functional slices. Those slices, when there are a lot of them, become very detailed. They are no longer describing the outcomes that the user wants, but the intended way of delivering those outcomes. When you discover that some of those outcomes are unimportant but others, not previously envisioned, are important, then it's very difficult to change the plan. Which of these stories can you pull out to affect only these outcomes?

You may discover a simpler design that's less work to implement. You may notice that things that don't work as smoothly as you'd like, and redesign to improve that. Or you may live with the existing design, and suffer delays from its inadequacies. Sometimes you get in the middle of the implementation and realize that your design won't quite accomplish the goals. Do you change the goals, or redesign?

There are a lot of scenarios where the system you'd like to write doesn't follow the design of the system you've assumed in your estimate. What happens when you discover that? If you've put a lot of effort into your breakdown, then you're likely to suffer from "Sunk Cost Fallacy" and "Anchoring Bias," (see Cognitive Biases, on page 72) and try to maintain that original breakdown even in the face of evidence that another approach will be superior. It's a natural human reaction to minimize the issues discovered with your initial approach, and magnify the risks of a different one. If this happens, it may be that your estimation technique leads us to build the wrong thing, or build it in a less effective way than you might. If so, it might be more expensive than a bad estimate.

On the other hand, if you don't build the little pieces you used to make the estimate, then how worthwhile is the estimate? Will it be close enough for your purposes, or will it lead you astray? Should you reestimate the new pieces you discover? If so, should you add the cost of reestimating, this time and probable future times, to your estimate?

Stepping Back for a Broader View

Decomposition of the anticipated work is a common approach to making estimation achievable. As with many things, there are pitfalls for the unwary. Being aware of the trade-offs of different variations can help us achieve better

Cognitive Biases

It's a very human tendency to fool ourselves. We often do so in very predictable ways. Some of these ways are so predictable that they've been given names.

Sunk Cost Fallacy This is sometimes known as "throwing good money after bad." The Sunk Cost Fallacy refers to holding onto something, such as a strategy, a plan, or a body of work, because you've already invested in it. Of course, sometimes it's better to cut your losses and abandon what has proved to be a bad investment. It takes a clear head to make that decision.

Anchoring Bias The initial information you have sets the stage, and sets your expectations in the future. The first person who names a price when haggling sets one end of the range of negotiations. The initial plan of action tends to encourage later plans to be variants of the first, not radically different. You can get beyond this influence if you're diligent, but it's easy, and human, to be unduly influenced by early information.

Confirmation Bias When we think we know the answer, it's easy to see proof in the data we examine. We expect the data to confirm our belief, and therefore it does.

Precision Bias Information with more precision, especially if it has a decimal point or a lot of significant digits, may be mistakenly thought to be more accurate or trustworthy. In actuality, much of that precision may be noise.

Numeracy Bias Numeracy Bias indicates a strong reliance on numbers. People often assume that something expressed in numbers is more accurate than a qualitative judgment. The use of numbers gives the illusion of accurate measurement and calculation.

results in our current context. As with most things, there is no single "best practice" that is guaranteed to work everywhere. There are some "pretty good practices" that will often be helpful. A mindful approach is recommended.

As you break the anticipated work down to estimate the pieces, consider the following:

- Am I creating too much detail?

- Am I creating the illusion of knowledge? Could I be overlooking some of the pieces, or the work that joins the pieces?

- Am I making the whole look bigger than it actually is?

- Am I breaking things down in a way that will be useful during implementation? Or will it be a hindrance?

- Am I concentrating too much on the mechanics of estimation and losing focus on my actual goals?

Also, think about what unknowns you still have. How will you get a handle on them? Or do you need to do so? Perhaps they're immaterial at this point in the grand scheme of things.

Think ahead to actually doing the work, too. Is the decomposition useful for planning and scheduling the work? If so, then the decomposition of work will allow us to track progress by which items are done, which are in progress, and which are not started. That's good, since as soon as we get started on a project, people will be wanting to know how things are going.

Now It's Your Turn

1. Think about your last major project, whether complete or current. If you were to break it down into a dozen, plus or minus a half-dozen, functional components, what would those components be? Which one is most central to the intent of the project? Could that component be used prior to developing the others?

2. Now think about how you would break down that first component down into smaller pieces. What's the simplest starting point that would connect input to output to give a Walking Skeleton? How long would it take to implement just that part? If that answer is more than a couple of weeks, how could you simplify that Walking Skeleton to get it to fit within a couple of weeks?

3. What would be the natural first enhancement to your Walking Skeleton to move you toward your goals? How would you decompose that to pieces where six to 18 of them would fit in a two-week period?

CHAPTER 4

Checking Progress

Once a project gets started, people start wondering if things are going well or not. What does "going well" mean and how can you tell? You *could* use a gut feel that things are OK or things are NOT OK. That might work in small startups or experimental pilot projects. It's also an easy way to fool yourself. Startups sometimes find they've spent their funding before they've reached a level of self-sustaining business. In general, successful project managers avoid fooling themselves; that's what makes them successful. So they want some way to verify that the rate of progress is sufficient.

First you need to figure out how to detect and measure progress. We'll look at several approaches before settling on one that seems to work well enough, most of the time. We'll visualize that progress, so you can perhaps spot things that look "a little funny" and not take all the numbers at face value. Your measurement of progress is, itself, an estimate and subject to error.

We'll also consider that you'll likely need to show this progress to others, in ways that make sense to them. The people with fiduciary responsibility for a project have a need to compare the costs with expected value.

It's hard to talk about the progress of a project without someone getting anxious about how fast or slow it's going. Perhaps that person is you. Perhaps you need to talk with that person. In either case, we'll look at how too much focus on speed can sabotage the goals of the project, and even its rate of progress. I'm not suggesting that you ignore the speed of progress, but we'll look at balancing that with other concerns.

Of course, if the project is small enough and you don't have to communicate with other people, you might get by with using your gut feel for progress. You might...if you don't fool yourself.

Casual Sense of Progress

You may remember I had estimated how long it might take me to get to the train station by comparison with other trips (in Everyday Estimation—Another Take, on page 27). This trip, though, is a little more complicated.

I've got a lot of little errands I need to run. And I should get some lunch before catching the train. I wonder how many things I can get done this morning. Let me make a list of what I might accomplish.

I'd better move these things to the top of the list, as they're the most important or most urgent. And I'll reorder some things because of geography. I want to clump errands in the same part of town and I want to end the list with the café near the train station. That way I can get lunch before catching the train.

I'm a quarter of the way through my list in a quarter of the time I have available. Things are looking pretty good. I'm glad of that, because I don't want to miss my train.

A gut feel won't be reassuring enough in most situations encountered in organizations of size. Executives of larger organizations have a fiduciary responsibility to spend money wisely. They may not be able to define what "wisely" means, but they need to show evidence to those with oversight of getting value for the cost.

When satisfied that things are going well, people turn to improvement. "Couldn't thing be going a little better? We want the optimum progress!" This is understandable, but you can get into some dangerous territory. If you're not careful, you can harm your progress in your attempts to optimize.

Getting Things Done

When wondering how things are progressing, one point of reference is the completion of the project. This doesn't give a very detailed view of the progress, though. It's either completed or not.

How's the Project Coming?

Ryan ducked into Sidney's office. "How's it coming with building the new call center? When can my customer service reps start using it?"

It's more useful if you can measure something besides whether the project is completed or not. Don't even rely on a percent complete measurement. Those are notoriously dangerous. When you say it's 50% complete, people will expect the next 50% to take the same amount of time. That's often a bad assumption.

Those most concerned with how things are progressing are the people focused on smoothing the path of the project and meeting the expectations of others. In most organizations, this focus falls onto the shoulders of the person with the role of *Project Manager*. The project manager is the primary point of contact for those outside of the project. When executives want to emphasize their needs, such as business goals and expected timelines, they contact the project manager. The project manager is expected to meet these needs, and an important part of meeting these needs is keeping the expectations reasonable. If the expectations are outside of the realm of possibility, then nobody wins the game.

As part of letting outside stakeholders know what is getting done and what can possibly get done, the project manager has to first answer these questions for themselves. But they are not the only member of the project team that can benefit from understanding these issues, though. Everyone should. Some people assume that project team members can do what's assigned to them without needing to know what's going on. I find that individuals taking a narrow view of just what's on their own plate, without a sense of what's going on around them, has a negative effect on the overall project. If we've bought into the common goal, we have an interest in seeing how we, as a whole, are progressing toward the accomplishment of that goal.

Detecting Progress

The desire for detecting progress clearly needs more than an estimate of the whole project. In the movie, *Captain Ron*, there's a great storm scene where the passengers are getting antsy about the voyage. Captain Ron reassures everyone that they're not lost; in fact, they're almost at their destination.

"When we left, we had just enough fuel to make it to San Juan. And now...we are out of fuel!"

Clearly it's desirable to have some earlier, and more reliable, indication of our progress or lack of progress. It's prudent to consider how circumstances might change. A sailboat in a storm gets pushed around a lot by the wind and the wind-driven currents. These invisibly push you off your intended course, requiring more fuel or more sailing time to reach your intended destination. We'd like to notice such a situation in time to take action, such as choosing a different destination for this passage. As we'll see in Danger Bearings, on page 167, we can set up some prior expectations to warn us when we're not making the desired progress.

Software development projects get pushed off their expected track, too. Unexpected hardships and side investigations come up. New goals get added and original goals get amended with more detail. Expectations change, sometimes implicitly rather than explicitly. "How we're doing" can be as difficult to ascertain in a software development project as it is in a sailboat making an offshore ocean passage.

So you need a good way to track progress. Progress toward what? Toward our goal. *Which* goal is that? Do we all have the same goal in mind? Do we have the same goal in mind from day to day? Even when we agree on a goal specified in a short phrase, we may have different pictures in our minds.

Then there are contextual goals surrounding the nominal goal on which we've agreed. The organization's mission statement likely expresses some high-minded organizational goals that may or may not give you some distinguishable direction. Realizing the capability intended for the system to provide is another goal. So is the desired impact from automating that capability, such as any expected profit or savings to the organization, or the effects of exercising a capability you didn't have before. Personal goals—for example, displaying our competence to ourselves and others, avoiding rebuke or blame, and taking home a paycheck—are mixed in with these.

Measuring progress toward a goal is tricky. You can see what you've done, but you have to estimate what you have yet to do. Sometimes you can't even tell what part of what you've done will help fulfill the intention of the project. You may have started some speculative work that didn't turn out to be as useful as you'd imagined. You may have made some mistakes that you'll need to correct. When you discover such things, you need to subtract from what you had perceived as progress and add to what you estimate as remaining work. In some cases, there is possibility that the goal is not possible to reach.

What to Measure

It's so hard to measure the things you really, *really* want. In *Software Engineering: An Idea Whose Time Has Come and Gone? [DeM09]* Tom DeMarco said, "Most things that really matter–honor, dignity, discipline, personality, grace under pressure, values, ethics, resourcefulness, loyalty, humor, kindness–aren't measurable." You'll generally need to track proxy measurements for your ultimate goals. You'll want proxies that tend to mirror success well, have enough variety to avoid blind spots, and give you early indication when things are going wonky.

Measuring Delight

You'd like to measure the impact that your work has on the lives of people or the finances of the organization. Michael J. Tardiff tweeted, "Completing requirements is not progress. Delivering delight to people who care about and value those outcomes: *that's* progress."[1] I love that sentiment, but how do

---

1. https://twitter.com/mjt/status/939203014333571072

you measure the delight of people using the system? By the number of people? By the sum of their delight? What about the people who are paying for the development so that they can make a profit off of that delight? Do you measure their delight in short-term profits? In long-term viability? And when people pay you to build a system while they continue to do whatever it is they do, is the delight in how well you anticipate their desires? Or in how little you interrupt their lives to do so?

You'd also like to measure progress in a way that proceeds somewhat smoothly, and helps you judge how far you've gone and how far you have to go. The delight may be zero for quite a while before something happens, something well after software development is finished, that triggers an incident of delight. Or you could measure the profit or cost savings from use of new functionality. These are trailing indicators and may take a while to accrue. They might also be affected by things outside your control. As steering indicators, they do poorly for early, small course corrections.

It's reasonable to measure impact when modifying a system which has already achieved basic functionality. In particular, you might release small changes to a working application and measure the impact it has on usage and profit. Ask questions like "When we automatically bring up the customer's call history in reverse chronological order, what impact does it have on the efficiency of handling a customer service call?" "When we add hooks to social media platforms, how often do users mention us to their friends?" "When we highlight a photo of the product, do people purchase it more often?" These are ways of checking progress on the impacts you wish to see.

There are caveats to be aware of when measuring impact. A reverse chronological listing might make some call handling more efficient but make the handling of other calls less efficient. It might even obscure some information vital to the correct handling of certain issues. Mentions on social media might or might not be beneficial to your purposes. What if people are using those links to make fun of your product? Purchase volume might be related to some impetus entirely unrelated to the change you made. Or, especially when people visit a site regularly, a change might draw attention for a little while, but mean little in the long term. And consider what purchases they might be foregoing to make the ones you're measuring.

For such reasons, few organizations rely solely on impact measurements to judge the progress of work. It's important to also check progress with measurements that are more directly related to the work, for quicker and more reliable feedback.

Measuring Effort

At the other end of the scale, measuring how much work we've put into something is almost the opposite of measuring delight. It certainly proceeds smoothly from the start but it's disconnected from the results you want to see. That's not to say such measurements are totally worthless. Sometimes, especially at the beginning of an endeavor, that's all you have to give you some sense of progress.

The Effort So Far

Sidney looked up at Ryan. "We've explored several new-to-us technologies and think we've found some frameworks and libraries that will save us significant time. We've examined the current system to see what it supports. We've found some confusing things in there, but it's not clear whether or not they're actually being used. We've got a plan of attack and are moving forward."

Measuring the effort expended gives you little assurance that you're making progress at all. This is the equivalent of measuring distance traveled through the ocean by the amount of fuel you've burned. Does the number of hours worked equate to progress? Perhaps it does for the goal of taking home a paycheck, but probably not for the project or organizational goals.

That's a problem with traditional Earned Value calculations. *Earned Value* is a traditional project management tool for measuring progress. For simplicity, Earned Value calculations, at least in software development projects with no tangible deliveries along the way, presume that the plan, expressed as a series of tasks, will result in value. Therefore, the cost expended indicates progress along that plan. In effect, it presumes that the value of the work is equal to its budgeted cost. That's not been true in my experience. Even measuring progress against plan is suspect if you can't measure, or at least observe, the value of what you produce along the way. If the value is "all or nothing" and realized only on completion, then progress is not assured until then, no matter what Captain Ron says.

Agile teams often fall into the trap of treating Story Points (see Story Points, on page xii) as their measure of progress. This suffers from the same problems as Earned Value calculations. Story points are merely an estimate of the time and effort it takes to do things. They can be useful for planning how long something will take, or how much work fits into a timespan, but not so much for measuring progress toward a goal. Doing something harder is not necessarily more valuable; it's just more expensive. In any event, our ultimate goal is not that to have more Story Points.

So what can we measure instead?

Measuring Output

Effort produces output. Measuring output can be valuable depending on *how* you measure it. Lines of code is a measure of output that was justifiably rejected by the software development industry at large because it's so meaningless. It's easy to add lines of code that contribute nothing to progress.

What We've Produced

"We're almost done with a minimal Automatic Call Distributor implementation," Sidney continued, "except it has no 'distributor' logic. It works only for a single agent's terminal. And only for a single customer."

"What use is that?" Ryan demanded.

Measuring progress by software component rarely makes sense, either. What value does a database schema have, by itself? How can you tell that the database schema is done if nothing is using it? Most useful functionality requires a number of components to collaborate. Working component by component often leaves gaps between them that isn't discovered until you try to integrate them. And when integration is left until late, you have a false sense of progress. While you may have completed big pieces of work, there's "undoneness" lurking between them that no one had noticed. Fixing that undoneness may require reworking some of those big pieces. This is where the saying, "We're 90 percent done and just have the 10 percent that takes 90 percent of the time left to do," comes from. Your progress meter is fooling you.

Measuring Functionality

When the pieces work together to give the desired functionality, then you've created potentially deliverable output. That's a better stick in the ground. If you can say "the system allows you to communicate in English, but not in other languages," then you have a measure of progress. We can't, perhaps, calculate the percentage complete, since you don't know how many languages there are to implement. And you don't know what overlap exists in the functionality between one language and another. We could try another, say French, and get an estimate of the incremental cost of adding a language. Is it the same for all languages? Perhaps Hebrew, Arabic, and Chinese would have less commonality than other European languages based on the Roman alphabet.

What It Does

"The system connects to the major interfaces and shows those connections are working. We're almost done with a 'Walking Skeleton' implementation," Sidney replied. "The system recognizes a call on a single incoming line and forwards it to a single agent's system. We've brought up a single customer's CRM screen, but that doesn't seem to add value to the implementation. We're thinking that enabling the agent to search the CRM system for the customer is the next priority. In the meantime, we've got a minimal call routing integration from the phone system to the agent. Then we can add support for multiple agents and have a rudimentary working system."

"Oh, OK. That sounds like progress." Ryan smiled and left.

I like to measure slices of usable functionality as the unit of progress, confirmed by automated tests that check examples of the desired behavior. This is similar to Ron Jeffries' Running Tested Features (RTF) metric[2], with the concept of feature being on the smaller side of the continuum.

Some projects are not about adding end-user functionality, though. If your project is to change an underlying technology, such as a database manager or a JavaScript framework, then you could use a measure of the slices of functionality that are currently working with the new technology. This works pretty well if you created automated tests of the functionality as we built the original. Then you can reuse the same tests, with modifications to interface with the new system, as your indicator of progress. If you didn't, then now is the time to start.

> "The best time to plant a tree was 20 years ago. The second best time is now." – ascribed to a Chinese proverb

This is the rationale behind developing, User Story by User Story (see User Stories, on page 53). Since a User Story is a thin slice of functionality, it can be tested to see if it works as desired or not. This leaves less room for things to be neglected and not completed. The functionality crosses components, and all the necessary components must work to the degree required by this small slice of functionality.

Reliably Measuring Functionality

Tracking our progress by what functions work is a great tool. Having a suite of automated tests that verify the functionality makes it easy to check that progress, and make sure we're not slipping backward. Beware, though, of using optimistic measurements that don't cover all the spaces where problems might hide.

Where does it work? Is this on a developer's machine in a local sandbox? There might be some undoneness lurking that you'll discover when the code is integrated with that of other developers. That's the advantage of continuous integration–you discover such issues early and often in small bits. Does it work when installed to a fresh, new environment? This discovers dependencies

---

2.   https://ronjeffries.com/xprog/articles/jatrtsmetric/

on elements that are not version-controlled. Does it work in an environment that mimics production? How well does this environment mimic production? The idea is to eliminate ways in which things could seem more finished than they are.

Is the functionality ready to deliver to production? How well can you know if it's ready? Unforeseen bugs represent hidden undoneness. What would be required to give you confidence to deliver the requested functionality to production? Actual use shines a light on a lot more places where undoneness can hide. If people are using it, it must be usable to some degree, and it must be meeting at least some of their needs. Production use will also generate more varied conditions of use, and that may uncover hidden bugs that testing didn't.

When you deliver the working system, you've given the users of that system capabilities they didn't have before. The outcomes are those derived from actual use of the capabilities you delivered. What do the users do that they couldn't do before? In what ways have the things they could already do changed? These are the outcomes that matter from the perspective of the whole organization, or the organization and its surrounding context. Are people actually achieving the benefits that were intended when you decided to create this? Are they delighted by it?

Not all organizations are capable of frequent delivery, yet. For that matter, not all organizations want frequent delivery of changes into production. There is also value in stability. But delivering frequently, however, is a powerful way to track progress.

Visualizing Progress

In order to gain a sense of progress and completion, it's helpful to do more than look at the numbers. Visualizing the numbers, and how they change over time, will give you a quick and clear sense of progress, at least to the extent that you're measuring actual progress.

The simplest and clearest way to make progress (or lack thereof) visible and understandable is to use a *BurnUp Chart*. We'll explore them more deeply in BurnUp Charts, on page 111. For now, let the X axis of a Cartesian chart represent time. On the Y axis, periodically plot the current value of the measure of progress you're using and the current estimate of the goal of that same measure.

What Progress Looks Like

"Have you got a minute?" Sidney asked.

"Sure, come in." Ryan replied.

"I just wanted to show you what the progress on our Walking Skeleton system looks like. I've sketched it on my whiteboard."

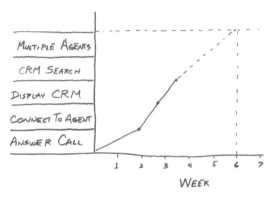

Sidney continued, "It's early yet, and given the nature of software development there are certainly time-consuming surprises waiting for us to discover them. I've projected out to the minimal system we talked about based on our current rate of progress."

"Oh, that looks good. I can't wait to see it."

This BurnUp Chart shows steady progress of the system's functional capability over time. Of course, it doesn't guarantee that progress is a steady as it looks. The sizing of the different functional slices is critical to the progress indication. If a function was shown as larger, it would make the progress look faster, but that might not be meaningful in the long run. And progress over time presumes a steady application of effort over that time. If the team were distracted by some other work, the progress would slow down. If both of these conditions were true, progress might look smooth and steady when it was anything but that.

In the short run, this can be deceiving. Over time, though, discrepancies tend to cancel each other out, and the visualization is reasonably accurate. Don't hesitate to dig deeper if something doesn't "seem right" about what is displayed, though. The visualization is a tool to help you spot things that don't match your other feelings about progress.

Showing Value for the Money

In most cases, somebody other than the software development team is paying the bills, and they want to know that their money is well-spent. They want to know that they're getting what they want or need, and at a fair price. There is, of course, considerable ambiguity in those wants and needs as well as in what constitutes a fair price. That does not change the desire for affirmation and assurance.

In very small organizations, it's possible for the senior leadership to perform the examinations discussed in Getting Things Done, on page 76 themselves. As the organization grows, high-level leaders get further removed from the work, and must depend more on indirect communications to verify things. At some point along that spectrum, the word "governance" is introduced.

Governance

Governance is a hard thing to define both concisely and in a way that communicates to people who don't know what it means. It's an expansive concept, and when we use the word, we're typically only considering a small portion of the whole.

At its simplest, governance is the ongoing setting of direction and priorities, and determining whether results are in alignment. This generally involves making sure the needs of the organization are being met in a timely and cost-effective manner. I think that covers it—but it leaves so much unsaid.

Imagine you're the CEO of a reasonably sized corporation. You confer with the board of directors regularly about the direction and priorities of the company, adjusting these as conditions warrant. You talk with your direct reports about these issues, plus the ongoing efforts to move the company in the desired direction and any potential new initiatives. They give you information about how the current efforts are doing, and the expected costs, risks, and returns of new ideas. These direct reports have similar conversations with their direct reports. How many levels does the flow of information pass through, passing downward and progressing upward? How much is it filtered and changed along the way? How do you know what's really going on in your company, so that you can make informed decisions? How can you tell if the results are going in the direction you want?

"Go to the gemba," you think. This Americanized admonition of Taiichi Ohno, creator of the Toyota Production System, means to observe the work actually done in the place where it's usually done. It's a good way to get insights about how things are going.

You visit a factory, and you can see the work flowing through it. Does it appear to be flowing smoothly? What is the rate at which completed units come off the line? How large are the stocks of parts and partially completed work?

Look at the history of inventories; how have these stocks changed over time? You walk away with a more visceral understanding of what's going on there.

Next you visit the IT department. Where is the work and how can you visualize it? How can you judge how fast things are going, or where bottlenecks might be? You walk away thinking there's little point in visiting here again.

What sort of things might you want to know, and how can you make them visible? For ongoing projects, you'd like to know if you should continue them. Are you still getting enough value to justify the cost? Perhaps you should scale them back now, or mothball new development. Can you justify the expenses to whatever governance body applies in the situation (e.g., Board of Directors, Congress, the GAO)? Is the money being spent wisely? Are you getting the expected value for the expenditure?

For every program that is in progress, you'd like a capsule view that gives you basic information. And you'd like a way to drill down from that to get more detailed data.

Earned Value

Earned Value Management (EVM) is a traditional tool, made popular by the U.S. Department of Defense, for assessing progress against plan. Progress is measured against a Work Breakdown Structure (WBS) created as an initial plan for the project. Within a work item, cost expended is often used as a proxy for progress.

If you consider the initial project plan as approved and funded by the powers that be, then demonstrably proceeding to accomplish that plan can pass for governance. The organization may get what they asked for, but they're unlikely to get what they want. And if there are any flaws in that plan—perhaps the WBS omitted some necessary things—then they are likely to not get what they asked for in the time and cost they expected. This is the source of so many "project overruns."

Again, we can turn to BurnUp Charts as a better Earned Value tool. Sure, it depends on a Work Breakdown Structure, but it can accommodate changes in that structure. Of course, if the goal line changes significantly, you'll want to communicate that with senior management. That's exactly what competent senior management would want, anyway. And that's the way the project manager will keep the executives' expectations realistic, which is necessary for any hope of appearing successful in their eyes.

Introducing a simple BurnUp Chart in an organization used to complex EVM calculations may be difficult. You'll likely want to produce numbers similar to their customary EVM numbers. The extra effort to calculate these numbers will be worth it, at least for a while. Many people tend to be suspicious of a solution radically simpler than their existing concept.

Efficiency and Effectiveness

It's hard to talk about measuring progress without raising the topic of efficiency. People being people, it's hard to be satisfied with the status quo of the progress you're making, particularly if you're waiting on someone else. There's always a nagging suspicion that more is possible. There seems to be no limit for demand. We want more, *more, MORE!* For customers internal to the organization, the needs and wants seem always to exceed the ability to build systems that satisfy.

It's hard to know, however, if you're producing these systems as fast as you could produce them. You can, after the fact, identify ways in which you "wasted" time without contributing to your desired outcomes. Why can't you identify which will be waste before the fact? We want to go as fast as possible!

Pushing for Speed

It's a short step from trying to optimize for speed to trying to push people to go faster. Sometimes people push for speed because they're worried about Parkinson's Law and sandbagging.

Parkinson's Law
   Work expands so as to fill the time available for its completion.

sandbag (verb)
   to deliberately underperform to gain an unfair advantage.

Sometimes, managers are worried that, without pressure, things won't get done in a timely fashion. Sometimes managers worry that they're not getting their money's worth out of their teams and will resort to pressuring them to do more. This, of course, comes at the expense of all other measures of value.

Even without an explicit push for speed, software development teams often feel an implicit push. They will often push themselves if no one else does.

Maneuvering in Heavy Traffic

I was thinking about the balance between speed and effectiveness recently as I was driving down the road. The four-lane road was crowded, and traffic was moving slower than the posted speed limit. The car behind me saw an opening and whipped over to the right lane, accelerating until it closed the gap with a two-ton truck ahead. There the driver, again, matched the speed of all the other vehicles, signaling their frustration by following close behind the truck. They had escaped one impediment briefly, and significantly increased their speed until they reached the next one.

The truck slowed for merging traffic ahead of it. As my lane accelerated slightly, I passed this car thinking about the parallels between this and many of our software development endeavors. We often focus on our peak speeds to the detriment of minimizing the time to reach our goal. The short-term speed increase is immediate and sure. The longer-term consequences are less certain.

I realize that I've driven similarly, at times. On this day, I was relaxed because I had started early enough that I was very likely to get where I was going in plenty of time, even considering the heavy traffic. I also knew that there was no critical penalty for being a little late. This lack of pressure contributed to my getting there faster. I could pay attention to the bigger picture and choose a strategy that made sense from that point of view.

When conversation revolves around speed and efficiency, then the participants will feel an implicit pressure to go faster. This happens reliably whether intended or not.

Side Effects of Speed

The effects of hurrying can often be seen in software development projects. The more schedule pressure, the less time you can take to look around at other factors than speed. Waste creeps in as:

- deferring attention to quality, and having to do work over.
- duplicating processes before we get them working well.
- accomplishing less with more work, often the result of team burnout.

Pushing harder often means arriving later at the destination.

Loss of Long-Term Focus

Focusing on short-term measurements tends to blind us to the longer-term progress. Sure, we want to make the team look good this Sprint, but not at the expense of the project. Sure, we want to make this project happen on time and under budget, but not at the expense of accomplishing the goals of the project. Sure, we want to be efficient and reduce waste, but not at the expense of the survival of the organization.

While we need to pay attention to what we're doing now, we also need to reserve some attention for the next larger context around it. And the next around that, too. And perhaps another, even larger. Consider also if there are smaller contexts within our current view that bear separate considerations. Don't maintain one view too long. Instead, work like a zoom lens, zooming in for details and zooming out for the big picture. No one picture tells the whole story.

Hiding Reality

Another issue that often comes up when focused on speed and efficiency is the tendency to fool yourself. Whether intentional, to look good to someone else, or unintentional, to reinforce your optimism, it's easy to pay attention to the data that supports your attempts to hit your target.

Goodhart's Law:
> When a measure becomes a target, it ceases to be a good measure.

Charles Goodhart was an economist who originally stated his law a bit more verbosely than that. This common restatement of his law has been applied to many fields. In terms of estimation, when you use meeting your estimates to be an indication that you're going fast enough, then you'll certainly find it affects either the estimates, the measurement of whether the estimated work is truly finished, or both. Either way, the self-deception hinders your effectiveness.

Cutting Safety Margins

We've all seen the guy who takes dangerous risks to pass one car, cutting into a tight space when the highway ahead is bumper to bumper as far as we can see. Why risk the entire endeavor for a brief sense of going faster? If you're not increasing overall flow, then you're not affecting the overall result.

In software development, people sometimes take huge risks in order to go faster, especially if they're behind the desired schedule. Maybe they don't take time to consider all the possible situations the system might face.

Everything looks great until one of those situations comes up in the production environment, perhaps crashing the system, losing a large amount of money, or tarnishing the company's brand for a long time to come.

More Than Speed

The way to avoid these side effects, of course, is to deemphasize raw speed. From a manager's perspective, it's not enough to reduce asking questions about how fast you're going. You need to ask other important questions, also. Ask questions that highlight other important considerations.

- As we do this work, is there anything we're neglecting that might come back to bite us later?

- Are there important measurements that we're overlooking?

- Are we building safety into the system we're building?

- Are we working in a safe manner that we can continue indefinitely?

And my favorite question,

- What have we learned recently?

Questions like these will help you maintain Situational Awareness, on page 97 that can keep you out of trouble. And keeping out of trouble might get you to your goal line earlier.

Optimization

People often talk about optimizing a work process. But optimizing for what dimension?

optimize (verb)
> 1844, "to act as an optimist," back-formation from optimist. Meaning "to make the most of" is first recorded 1857.

Often, people try to go as fast and/or cheaply as possible. So they ask for optimistic estimates, build a plan based on them, and then try to stick to that plan. In the process, they forget about determining how things are progressing by other measures. We've just looked at some of the many ways that optimizing for speed is suboptimal for some other measures you might care about.

There's more to speed than trying to do things faster, though. There are other ways of approaching the issue.

Managing Work to Capacity

Achieving a smooth flow optimizes your process better than getting faster on a few individual activities. And one of the biggest flow disrupters is trying to do more than you can in a period of time. This results in bottlenecks that inhibit progress, or starting more tasks than you can finish and wasting time multitasking between them.

Getting a Handle on Incoming Work

The Ops Team worked hard to keep their systems up-to-date, reliable, and ready to meet the needs of the organization. They were frustrated, though. As hard as they worked, management was always disappointed that they didn't accomplish more. There was too much to do. And on top of that, the people using the systems created emergency work. "This terabyte dataset won't fit in my directory!" Things like that. And management often got new ideas that weren't in the two-week plan.

"How much unplanned work gets added to your two-week plan?"

They didn't know, so for two weeks they kept notes on how much time they spent on different types of work. Of course, there were also scheduled and ad-hoc meetings that took up time. They kept track of that as well.

"OK, now we have a better idea how much time you have for planned work. Each planning cycle, estimate how much work fits that amount of time."

That worked much better. Of course, it took some explaining to management to get them to understand, but these drawings helped. And they didn't always get it exactly right. Sometimes their estimates were off. Sometimes the amount of unplanned work varied. And sometimes someone was out sick. When these things happened, they asked their management to explicitly choose which items they should postpone.

Overall, they got more done with less drama. And they slowly adjusted their expected capacity over time, when actual results tended in one direction for a while.

By limiting their work to their actual, rather than desired, capacity, the Ops Team got a lot more done. There was less delay, also, as they hadn't stacked up a lot of commitments ahead of any new work. The expectations of their throughput became more realistic, and less pressure was added to get more done. This allowed them to focus on doing their work better.

Balancing Speed and Risk

When you take multiple measures and aspects into account, you're no longer optimizing. Instead, you're making trade-offs.

The Washington, D.C. area has some world-class traffic problems, especially on a weekday morning or Friday afternoon. The travel demand often exceeds the capacity of the roads, and flow comes to a halt. When I have a meeting in the area, I sometimes start the trip extra early, hoping to avoid peak traffic and spend less time in a traffic jam. I use a GPS app on my phone that has access to the actual speeds of other users. Knowing both the road segment lengths and speeds on those segments, the GPS model estimates my travel duration. As conditions change, it may reroute to avoid known traffic jams and suggest a route that it estimates will get me to my destination earlier.

Sometimes those alternate routes are a foolish choice. The routing algorithm can't know the speed of a road segment in the future, when I will reach that road segment. Nor does it apparently model the ebb and flow of traffic conditions. The estimation doesn't seem to take the risk of slowdowns at chronic bottlenecks into account. I've had many experiences where following a route that was supposed to save me a few minutes ended up costing me 15 to 20 minutes, instead. For trips I take repeatedly, I've learned to avoid some of the "shortcuts" and stay on routes where I've experienced less variability in the trip duration, or have more alternatives if the road is clogged.

Likewise, in software development, you should manage risk over maximizing possible speed. Many practices are tuned to that trade-off. Continuous integration is less risky than feature branches, even if it requires a bit more work collaborating between developers. It avoids the potential of a big merge later. Developing small functional slices needed now, and then enhancing that functionality later is less risky than designing and developing the more complex functionality all at once. This is true even though, when viewed mechanically, going back over the same chunk of code looks like additional work.

Similarly, it may be tempting to graft a large framework of functionality onto your project. The framework surely promises to do everything that you might need. This can be a boon for development, or, if something you need hasn't been anticipated by the framework, it could be a painful dead end. Watch out for painting yourself into a corner. If possible, experiment to identify such technical risks as early as possible.

Taking the more reliable path gives you more predictability, and therefore better estimates. More reliable estimates let you better track your progress.

Are We Going Fast Enough?

How do we know how fast we *should* be able to go? After all, given the current circumstances, we're going at exactly the right speed. That's a tautology. But is there some small thing that's holding us back, something that's within our control?

When tracking progress over a significant period of time, it's naive to think that the rate of accomplishment will remain constant. The only way that's likely to happen is if someone is managing the data to make it look constant because they think that it will reflect better on them. (See Hiding Reality, on page 89.) Things change. People and teams of people cycle through better times and tougher times. On something as hard to measure as software development, even the measurement is unlikely to remain consistent over time. Expect uncertainty and learn to live with it.

In spite of the uncertainty, you can use this information to guide your exploration of what may be happening. Ask not only how fast have you been going, but how that rate has been changing. Look for trends and patterns. Don't jump to assumptions about the competence, motivation, or individual performance of people. The more likely causes are systemic effects.

What are the components that affect changes in velocity? These lists are surely not complete, but they are some of the common contributors that I've seen.

Slowing Down

When the data tells you that work is slowing down, the first thing you should look for is bottlenecks in the process. Are work items building up at some stage in the process? A Cumulative Flow Diagram, on page 118 can make such a buildup obvious. Watching the flow of work items in a visual management tool can reveal bottlenecks just as well, if you look for them.

Also, check if the pressure to deliver is driving teams to leave technical debt in the code:

- The code diverges from clearly expressing the problem domain.

- Small messes get left behind for "someday" when there's time to clean them up.

- Code gets more and more complex, and therefore harder and harder to expand and enhance.

- Duplication grows when there are areas that people are afraid to touch, or can't easily know about as they're writing code.

- Code gets harder to read, and therefore it takes longer to find where to change it and how the change should happen.

One of the key telltales of this situation is a rising bug count. If you have an honest relationship with the programmers, though, they can likely tell you about this. Some programmers may not be aware of techniques of keeping code well-factored with lots of easily rearranged modules instead of a few rigid ones.

As the bug reports come in, at some point effort needs to be spent addressing them. This points out hidden undoneness of the functionality that's been shipped so far. It wasn't really completed as it didn't do everything expected of it. You might not have discovered these deficiencies at the time, so you congratulated yourself on completing the functionality. Now, going back to complete it is taking away from your capacity to implement new functionality. If you're not careful, this can lead to a runaway spiral of less and less completion plus more and more bugs.

Maybe the work environment has become less conducive to working together. There may be increased friction in communicating information and ideas between people. Or unrelated noise is distracting people. Perhaps an increase in the number of people working on the project has increased the number of relationships and communication paths beyond what can be handled. Maybe the communication has become more point-to-point rather than many-to-many among the group.

Could it be that changes in the oversight or evaluation of the group is causing them to do more overhead work at the expense of development? Are there more reports? Is there more fear of blame, resulting in more CYA documentation that eats away at the team capacity? Is micromanagement interrupting the flow of work?

Perhaps you've been doing the easier work to make a good show of progress and have deferred the harder or riskier work until now. Or maybe you're just counting your progress in larger units of work. Maybe you're estimating more optimistically? It could be that your unit of measurement has changed more than your rate of doing work.

Speeding Up

If things seem to be speeding up, perhaps you're getting better at what you're doing. It's relatively rare that you get better at programming in a time short enough to be a noticeable productivity boost, but it's possible. Maybe you've all learned some clever techniques from each other and that's boosted your output. Or you've become better at working together as a group, gaining synergy from the best skills of each person combining into a group effort.

Sometimes teams start off with a lot of speculative framework development. If they guessed right about their needs, then maybe it's paying off now. Conversely, perhaps they've started postponing the hard work until later, creating a false sense of progress. Could they be taking shortcuts that will later show up as technical debt, unfinished functionality, and bugs?

Or maybe it's an illusion of measurement. It could be the team has gotten better at splitting User Stories, and are counting smaller units of work. Or maybe, having been burned before, they're now estimating more pessimistically. This is especially likely to be true if there is pressure to increase velocity.

Oscillating

If rate of accomplishment seems to be alternately speeding up and slowing down, then it could be that the development team is correcting based on feedback that is delayed. Systems engineering shows that delays in a feedback loop result in a late start to correction and subsequent overcorrection, causing oscillations. The delay in feedback can be external, or it can be created within the team's work system. For example, if the work items take longer than the measurement interval, the feedback on accomplishments gets delayed until the next measurement interval. Reducing the size of the work items will help the data reflect reality more clearly.

It could also be that the division of work is inconsistent in sizing. Or that estimation is haphazard. Either would affect your data measurement. It might also be that there is noise in the collection of the data. Or that frequent perturbations in the team makeup or environment make a steady pace impossible.

None of these patterns are necessarily indicators of a problem, but it's definitely good to notice the variability of velocity if you're projecting it into the future.

Pushing Our Limits

If development speed *is* the critical bottleneck, how can you determine how fast you can go unless you push as hard as you can? How can you be sure the development team is not loafing if you don't keep pushing for more speed?

I was discussing this topic with a colleague, and she described how a runner learns to go further, faster, by using a technique known as interval running. As a beginner to long-distance running, she could improve her time and endurance by running for two minutes and walking for one. As she got in better shape, she could reduce the length of the walking interval, or replace it with jogging. She emphasized that even the best conditioned long-distance runners do not try to maintain the same speed all the time. Pushing the limit for short periods of time, though, can condition you for faster performance in the future.

In project work, the same principles hold true. People burn out faster when they're pushed to go at top speed all the time. If they're trying to maintain a constant speed, they also don't hit the highest speeds of which they're capable.

Certainly, people can decide to push themselves harder from time to time, usually in response to some triggering event. But they will need recovery time from short pushes.

Short pushes of increased effort can increase your capability. It helps you stretch your abilities. It can't do that, though, if you're in a panic. Learning happens best when it's safe to fail, and when you're thoughtful about what you're doing. You can look at the need for a speedup, talk about ways you can do that, and try it out. If you have some historical data for comparison, you can check whether your attempts to speed up are working or not. This

gives you new tools for times that require more speed, and other tools that might help you speed up, on average.

When moving at a steady pace, it's difficult to judge whether or not you are proceeding at a pace that's fast enough, but not too fast. Our ability to judge differences is much better than our ability to judge absolute conditions. We can compare our progress during a slower interval with our progress with a faster one. Which gets more done? Which has fewer problems?

You should be vigilant and sensitive to the potential for burnout or other byproducts of schedule pressure. These can quickly eliminate any advantage of going faster. By the time you notice them, it's usually too late to avoid a significantly long recovery period. Short experiments, starting with *very* short, are the best way to avoid overstressing.

These short experiments shouldn't be restricted to trying to go faster doing the same things. Try some different techniques, too. We mentioned in Balancing Speed and Risk, on page 92 that trying shortcuts can increase variability and decrease predictability. If we're trying experiments, then we are seeking decreased predictability intentionally, in the hope that we find other things of value. Some of that value might be increased speed, but you should also be on the lookout for other ways to increase effectiveness.

By observing performance under a variety of conditions, you can tune the pace to maximize overall performance. Maximizing overall performance, however, will never be reached by trying to maintain peak performance. If trying to improve on performance, never focus solely on speed.

Situational Awareness

In the end, it's not about the number, but situational awareness. Discover what the possibilities are and where the dangers lie. Use your estimates to sense the world around you and make visible the intangible and ineffable. Mark the areas you want to avoid. But whatever you do, do not fool yourself into believing that estimates are truth. Especially do not believe a simple number.

When the Depth Sounder Broke

Our sailboat, when we bought her, had an electronic depth sounder that measured the water depth by bouncing sound waves off the bottom. In spite of this tool, we often ran aground. The tributaries of the Chesapeake Bay have a lot of shallow water, irregularly shaped and often unmarked. When the depth sounder showed that I was venturing into shallow water, I often didn't know which side had the deeper water. I had been watching the number on the dial. I frequently turned the wrong way and went promptly aground.

One day while entering a notoriously difficult passage, both narrow and shallow, the depth sounder showed no less than 80 feet all the way in. That was particularly noteworthy given that the water was about six feet deep. It turned out that the wire to the transducer had chafed through, so no signal was returning.

A remarkable thing happened after that, though. I ran aground much less frequently. Instead of looking at a number, I was looking around me. I was noticing the shape of the land and inferring the shape of the bottom from that. I was picking up clues from the color and texture of the surface of the water, from the activity of birds and fish, and from the locations of crab pots and twigs. I was paying attention to the world instead of trusting a number. For those times when I really did need to measure, I bought a leadline. It's a lot less convenient and has a less precise readout, but it's generally enough.

Keep your eye on the prize. What made you, or the organization, want to undertake this in the first place? How can you reach that goal? How can you tell that you're on track? The prudent mariner will not rely solely on any single aid to navigation. Take what you learn and try to confirm it in a completely independent way. Even if these assessments agree, trust them tentatively. It's far too easy to have a single assumption affect them both without noticing.

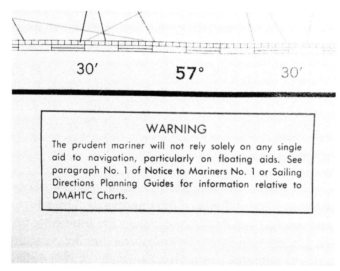

Steering and Prioritizing

Once you've reached the point where you can confidently track progress within a project, then you can apply a lot of the trade-offs pertaining to choosing between projects to choosing between capabilities or implementations. You can select between options based on estimated benefit, cost, and time. Should you cancel or postpone the current effort to start on this new idea now, or would it be better to let it run to a logical conclusion point? You can select urgent things that can be done before items that have a hard deadline, without running undue risk. For example, can this bug that is annoying our biggest customer be fixed without endangering a critical integration date? You can determine if sufficient value can be reached by a deadline to make the effort worth attempting: for example, can this feature be added in time to show it at the big industry trade show? You can monitor the risk of not meeting a hard deadline, such as the Christmas market, or a regulatory deadline. Are you still on the "safe side" of this hazard? See Danger Bearings, on page 167 for more on this.

Confidently tracking and predicting progress allow you to make smart business decisions. You can compare the cash flow of projected expenses and income to determine your break-even point. Ultimate ROI may not be the best criteria for your current decision. What about cost of delay? A lower ROI project that can start generating revenue sooner may be a better choice. What is your need for cash flow? Do you have the reserves for expenses prior to break-even? Is this the best use of those reserves? Consider the time value of money. A dollar today is worth more than a dollar next year. Identify "low-hanging fruit" that can provide near-term benefit for little cost. Fix "broken windows" that consistently cost money without benefit. This includes both things that slow down the user and those that slow down the development team.

You may have several approaches you can take on a single project, and you want to choose the best one given your constraints. Which of these approaches is more likely to be shorter or cheaper? Do you have the information to estimate that? Can you develop a little each way to confirm or refute those estimates?

Picture the situation where a version upgrade of a third-party framework had an unexpected change of some minor functionality, and a feature depending on that functionality was broken. As of this writing, work was ongoing to resolve that problem. Consider the uncertainty of the situation and the questions you might have. Is there similar functionality in the new version of the framework that the feature can use? Does the feature need to be rewritten to work around the framework? Can we afford to try both approaches in parallel?

Managers requested an estimate of when that work might complete relative the scheduled production release. This estimate might be a date if the fix looks possible and progress is being made. It might be "unknown" if the possibility of success can't be judged. Or it might yield "unlikely" as the possibilities of a simple resolution are dwindling. Based on this estimate, the managers might decide to authorize reworking the feature to avoid that functionality. They might also consider rescheduling the production release.

Are we on track, or should we reexamine our assumptions? When we estimate how much time, effort, and money it will take to do something, we've wrapped up a bunch of assumptions into those estimates—whether we chose those assumptions explicitly or not. If the actuals differ from the estimate, it calls those assumptions into question.

We'll want to identify any problems well before our final deliverable date, when there's still time to take action. This implies that we want to estimate intermediate or short-range milestones to give us early warning. Perhaps we discover that costs are going up or that we won't make a necessary target date. The action might be corrective, such as cutting scope, or it might be to cancel the project because it's unlikely to meet our goals. The urgent question is, how soon can we know things are not as we planned?

Stepping Back for a Broader View

A common driver of the need to know "how you're doing" is based on a vague fear that you should be doing better. Sometimes it's your own fear and sometimes it's the fear of someone who is responsible for the work, but is not doing it themselves. Either way, this fear is not helpful for either accomplishing your goals or for doing the work better. In fact, chasing speed for safety can have some serious negative effects.

That's not to say that you can't work to improve your speed, but you need to do so while remaining cognizant of all the other aspects that are important about the way you're working. Whenever you're trying to go fast, you'll do well to be wary of negative side effects. Our ability to measure "progress" will always be biased toward one aspect at the expense of another. Watch out for things, like burnout, team attrition, and hidden problems in the code, that might cost you more in the long run, even though you're making your progress look good at the moment.

You can track your rate of progress as accurately as you can measure what "progress" is. And you can try experiments to see what effect different strategies and tactics have on your rate of progress. Visual tracking tools, such as BurnUp Charts, help you relate your measured progress to time, and therefore to other aspects you may be noticing, such as latent defect rate or team mood.

Beware of proxy measures of progress that may mislead you into a false sense of how you're doing. It's easy to spot the fallacy of measuring hours worked

or lines of code written as indicators of progress. It's hard to find tangible value to track. Tracking story count or Story Points completed is only useful to the extent that those stories are coming together to produce the results intended for the system. Tracking features completed is only useful to the extent those features are furthering the business or mission goals of the organization, or inducing delight in the people associated with the result.

In most development efforts, we need to demonstrate the value being produced to those paying the bills, or to those delegated by them for overseeing the effort. This requires not only measuring the progress so far, but using that empirical data to create forward-looking estimates of the future, when some desired capability will be available. We'll next examine ways to look forward in time.

Now It's Your Turn

1. How do you measure progress on your projects? Is it progress along your plan, or progress toward your goal? Are you measuring progress in terms of effort, output, functionality, or delight? In what ways might your measurements be giving you a false sense of progress?

2. When people in your organization talk about project progress, is the emphasis on speed and going faster? What other aspects of progress (e.g., needs met, lessons learned, risks mitigated, benefits of system use) do you hear in conversations about your project?

3. In what ways are your measurements of progress helping you improve the outcomes from the project? In what ways are they designed to help it look good in the eyes of others? In what ways are your measurements helping you keep an eye on things that could affect your project?

CHAPTER 5

Model-Based Estimation

It's pretty simple to model when a software development project will be completed. All you need is to know the size of the project and the rate at which progress will be made. If you divide the size by the rate, you get the elapsed time. If you want to know the cost, just multiply the elapsed time by the per time-unit cost. It's simple, right?

$$\frac{\text{Size}}{\text{Rate}} = \text{Time}$$

If your size is "1 Project" and your rate of progress is "1 Project per Year" then your estimated duration is "1 Year." Just translate all your measurements to these units.

Perhaps that's too simple to be useful for you. The equation is surely true, but modeling the real world *size* and *rate* in terms of what you know and can observe about your project is more complicated. You generally want a model that is "as simple as possible, but no simpler."[1]

In Chapter 2, Comparison-Based Estimation, on page 27, we looked at ways to model the duration of software development by comparing it with prior software development. Here we look to model it by comparing *attributes* of this software development with prior. Whereas you might lump size and rate together when you estimate by comparison, when modeling it's natural to start with dividing those two fundamental attributes.

Let's take a look at how we can model the size and rate variables in terms of things we know, or think we know. Then we'll consider the type of construction of the model as a whole.

---

1. Generally attributed to Alfred Einstein. See http://quoteinvestigator.com/2011/05/13/einstein-simple/

Modeling the Size

Modeling the size of the work as "1 Project" is obviously not very useful for estimating the duration. There are no bounds on the size of a project. What else do you know about the project that might be useful for modeling the size?

I've known some projects that were sized by the number of screens needed for user interaction. The user's workflow was envisioned in terms of data provided to the program, choices made by the user, and results displayed to the user. The number of screens required to support that workflow was counted, and then treated as a proxy for the size of the application.

This makes a lot of sense for relatively simple applications, many of which are mostly a front end for manipulating data in a database. For each input screen, there is some code needed to insert or update data in the database. For each user choice, there is some code needed to do calculations based on the data. For each output screen, there is some code needed to retrieve and display the data, either from the database or from the results of the calculation. For such applications, a count of the screens makes an excellent proxy for size.

Capers Jones, in *Estimating Software Costs [Jon07]* recommends the use of Function Points (FP) as the gold standard for sizing software. This is a proprietary model of sizing, maintained by the International Function Point Users Group (IFPUG), that depends on counting

- inputs,
- outputs,
- queries to the system,
- logical files maintained within the system, and
- interfaces to other systems.

These inputs are combined with some weighting factors and then adjusted according to "general system characteristics," including the perceived complexity of the processing.

This is similar to sizing by number of screens, but more complicated. There are many more sizing variables, each with their own definition to count them correctly. These attributes are combined in accord with their effect on the system size. The type of system being produced also affects the size, as not all systems are simply reading and writing a database.

Jones' book doesn't give instructions on how to calculate Function Points. For that, you need expensive training and access to the proprietary weighting coefficients produced by crunching the numbers on hundreds or thousands of projects. In addition, Jones notes, "It is very difficult to produce a reasonable software cost estimate prior to the completion of the requirements, which comprise the first software document with enough information to derive Function Point totals." He then goes on to describe some rules of thumb for estimating Function Point totals prior to complete requirements, while warning that they have "a high margin of error."

Most agile software development projects decompose the work into User Stories and use either the sum of their estimated sizes or a simple count of them to account for the size of the project. This appears at first glance to be the opposite end of the complexity spectrum from Function Points, but it's not without problems. As noted in Chapter 3, Decomposition for Estimation, on page 49, this can be an overwhelming number of stories if you decompose to the level normally used for development.

Using a count of User Stories, or estimated Story Points of them, as a proxy for size runs into the same problem as Function Points. It requires a complete list of stories or requirements in order to calculate the size. If you're doing agile software development, you don't have a phase where you list all the User Stories at the beginning, because you're expecting to learn and steer the project along the way. That's a motivation for using functional chunks larger than User Stories for your model.

This, too, has disadvantages. User Stories tend to regress to a mean size, because they are small and there are many of them. When decomposing to a larger chunks, there's less confidence that they are of similar size or that there are enough of them to make their variance negligible for estimation. Many people resort to sorting these larger stories into small, medium, and large for their sizing model.

Note that these size measurements only concern themselves with code. There are often other deliverables in addition to code that will require time and effort. Capers Jones recommends cataloging all of these non-software deliverables and estimating them also. In Agile projects, it's common to specify infrequent deliverables as if they were User Stories. The frequent deliverables, and the non-software activities associated with development, can be treated as overhead in the production of functional code. They'll affect the apparent rate of progress without having to explicitly account for them.

Another approach to non-software deliverables is to produce them in tandem with the software. If you're measuring size in functional User Stories, you might amortize the work of creating the user manual over all of the stories.

Velocity vs. Cycle Time

People use two common ways to measure the speed at which User Stories are completed. These are *velocity* and *cycle time*.

Velocity is the number of stories (or the number of Story Points) completed within a fixed timebox. It's easy to compare one timebox with another, and the timeboxes give a natural point to notice how you're doing.

$$Y = 2X$$

Cycle time is the average time from starting work on a story to completing it. If a team if working on multiple stories in parallel, the cycle time may be shorter than the calendar time to complete a story.

$$Y_1 + Y_2 + Y_3 + \ldots + Y_n = 2X$$

While people may prefer one of these measurements over the other, they are fundamentally measuring the same thing and are comparable. Velocity is work per unit of time. Cycle time is time per unit of work. This means that they are reciprocals, though you may have to adjust for different units of measurement.

$$Y_{avg} = \frac{Y_1 + Y_2 + Y_3 + \ldots + Y_n}{n}$$

$$nY_{avg} = 2X$$

The most honest way to do this, that is, the least likely way to fool yourself, is to write that part of the manual relating to each story at the time of implementing the story. That keeps the manual and the functionality in sync, easing the estimation and measurement of progress.

Modeling the Rate

The rate at which software is developed also needs more precision than "Projects per Year." Whatever your measurement of "size," you need some idea of progress over time. If you're using a simple one-dimensional sizing model, such as the count of user screens or User Stories, then you can use the average time per screen or story as your rate, assuming the effort applied remains constant.

Advantage of Functional Slices

 One of the advantages of decomposing the project into functional slices (see Which Way to Slice?, on page 49) is that you can test whether that slice works or not. This gives you a measurable indicator of progress that you can check at intervals to calculate your rate of progress. Whether you measure your progress by Story Points per Sprint, as many Scrum teams do, or Count of Stories per Iteration or per unit of calendar time, as I prefer, you've got a reliable if imprecise indicator of your development rate. This works well as long as you maintain the same team working in the same fashion.

Some organizations try to optimize employee utilization by swapping developers in and out of the team based on perceived need for their particular skills, or relative priorities of different projects in progress at the same time. This throws a monkey wrench into the presumption of a constant rate of accomplishing work. If you do this, you now need a parameter in your model for how many people are working on the project.

There are many confounding factors in modeling a changing makeup of the development team. Programmers are not fungible and interchangeable. Changing the number of programmers, or even replacing one with another, is not an easily calculated effect. Consider also that a well-functioning team is more than the sum of its members. Every time you change the membership of the team, it has to revisit the process of team formation to some degree. Of course, if you reshuffle the team frequently enough, you'll inhibit the team formation and the rate will become more predictable again, although slower than you might otherwise achieve.

Unavoidable Subjectivity

There is a school of thought that if we make mathematical projections into the future, that we're not estimating—that we're projecting or forecasting, instead. We may be forecasting the future by projecting the current trend, that's true. But as noted in the Definitions, on page xiv, that's a subset of estimation, not distinct from it.

Why would people make this distinction? One influence is to characterize this forecasting as rational and objective, rather than an emotional and subjective activity. Many people attracted to technical fields have the opinion that rational actions are inherently superior to emotional ones. Study of psychology will show that, at the very least, the rational and emotional aspects of humans are tangled together and ultimately inseparable. One of those emotional aspects is believing that decisions based on numerical calculations are superior to other ways of empowering decisions. This is an example of the Numeracy Bias. (See Cognitive Biases, on page 72.)

Even if you carefully avoid estimating based on opinion, there are still components of subjectivity that, if you're not careful, can fool you. First is the choice of model. Even the simplest model is biased by the structure of the model. You may choose a model that seems to agree with the results you've seen in the past, or that worked in a different context. You might design or pick a model that gives you the answer you want or that "seems right." The choice of data to feed into the model is another subjective choice. The model cannot correct for data that is missing or incorrect or biased in some manner.

There are cases where subjectivity has advantages over objectivity. Have you ever had a feeling, without any specific data you could use to prove your hunch, that something was about to change in a project? Perhaps you sense a change in mood of the development team or of someone associated with the project. People can subconsciously observe small nuances that they don't explicitly notice. Don't entirely discount the power of subjectivity.

Whatever model you use, you should check its calibration against your past experience. If you put the data from a past project into your model, do you get answers that accurately reflect what happened? Are those answers within the precision limits that you need?

Given the need to calibrate your model, you'll notice that it's still a form of estimating by comparison. The comparison has been broken down into two components, measuring the comparison reference and comparing your upcoming work to the measurements. In between, you can break the measurements down into components that are used to model the factors that affect the estimate.

While not fundamentally different from comparison estimation, a model can give you a good starting point with relatively little effort beyond creating the model. And as long as it's giving you "good enough" estimates, it's a cheap and easy way to go. It allows you to estimate arbitrary points in the future without a lot of reanalysis. And it should help you with work that doesn't seem to resemble your past experience.

You should be safe as long as you don't fall into the trap of believing that the answers your model gives are "the truth." I find the concept of a singular knowable truth to be a bit slippery in the best of circumstances. It's a seductive concept, but I find less risk by holding assertions lightly, keeping an eye open for observations that seem to contradict. It should be obvious that, particularly for estimating or forecasting the future, we cannot know "the truth."

You will be prudent to compare your estimates with your actuals to check the continued validity of your model. Even if you calibrated the model with past data, things might have changed since that data was recorded. There may be factors that the model doesn't take into account. There may be factors that the model seems to take into account, but not accurately. When the map and the territory disagree, believe the territory.

Armed with that disclaimer, let's examine some of the different modeling approaches you might use.

The Linear Model Approach

Barring some fundamental change, it's reasonable to assume that things will continue the way they are going. What you've done is what you'll do. If we project that our achievement will continue at the same rate, then we're using a *linear model*. The accomplishment over time is a straight line on a graph. Ignoring all other influences, a linear model assumes that time is the dominant variable in calculating progress.

In Extreme Programming, this assumption was given the name Yesterday's Weather based on the idea that today's weather is likely to be substantially like yesterday's. If you use that to make your morning prediction, you'll be correct about two-thirds of the time. That's pretty good for such a cheap and easy prediction model. The weather services spend lots of time and money trying to improve on that, and sometime fail spectacularly, to the delight of homespun meteorologists. The caveat in Calibrating to Unknown Context, on page 44 that there is long-term variability still applies, but sudden changes in speed should be rare.

We talked in Getting Things Done, on page 76 about how tricky it is to measure the progress of software development. The same problems apply in developing a model for estimating future progress. If you measure effort, you'll extrapolate the future effort required. But extrapolating effort, say in terms of team-weeks, is a tautology when you extrapolate over time. "The next 12 weeks will require 12 team-weeks of effort." How is that helpful? To make sense of the forecast, you need to relate that effort to some accomplishment.

The most common approach of measuring accomplishment is in terms of output. Most teams use Story Points or the count of stories completed as their output measurement, and these should be relatively linear in terms of effort. That's what makes them a reasonable choice.

If you're using multiple levels of decomposition (Multi-Level Decomposition, on page 62), you might consider sizing the larger components and counting the smaller ones. The smaller the component, the less the effect from the difference of actual and average size.

For the Mathematically Inclined

Remember in Chapter 2, Comparison-Based Estimation, on page 27 when we talked about judging that this work was about twice the amount of some work we'd previously done? If X is the reference work and Y is the work we're estimating, we can express this judgment as a mathematical model.

$$Y = 2X$$

Then we decompose Y for estimation (See Chapter 3, Decomposition for Estimation, on page 49.) and model the estimate of the smaller pieces.

$$Y_1 + Y_2 + Y_3 + ... + Y_n = 2X$$

If we have a small number of components (as in A Small Number of Large Parts, on page 58), then you can do relative sizing of all the components of Y and add them up like that. You can see how unwieldy that will get for more than a few components (A Large Number of Small Parts, on page 57). Another approach is to simply count the components of Y and treat them all as if they're the average size.

$$Y_{avg} = \frac{Y_1 + Y_2 + Y_3 + ... + Y_n}{n}$$

Therefore

$$nY_{avg} = 2X$$

Counting Stories

I have long recommended that teams estimate their User Stories in using the Abbreviated Fibonacci Series of {1, "too big"}. In other words, just split the stories until they seem "story sized" and count them. For short-term estimates of how much work is likely to fit into the next iteration, I find this works just fine. For the medium term it can work pretty well, too. If you've got a stable rate of stories completed over time, then naming which remaining stories go in the next release may be sufficient for counting a "close enough" precision.

Making Stories Small Enough

Note that the approach of counting stories still requires estimating whether or not a story is "too big." When I'm doing the work, I find this pretty easy. When I look at work that others are doing, I sometimes struggle, as they break the work down differently than I would. They envision the natural boundaries of the work differently than I do. I strongly recommend that you split to functional slices, even if they're less complete than you want to put in the hands of an actual user. As a rough rule of thumb, if you're working in two-week iterations, I would try to size the stories for completion within about two days' time, with as many team members working together as can productively do so. That will give you at least five completed stories at the end of the iteration, and a sense of progress during it.

Counting the stories has the same problems of decomposition that estimating the stories has. How many stories will it take to build some large feature you have in mind? If you break it all down into stories at the beginning, you're committing to a plan when you know the least. If you estimate how many stories it will take...well, you're estimating. Not that estimating how many stories a feature will take is a bad thing, but it gives the lie to statements that projections are not estimates. Projecting based on the historic rate of story completion is great for approximating how many stories you can do in the future, if that's what you want to know. It's less great for knowing the things you may really want to know, such as when a particular functionality will be ready for production use.

BurnUp Charts

Whether counting components or using individual component sizes, this linear approach assumes that the effort or duration is proportional to the size of the work being done. As suggested in Visualizing Progress, on page 83, one of the simplest approaches for tracking your progress is the lowly BurnUp Chart. This is a simple chart with progress on the Y axis and time on the X axis. The progress can be measured in many ways. I prefer counting User Stories, if they're being used at all. (I've also considered using the count of passing automated test scenarios, but I fear that might induce people to write a lot of useless tests.) At intervals in time, mark how much you've done and how much total there is to do. Then connect this mark with the previous one.

As a tool for estimating into the future, you can look at the progress made so far and extend that line into the future. Where that extension meets your scope milestone indicates the date that scope will be completed.

Alternatively, you can set a target date and see what scope can be completed by that date. Either way, the future is modeled as a linear extension of the past.

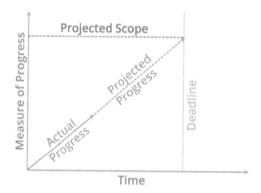

Our past progress is not likely to have been straight and smooth, but you can easily eyeball the extension on your BurnUp Chart.

Beware of Calculating the Extension

Instead of eyeballing the extension, you can also fit a line to the data points and calculate it. Be careful about this. Your input data may be a little "dirty" and you might choose the wrong line fitting procedure to represent the data without those discrepancies. At the very least, double-check your extension visually. If the extension line doesn't look reasonable with all of the prior history, don't trust it too much.

Advanced Linear Model Techniques

By now, you can probably model your current project on a BurnUp Chart and have a pretty good idea of what will be done by when, as long as things progress the way they have been. But what if we run into some bad luck? Or what if our efforts to improve are paying off? This versatile chart can let you model other *what-ifs*, too, and help you keep a reasonable sense of how things are progressing based on a fuller picture of the situation. Let's look at some techniques that can help you model what you know or suspect on a simple BurnUp Chart.

Optimistic and Pessimistic Projections

We started our estimation asking ourselves What Question Are We Answering?, on page 5, but we might also look at the impression we're trying to make. Are you looking to impress people with your progress and your software development skills? Are you looking to lower expectations, to avoid future disappointment? Are you considering the bounds of what is likely to happen, in both optimistic and pessimistic futures? The BurnUp Chart can represent all of these and at the same time make clear the future you've decided to believe.

As you look into the future, you might be tempted to extend the latest iteration's rate of progress, especially if it shows a greater slope. You might convince yourself that the problems experienced during prior time periods have been solved. Some people take a slightly more conservative approach and average the rate of the last three iterations and use that as the assumed future rate of progress. Others extend the straight line from the beginning of the project to the latest data point, averaging together all of the ups and downs of past experience. I prefer to eyeball it and draw both optimistic and pessimistic projections, taking into account any other things I know about the past and future rate of work. I know that the worst performance could easily return and the best performance is unlikely to be maintained. All of these are valid approaches and all have potential to fool us. Question your choices, and get a second opinion if you're unsure.

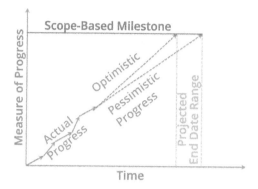

Scope Uncertainty

As much as you'd like to think you know exactly where you're going, your goal line is an estimate of how much you need to build in order to accomplish what you want. You may want to indicate this scope uncertainty in your BurnUp Chart, as it widens the projected end-date range that you can expect. You can do so by marking optimistic and pessimistic scope lines.

If you have estimated a single value of scope, take a quick guess at the error bars around that value. It's far more likely that you left something out than you will achieve your goals with less, but both are possible. Because of this, you should opt to draw the optimistic scope line closer to your single-value estimate than your pessimistic scope line. I usually expect two or three times the error in the pessimistic direction as in the optimistic, but that's just a rule of thumb.

When you plot optimistic and pessimistic scope lines as well as optimistic and pessimistic projection lines, these pairs cross each other and bound a trapezoidal space. I call the area in this space the "zone of probability," as it's your most probable prediction of scope and schedule. This technique tends to give a reasonably honest amount of precision, as shown in the figure on page 115.

Don't forget that there are numerous estimations contributing to this projection. You've estimated the scope you think you need. You've estimated the rate at which you think you can implement that scope. You've based that estimated rate on your historical measurements of accomplishment. These measurements have their own inaccuracies and uncertainties, and are therefore also estimates. That zone of probability is not a sharply defined

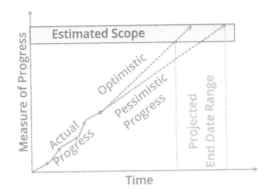

trapezoid, after all. It's an approximate probability. Keep that in mind, even if you don't model it in your BurnUp Chart.

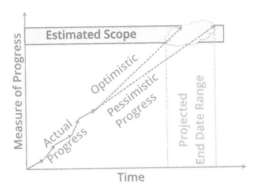

Despite the caveats about imprecision, it's pretty easy to get a gut feel for the progress being made toward time and scope goals when looking at such a chart. You can easily reason about scope versus time trade-offs. You can see some of the components that go into the projections, and can question them individually. At the same time, you get a clear overview of the entire situation.

Moving the Goal Line

With agile software development, it's generally assumed that the scope of work may be variable in achieving more valuable goals. There may be a hard deadline to hit, either to take advantage of an opportunity such as a trade show, or to avoid a penalty, such as a legal requirement. Or the focus might be on achieving a business goal, such as better market penetration, or a certain amount of cost savings, and both scope and schedule are secondary to that.

A BurnUp Chart has advantages over the more widely known BurnDown chart in that it easily displays changes in your goal. If you decide you need, or can afford, more scope, then move the horizontal line at the top of the chart up. If you trim scope, perhaps to meet a deadline, then move it down. Do this at the point the decision was made so the BurnUp Chart gives a record of the scope changes during the life of the project.

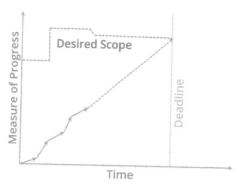

Such a chart gives you a clear visual display of how you're doing, and what adjustments you've made. Few people need much explanation about what it's saying. The rub, of course, is how to measure the total scope and the amount you've done so far. These "measurements" amount to estimates of what you really want. As previously mentioned, you'll probably end up quantifying this in terms of outcomes—the capabilities that the system gives you. You choose outcomes because it's the closest you can get to the things you really want, without significant measurement delay from when you do the work.

When the BurnUp Lines Don't Cross

I once worked with a project that was going to be done in an agile fashion, with my help, but the manager decided at the last moment not to risk introducing a new methodology. They still wanted my help in running the project, however. One of the things I did was create functional slices from the requirements document, and write them on 3x5 cards. From that, I created a simple BurnUp Chart showing the total number of cards and how many the development team reported were done. Each week, I updated this chart with the progress the team had made, as shown in the figure on page 117.

It wasn't long, though, before we started to get changes in requirements from the business. Sometimes these replaced future cards, but most of the time these changes added new cards. Sometimes the development team was able to make progress against this inflation of expectations, but it was quite easy to lose ground. After a few months, it was easy to spot that the line representing the total amount of work was going up at a greater rate than the work completed line. It was obvious that this was a project that would not accomplish the goals given to it. We didn't need an estimated completion date to see that.

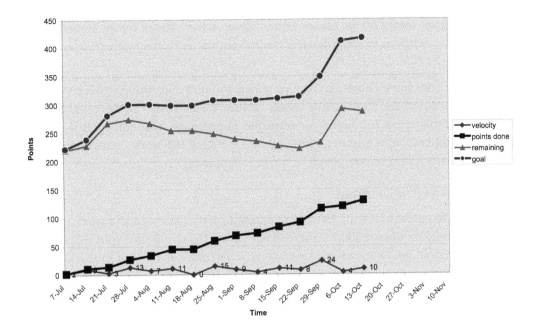

Multiple Milestones

You can do fancy things on one chart, such as track progress toward multiple milestones. We'll take a deeper look at what some of these milestones might be in Chapter 6, Estimating Milestones, on page 133, but one of the most obvious uses is estimating successive releases of the same product.

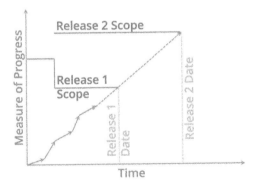

In this chart, you can see that the goals for the first release were lowered at the same time that the second release was planned. Perhaps the addition of additional goals prompted the decision to have a second release. Adding those goals to a single release would have delayed the release date. Instead, some of the original goals were postponed for the second release in order to move the first release earlier. This allows accruing value from the development effort of Release 1 without waiting for the additional value that's been postponed to Release 2.

A multiple-milestone BurnUp Chart provides you more situational awareness in a complicated context than does an ordinary BurnUp. You can see how today's efforts affect the plans for multiple milestones. You can shift scope from one milestone to another. And you can see how the work contributes to larger goals which are composed of those milestones.

Cumulative Flow Diagram

You can also enhance your BurnUp Charts to look inside of the work processes. The *Cumulative Flow Diagram* (CFD) is effectively multiple BurnUp Charts overlaid, showing what work has reached each stage in a multi-stage process.

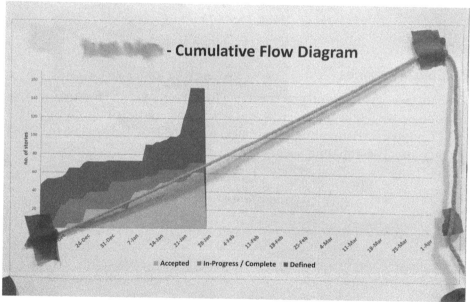

Here we see a simple CFD with three stages. The light color at the bottom indicates work that has been accepted as finished; the middle is work in progress or waiting for acceptance, and the top is work that has been defined. The chart of accepted work is the same as the progress marked on a typical BurnUp Chart, and the chart of defined work is the same as the scope goal on the same. The area in between gives us a bit more information. It represents work that has been started but has not been accepted as complete. Where this region widens (top to bottom), the CFD is telling you that there's a bottleneck. Work is arriving at this stage faster than it's leaving. The natural consequence is that it creates a buffer of unfinished work. Most teams try to minimize such work in progress (WIP), as it is considered "inventory" in lean terms. It's work that has cost, but not yet value.

In this particular chart, you can't tell whether the development team is diligently working on these User Stories, or if they're waiting for someone to accept them. Separating these two stages out into separate areas on the CFD would let you see which is typically the bottleneck, or when each constrains the progress. This extra information gives you insight on how to smooth the flow of work.

Of course, when working with a single team, the team members likely have a good understanding of where the bottleneck is. You can ask them. If they have a habit of starting all the work at once, even though they can't reasonably get it to done for some time, putting this in a picture might be the illustration that helps them decide to change their behavior.

On a larger scale, it may be very hard to judge if WIP is growing overall. A CFD such as this will let you clearly see when it's happening.

The Parametric Model Approach

Sometimes a linear model seems too simplistic. Progress depends on more than the passage of time. There are so many variables that a linear model ignores, and surely these variables have an effect. Of course, if the variables are constant in the reference system and the system being estimated, they don't need to be explicitly modeled. They're implicitly included in the reference system.

If some of the variables differ between your reference system and the system being estimated, though, then it may well be worthwhile to account for them. That's especially true if these variables change over time during the project. If you double the number of people working on the project halfway through, you don't expect your rate of progress to remain the same. Nor do you likely expect your rate to double. The overhead of people working together goes up, too, so you'll want to figure out what coefficient to multiply "number of people" by to accurately express the average rate of work. (You might even want to account for the initial drop in efficiency when suddenly adding people to the project. Or not—by the time you calculate that, it may be too late to worry about it.)

A *parametric model* calculates progress based on other parameters in addition to time. To make our past and projected progress fit a simple linear model, we presumed a known set of small functional slices of work that could be completed at a constant rate. Even when you consider "estimated story size" in your model, you're starting to tread on the boundary of the basic linear model. You're modulating it with a subjective sense of size or difficulty. The objective components of this subjective composite may be hard to isolate. What makes this story seem like a "5" rather than a "2" to you? Can you identify and use some of these components rather than the more subjective Story Point estimate?

Perhaps this story requires implementing a complicated algorithm that makes it seem bigger. And that one might have an unusually high number of permutations that need to be checked. And another has a lot of potential error conditions. Such things can make a story seem bigger. What parameters would you add to your model to let it calculate how much bigger the story could be? How can you quantify how complicated is the algorithm? Do you determine and count the number of permutations to check, or just use the factorial of the number of inputs? Can you be sure to count all of the error conditions?

You can build a sophisticated parametric model based on things you can count. Think back to the aspects of the work mentioned in Aspects of the System to Consider, on page 35. What can influence the size of a system? There are things like the number of user input screens, the number of database tables to hold the domain schema, the number of external interfaces to other systems (perhaps divided into input, output, and bidirectional interfaces), and other aspects of the system you're building. These parameters may have a nonlinear effect, so the model may get quite complicated. What effect might each parameter have on the system size?

Estimating an Online Storefront

Jules greeted Kai enthusiastically. "Come into my office. I'm really excited to put our stationery store online, and I'm told that Riffle & Sort has good experience helping stores of our size."

"We can certainly build your online presence for you. The critical part is helping you decide what you want to build. I've got a laundry list of common options to help you think it through. Then we can use your choices to estimate how much work it will be and, therefore, the cost. Bear in mind that the estimate will cover typical needs within each list item selected, but something special or high-performance might cost more. We'll alert you if anything sounds like it might cross that line."

Jules looked at the list.

- Home Page:

    - ☐ Aesthetically pleasing design (up to 20 designer hours)

    - ☐ Additional design (time and materials)

    - ☐ Rotating capsule for special offers, highlighted products

- Static Pages:
    - ☐ About Us
    - ☐ Shipping
    - ☐ Special Orders
    - ☐ Other _____
- Product Catalog:
    - ☐ Up to 5 (five) product page templates
    - ☐ Additional templates (time and materials)
    - ☐ Cross-selling capsule
- Shopping Cart/Checkout:
    - ☐ "Save for Later"
    - ☐ Drop-ship to different address
- Payment Options:
    - ☐ VISA merchant account
    - ☐ Stripe credit card processing
    - ☐ PayPal
    - ☐ Other _____
- Warehouse:
    - ☐ Packing List
    - ☐ Interface to warehousing system (Specify: _____)
    - ☐ Interface to drop-ship system (Specify: _____)

"Walk me through each of these so I'm sure I understand what they mean."

"Our designers have done a lot of storefront sites, and can have a conversation with you, show you a lot of samples, and come up with a suitable design for you. That's standard service. Some clients want to be highly involved in the design, though, making detailed decisions. We can't tell how much extra that will cost, so we charge by the hour for the extra work. They also have some standard extra features they can add that are priced by the feature." Kai continued describing the listed options, explaining which ones added costs by the number of them, which added costs by the complexity, and which were just measured by the hour. He concluded, "Of course, if we're interfacing to a system that's totally new to us, it will ultimately be a per-hour charge, but we can give you some educated guesses once we learn something about the system."

In our linear model, we assumed a constant rate of progress that we'd seen in the past. It could be that aspects of the system context (see Aspects of the System Context to Consider, on page 36) affect the rate of progress and could be different from our reference data. Does the number of teams or people working on the implementation vary? Are parts of the system similar to what you've already built and other parts unfamiliar territory? Does the system specifier sometimes change their mind, or delay in answering questions that are blocking the completion of work? There are many parameters that affect development rate.

Anticipating Delays Outside Your Control

Casey was getting frustrated. "Brook, the content you've written for these products doesn't match the template. We need to change the content or create a new template."

Brook sighed. "I know. I've called the customer, and they don't want to add templates. Jules is out of town this week, so is even slower about getting back to me than normal. Can't you just go onto other products?"

"That's what I've been doing, but that means that so much has to be revisited in the future, when it's not so fresh in my mind. That makes it more work and it takes longer."

Just then Kai happened down the hall.

"Kai," Casey called, "I think we need to change our online store estimation form. We need a count of products, too. The more products we have to load, the more delays we run into. Our current pricing model doesn't account for these delays on the customer side."

Capers Jones' model uses many inputs related to either size or development rate, and sometimes to both. The principle size measurement starts with Function Points, themselves a model counting the system's inputs, outputs, inquiries, logical files, and interfaces to other systems. Defect insertion rate both increases the size of the effort and slows it down, as finding the origin of defects is time-consuming. On top of that is the defect removal efficiency and the bad fix rate, or new defects injected in the process of fixing a defect. The capabilities and experience of the people involved has a great deal of influence on the rate of accomplishment. Typically, creeping requirements increase the size of the work over the lifetime of the project.

The development methodology used will also affect the rate of development and perhaps the size, also, though in ways that are not easily quantified. Capers Jones' model is clearly built with a phased serial process in mind, separately sizing the work products of requirements, analysis, design, coding, testing and installation phases, plus ancillary efforts such as project management, documentation, change management, and clerical support. The model offers a parameter to adjust for other methodologies in relation to this base assumption. There are also model dependencies on type of system being developed, quality level desired, implementation language, and software complexity. These are most of the items in the big picture, though there is much detail for each of them.

Capers Jones warns that the estimate you produce should be very conservative, to avoid litigation or protect yourself if you fail to avoid it. This suggests estimating to extremely high confidence levels, and therefore on the long and expensive side of every question.

How are these variables used to produce an estimating model? By analyzing a very large number of projects in a number of industries by a number of companies. By determining a best fit of all the input data of those projects to the corresponding actual results, a mathematical model is constructed to cover any potential project, to the extent that the data is known.

Models Are Only as Good as the Data They Model

 Unpleasant details of troubled projects are often omitted from public descriptions of them to protect the reputations of people and companies. Perhaps the model is also adjusted for the estimated amount of inaccuracy in the calibration data; perhaps not. We noted the problem of Inaccurate Recorded Data, on page 33 when considering Comparison-Based Estimation. The same issues apply when the comparison is encoded into a mathematical model.

You can buy this model as part of an automated estimation tool. Do you think it will match your actual results? Perhaps it will, especially if you're in the business of contract software development for government or large corporate customers. If you think it will help, and you can afford both the tool and the effort to collect and calculate the input data, then a commercial tool calibrated by someone else may be a good way to go.

The further your situation from the context in which such a commercial estimating tool was developed, the more it seems better to roll your own model. You don't need to model every possible type of system by every possible way of building it. Instead, many of these inputs are relatively stable between the reference systems they use to construct the model and the system development they are estimating. These things that don't change don't need to be explicitly modeled. That is, as long as they truly don't change.

Rolling your own model has some advantages. It lets you take into account the aspects you think are important. Beware of trusting models built for a different situation. They would likely be less helpful than a commercial model in terms of appropriately modeling your situation. Consider the inputs used by the commercial models and any other aspects that you think may be appropriate. Build your model slowly, as modifications to a linear model where that seems insufficient. Calibrate often and check against the results. Make sure your model is actually better for your needs than a simple linear model.

The Stochastic Model Approach

If a parametric model is too static, or you'd rather see the basis for the parametric coefficients in use, you can use a stochastic model. A stochastic model takes into account the random variations and gives you a probability distribution for an answer.

Perhaps you estimate (or assume a constant) the duration of each story, and then you model a random delta around that. Or you estimate the minimum duration of each story and model a random delay added to that. Either gives you a probability distribution for completion of that story. And if you add up the probability distributions for all the stories, you get a probability distribution for the release. In some environments, the contributions of delays swamp the amount of time actually building the product.

> **Modeling Delays**
>
> Casey stopped by Kai's office. "I've got an idea of how we can better model the delays when we need information from the client. Most of the requests for more information go through you, so I was thinking that we could mine your email archives for the data. If you can go through measuring the length of time between when you contact them and when they respond with the information, I can do some analysis on the distribution of those delays. And if you can separate those according to client, I can also analyze how the distribution varies from client to client."
>
> Kai looked worried. "That would be really useful information to have, wouldn't it. But I don't know how to collect that information without scanning through all my emails manually. I'm worried I won't have time to do that. When do you need it?"
>
> "Oh, there's no deadline. This can be an ongoing project between us. How about I set up a spreadsheet on a network drive where you can enter data in three columns: company name, query date, and response date? I can use this as input to determine the distribution of response times across all queries, and if there's enough data, perhaps get a distribution of the median response time from company to company. You could work on this when you have time to kill. I'll crunch the numbers periodically, and we can take a look at them. I think it would help us characterize the uncertainty we currently have in our quote estimates."
>
> "I'm in! Some companies really keep us waiting, and it's been a problem several times in the past year."

Be careful about the model of randomness you choose. Those of us who only studied a little bit of probability in school probably default to a normal distribution. This is generally fine for phenomena in the natural sciences where the sum of variances is evenly matched in both directions. The range of time it takes to accomplish a task is not evenly distributed, however. It's much easier to have an unanticipated delay than an early completion. The task can never be less than zero time, but can be arbitrarily long.

If we model our work as a series of tasks of known duration with normally distributed random delays between them, then we end up with a probability distribution that has a long tail to the right. Troy Magennis demonstrates that this behavior in *The Economic Impact of Software Development Process Choice – Cycle-Time Analysis and Monte Carlo Simulation Results [Mag15]* produces a Weibull Distribution.

Troy Magennis describes how he uses Monte-Carlo simulation to estimate Scrum (timeboxed) and Kanban (non-timeboxed) software development projects in *Forecasting and Simulating Software Development Projects: Effective Modeling of Kanban Scrum Projects using Monte-carlo Simulation [Mag11]*. Note that you still have to build the mathematical model to be simulated. For example, in a Kanban simulation, you'll need to provide upper and lower bounds of cycle-times for a unit of work for each work stage in your process. If your work queue has multiple sizes of items or dependency on certain specialties in the work process, you'll need to multiply your cycle-time estimates by the number of categories you use. You can also specify the frequency and range of impact of events such as added scope, work blockages for external events, and remediation of defects. When you run the simulation, the simulator goes through many iterations using random values within the ranges of your model. The result is a probability density of your completion date. If your model specification is accurate, this will tell you the probability of hitting a particular date, or the most probable completion date. It can also tell you what which events likely have the most impact on that date.

So, if we have to estimate the sizes of our stories, ranges of cycle times, and frequency of events, what's the advantage of stochastic forecasting? It combines all of these individual estimates into probabilities. When actual events are outside the expected ranges, you can adjust your parameters and recalculate. You also know in more detail what aspect is outside your expectations. For example, if the defect rate is higher than what you modeled, you can measure the impact by adjusting the model, and you can focus on behavioral changes to bring the defect rate within your expected tolerances. You might, for example, increase your cycle-time estimates to allow more development time for preventing defects, and see the probable results of that intervention.

Comparison-Model Hybrid

You can also use a combination of comparison estimation and mathematical models. Even a linear model of counting User Stories depends on the estimation of whether a User Story is "story size" by comparing with past experience and other stories. A linear model using Story Points nudges the comparison-model hybrid boundary in that it uses comparison-based sizes as input to a model calculation. Even the expensive commercial parametric models depending on Function Points can be adjusted by subjective factors.

Linear Projection of Affinity Estimates

I've used this approach when performing long-term estimation of requirements that are being detailed iteratively. It dovetails with the Multi-Level Decomposition, on page 62 approach of breaking the planned work down to a few large chunks, and then breaking each of those chunks down into User Stories as time gets near to implementing them. This is a healthy agile software development practice, as it defers work until the "last responsible moment," when the most knowledge is available.

The estimating problem is that you don't know the number of User Stories ahead of time, so you can't estimate long-term with fine-grained estimates. Nor do you want to do so, as discussed in Decomposing into an Unmanageable Number of Pieces, on page 66.

The procedure is fairly simple. Start by Decomposing by Functionality, on page 52 into A Small Number of Large Parts, on page 58. Use Affinity Estimation, on page 58 to sort these parts by perceived size and then label them with T-shirt sizes or some other non-numerical scheme. Take a rough guess as to how much bigger the items are in one grouping than those in the next smaller.

Order the parts by priority (see Ordering the Parts, on page 60). You don't have to get this perfect, but you do need to determine which part you want to build first. Split that part into smaller functional parts. If these are "story sized" then you've gone far enough, otherwise repeat the process followed so far, but with a different range of size names.

Once you've reached story sized parts, then order them by priority as well. Consider whether you need them all within the priority of this larger part. You will likely find that some of them are less urgent than some parts of the next large chunk of functionality. Split this chunk into the high-priority stories and the ones to be deferred.

Take a look at the chunk of high-priority stories. Is it still the same size category as before? If not, give it (and the deferred chunk) the appropriate size names.

Develop these high-priority stories. How long did that take? You now have some data for the time it takes for that size grouping.

If this is not the first group of stories to be completed, then compare the sizing with the others previously completed. For ones in the same grouping, does this seem close enough to the others to be the same group? Perhaps you need to split the group, or reconsider which group different chunks belong in. You have some information now that you didn't have when you performed the original affinity grouping.

For stories in other groups, does the factor between group sizes seem right? If a "medium" chunk was estimated as twice the size of a "small," but the time to implement is a factor of three, then consider what that might be telling you. Is this a problem with the affinity grouping or the assumed factor between groups? Or, possibly but not probably, has the rate of development changed? In general, you should assume that the same people working in the same fashion within the same context will have a pretty constant rate of progress. It could be, though, that the development team has changed significantly. Or that they've changed the way they're working. Or that the context around the team has impacted their progress.

Each time you complete a chunk of work, revisit your sizing estimates. Think what the new information means and how it affects that sizing.

An Early Forecast

Sidney, Marion, and Blaise were in the Empire Enterprise hallway, decorating a big whiteboard outside the call center development team room. Marion and Blaise were taping cards labeled with the feature decomposition they'd made when planning the project. The cards were different heights, depending on whether the feature was deemed small, medium, or large. They'd made the "medium" cards twice the height of the "small," and the "large" twice the height of the "medium." That was, at this point, an arbitrary choice, but it was easy to measure, as shown in the figure on page 128.

Sidney had taped a horizontal line along the bottom of the whiteboard, and was now marking it at regular intervals. "Hmmm..." he muttered. "Forty intervals." Louder, he asked, "Hey Blaise, how long is 80 weeks?"

Blaise pulled out their calculator. "Just over 18 months."

"That'll be good enough, at least for now."

Blaise drew a box corresponding to the Walking Skeleton they'd just finished developing.

Marion called out to Ryan who was approaching down the hall. "Ryan, would you take a look at the order of these features? We've taken our best guess at doing them from bottom to top, but it's easy to rearrange them if you'd like."

Ryan stopped and looked at the whiteboard. "When do you need an answer?"

"No time in particular. We'll continue next with the capability of bringing up the right customer in the CRM system by letting the rep search on various attributes. That seemed to be the most

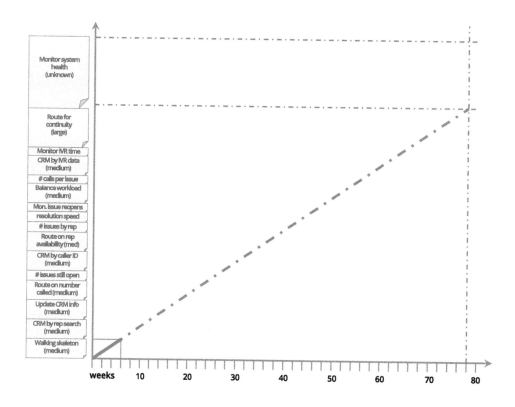

general case covering any circumstance, even if it's not the most convenient. Beyond that, we'll go in whatever order makes sense by that time."

Ryan watched Blaise and Sidney taping a piece of yarn on the whiteboard. "What's that for?"

"That's a straight line projection based on the rudimentary functionality completed so far."

"It looks like we won't have the monitoring system to catch our current problem in over a year and a half."

"There's a lot of uncertainty in the data, of course. The features could be bigger or smaller than shown on here. There might even be other features that take precedence over these. The rate of development is pretty uncertain, too. A lot of times there are one-time delays when starting a project. Of course, we might lose someone on the team and slow down, too. It's all pretty loose, but it lets us visualize if we're in the ballpark. And it shows why the order of development is an important business decision. When we have enough functionality that it's worth putting into production, for at least one product line, we can find out how well it works for you. And that'll be a lot sooner than 18 months."

Sure enough, when the second feature was finished, it looked a bit more optimistic. The search of the CRM database from the Customer Service Rep screen was finished in four weeks, compared to the six it took for the initial

Walking Skeleton. Both had been rated as medium-sized features. Were they really the same size and the rate of development had improved? Or had the start-up work of the Walking Skeleton invisibly made it larger than the CRM Search feature? You could go with gut feel, but two data points is hardly enough to define a trend.

To stay on the conservative side, Marion decided to project using the average rate of the two features rather than projecting with the faster rate of the second feature. Of course, projecting using the rate of the first feature would have been more conservative, but Marion had a couple reasons to not do that:

1. The second feature, being more recent, seemed a better choice for the team's *current* rate of development.

2. The second feature, not having any project start-up activities, seemed more like the future work.

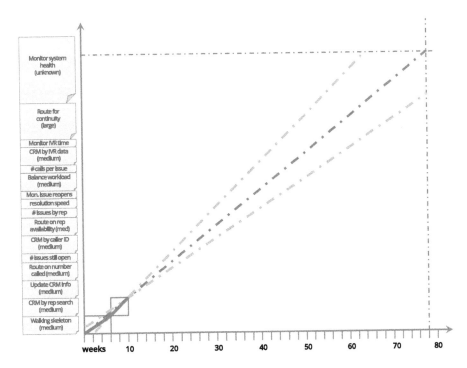

On the other hand, the rate of development indicated by the second feature seemed too optimistic. What did they have to let them presume it was more representative of the future than the first one was? Perhaps they just got lucky. Or perhaps the feature was slightly smaller than it initially appeared.

Given there was very little data so far and a long way to go in the project, it seemed premature to Marion to decide which data was biased. It's a judgment call, and Marion made a decision. The BurnUp Chart showed the decision clearly, rather than hiding it in some mathematical formula. Every time Marion looked at the BurnUp, that decision was visible. They could accept or reevaluate that decision as appropriate with current knowledge.

The start of a project has a lot of uncertainty. Unless it's an extension of a previous project, the work is different. Unless you maintain durable teams working together, the rate of the work is almost certainly different. The rate may be different even if you maintain durable teams, as they may not be as proficient, or may be more proficient, at the new work.

Functions Applied to Affinity Estimates

Technical people like to build tools, and the temptation is strong to build your own model using subjective measures and objective measures of the work, the workers, and the context. These measures are combined using mathematical coefficients representing their contribution to the development times.

Effectively they roll their own parametric model with the "T-shirt sizes" of work items as one of the inputs. Sometimes they go further and start building something approaching the complexity of the commercially available estimation models. The difference, though, is that these models are usually based on much less historical data, and the model is not usually tested on a wide variety of situations.

Stepping Back for a Broader View

We've looked at three basic approaches to modeling the time it will take to accomplish some planned work, as well as a hybrid approach that mixes elements from these three. All conform to some approximation of the amount of work and the rate of progress.

- Linear:
    - amount of expected work
    - historical rate of accomplishing work

Building the "Super Model"

I've seen a quite complex model that used a list of project sub-features developed early in the project by analysts, rating those sub-features by

- perceived difficulty
- number of dependencies on other systems
- whether they represented new, similar, or same functionality compared to prior work

and calculated optimistic and pessimistic durations based on expected number of teams working and historic average team throughputs. I could tell that this model was not based on empirical data as the coefficients tended to be nice neat figures such as 0.25, 0.5, and 1.0.

Alas, I cannot tell you how well this worked, as no one ever compared the model's prediction with actuals. Applying detailed adjustments based on individual characteristics of work items is a difficult thing to do well. Each coefficient needs to be evaluated and calibrated separately for the model to have true validity. This is perhaps worthwhile when there is a great deal of similar work being done by a stable workforce, but seems unreliable in the practice I've observed.

Seat-of-the-pants coefficients can work, but I would caution you to check your model both against historical data that wasn't used to derive the model, and against actuals in the future. Remember, the actuals are the real data. The model is a hypothesis.

- Parametric:
  - various parameters expected to correlate with or affect the amount of expected work
  - various parameters expected to correlate with or affect the rate of accomplishing work

- Stochastic:
  - nominal amount of expected work plus range of work growth
  - nominal rate of accomplishing work plus range of variation (including delays)

Models are a way of simplifying your view of the world around you. They give you a map for navigating that world. This lets you emphasize the points that are salient and ignore the noise. What is salient and what is noise, of course, is a judgment call on your part.

Using models to calculate estimates is a great time and cognitive energy-saver. They allow you to repeatedly apply the same criteria to different situations. This is both a blessing and a curse. You need to keep an eye out for situations where your usual criteria doesn't apply. If you question your model frequently, you should be able to stay out of trouble. If you double-check periodically with a different model, that's even better. And, as always, when the map and the territory don't agree, trust the territory. This tells you that there's something your map doesn't know.

As we've seen, no matter how sophisticated the model you're using, it needs to be calibrated to your context in order to give answers appropriate to that context. The advice to have lots of accurate historical data is repeated in every tome about accurate software development estimation. The assumption is that things have remained static enough that this historical data will be representative of your current context and useful to calibrate your estimation process.

Now It's Your Turn

1. If you use a model to predict progress on your software development project, what sort of model is it? What are the inputs? What are some significant contributors to development time that are not modeled explicitly?

2. How well does your model match the actual results you get? Is this close enough for your needs? If not, which decisions would be better with higher accuracy or precision?

3. When was the last time you calibrated your model with your actual results? What sort of changes did you make to the model?

CHAPTER 6

Estimating Milestones

Up to this point, we've mostly focused on estimating the end of a project. That's a natural point of curiosity, but it's not the only point that matters. In fact, once a project is started, we can control when it ends with certainty. We can end it at any time. The question is predicting what gets completed before we end it. And there are questions about when particular parts might get completed along the way.

A software development project is a journey. We've previously looked at Chapter 4, Checking Progress, on page 75 along that journey, but you might also like to anticipate when you'll reach certain points in that journey. These points may be arbitrarily assigned, like a milestone, or a natural landmark. In software development terms, an arbitrary milestone might be a release date, or the completion of some intermediate work product such as a document or a task that, by itself, doesn't create or enhance usable functionality. A natural landmark might be the release of a new or enhanced feature to production. For simplicity, I'll refer to both of these, and the continuum between them, as milestones.

Deadlines

Combine a milestone with a point in time, and you create a deadline. "I want to be at the 20-mile mark before noon." Or "I want to cross the mountain ridge before sunset." These are aspirational deadlines. Sometimes in group situations, the speaker may be one person and the doer may be another. Then they become imperative deadlines. "I want *you* to get us to the 20-mile mark before noon." That leads quickly to the interpersonal aspects of estimation that we'll explore in Chapter 9, When People Clash, on page 177.

People often talk about imperative deadlines as if someone dies if you cross them. Indeed, the earliest documented use of the word refers to a line demarcated about 20 feet within the stockade walls of the Andersonville Confederate military prison. Prisoners of war who crossed that line, or even reached across it, were liable to be shot by guards.

Sometimes people *act* like someone dies when you cross a deadline. Rarely is that true.

When My Mother Got a Digital Clock

When I was a teenager, my mother got a "digital" clock radio for her bedside table. It wasn't really digital. It was an analog clock run by a motor, the same as the one with minute and hour hands, but the output was digital, with a "split flap" display. Each number was on a divided flap. As the display rotated, the top half of the flap would fall down and display as the bottom half of the next number, revealing the top half of the next number that was behind it.

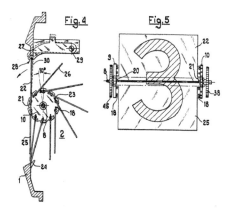

It wasn't any more accurate than her old clock, but it had a very precise output. And it had a built-in radio. She was very pleased with it.

Shortly after she got it, on a night when I was told to be home by midnight, it said "12:04" when I got home. She was furious! I had missed the deadline!

Nobody died because I was four minutes late getting home, though a bystander might have thought so by the tone of my mother's voice. It was an arbitrary boundary and I had hit it pretty precisely, if on the wrong side from my mother's point of view.

You may have seen similar reactions to missed deadlines in your career. We'll take a deeper look at these behavioral issues in Chapter 9, When People Clash, on page 177.

After the 1865 trial of the Andersonville Prison commander, Henry Wirz, the word "deadline" faded from use for a few decades.

When the word "deadline" reappeared in 1917, it had an entirely different meaning. This deadline was a mark on the bed of a printing press beyond which the type would not print. Soon after that it acquired another printing related meaning—the time after which material would not make it into a printed newspaper or publication. It is this definition of a time limit that most represents current usage in software development.

Sometimes deadlines are real, and if you miss them, you're not going to be included.

When I Missed the Boat

When I first started sailing keel sailboats, a friend invited me to join him as racing crew on another friend's boat. We'd leave slightly early on Wednesday afternoons to drive to the boat. There we'd join the boat owner and a few others to go out on the river to chase other sailboats around the racing marks. I started getting more useful than merely moveable ballast, and got invited for a longer race one weekend. The skipper told the crew, "The boat is leaving the dock at 0800 Saturday morning."

On Saturday morning I drove to the boat without my friend, who had other things to do. I wasn't in a particular hurry, as I had plenty of time. When I pulled up at the marina, though, there was something wrong. Even though it was only 7:55, I could see the boat turning the corner of the creek to the river. I had missed the boat, *even though I was before the announced deadline.* I was terribly disappointed.

I learned that day, if I wanted to join a racing crew, that I should be there well before the time the boat left the dock.

Many software development deadlines are like these. Some are target dates, and if they're not met then things are merely delayed. Some are fixed, and if you miss them, you miss the figurative boat. The release date comes, and the software is released, but your work is not included in the release. You may be terribly disappointed. Other people may be disappointed, too, but if the timing of the release matters more than the content, that's what happens. And you may be trusting the deadline to be more precise than you should. "Close of business" may mean "when Operations starts the deployment process" rather than "by 5:00 p.m."

> **Don't Bet the Farm on a Precise Estimate**
>
> Of course, missing a deadline can derail a whole release if you've mingled nonreleasable, unfinished work with releasable work. That's going to disappoint everybody and satisfy neither people focused on the date nor people focused on the content of the release. Don't do that—use safe mainline development practices, feature toggles, or even feature branches instead. There's no point in making your estimate the most critical component of a release.

Let's consider some of the needs people may have for estimating milestones.

Early Release

There is a time value to money. A dollar today is, theoretically, worth more than a dollar tomorrow because we can make use of it. If we invest it, then it becomes more than a dollar. We might not see that value in a single day, of course. And we might not take advantage of having the dollar in our pocket. If it just sits there, unused, we've squandered that time value.

What happens, though, if you release a little bit of new functionality and it starts earning a little bit of income while you continue to develop the rest of the functionality you ultimately want? You'll still be spending for development at the same rate, but a tiny bit of that cost will be offset by the value earned by the early release. If you keep doing that, the functionality grows and so does the rate of early value. That is, the rate of value grows if you take advantage of it, and don't just keep it in your pocket.

Let's compare the differences between waiting until you've built "the entire thing" before putting it in production and releasing incrementally as you can gain value. What's the estimated income from "the entire thing?" If you wait until a final release, you'll spend for development until that point and then start seeing that income.

If you can release something valuable earlier, you can estimate you'll earn a small portion of that income sooner. Each time you release, you presumably increase the amount of current income from the project. By the time you build "the entire thing," you are earning the same income as if you'd waited to release. The current net cost, development costs minus current income from the project, decreases over the life of the project. The accrued value doesn't go as far negative and reaches the break-even point earlier as shown in the figure on page 137.

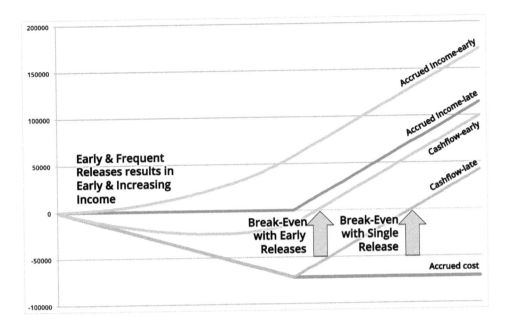

It's possible you'll reach a break-even point before you finish developing. The income might become more than the cost of development, and the project becomes self-sustaining. If this is the core of your business, that's exactly what you want. This lets you continue to develop revenue-producing function-ality forever. Even with very conservative returns on a fixed-scope project, delivering some functionality early and starting to accrue some value from it makes a considerable difference in the time to a break-even point.

IT projects can also accrue value earlier. Even when there's no customer paying money, presumably there is benefit in the new system or the project wouldn't have been undertaken. Perhaps there are cost savings from the new system. It may be easier and quicker to do some type of work, or the operation and maintenance is cheaper or easier than an older system that is being replaced. Perhaps the new system provides the capability to do some work that wasn't previously feasible. It may be harder to quantify the value accrued when it's not income, but it's still accruing value.

Minimum Releasable Value

Ryan stood in the hallway looking at the whiteboard with the big BurnUp Chart. Sidney walked up and asked, "What are you thinking?"

"I'm thinking about the order of these features, and what it would take to start seeing the value before it's all built."

"Great! Would you like to change the order?"

"I'm thinking that we can put a limited version of this new call center into production with just a single division, and we won't need all the features. If we direct only the customer service number of the Applied Magnetics division, we won't need any of the advanced call-routing features. Their call volume is low enough that they don't use the Interactive Voice Response feature. And the customer search feature on the agent console will be good enough for now."

The two of them started moving cards as Ryan talked. They moved everything that Ryan thought essential downwards and filled in the space above with the cards they'd taken off to make room.

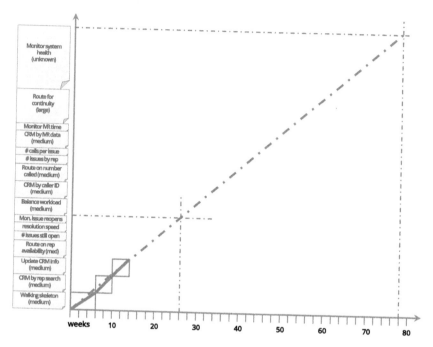

Ryan stepped back with a look of satisfaction. "I think that's better. I'm looking forward to seeing it actually used."

Sidney replied, "We can always change it again. But looking at it now, it looks like approximately three more months to that minimal releasable version. Thanks for your help."

Ryan looked up. "Thank you. It wasn't like this when we built the last system."

Releasing multiple times throughout the project effectively turns it into a series of mini-projects. Each of these will have a release date that will interest someone, and they'll want to know when that is. We have an advantage, however, in judging these interim release milestones. As when you are Chapter 4, Checking Progress, on page 75, you have some recent historical data with the same context as you'll have going forward. Earlier milestones give feedback on the validity and accuracy of assumptions made in estimating, and that feedback will help you correct estimates of future milestones.

Deciding to release early is one reason to look at milestones prior to the end of your project, but it's not the only one.

Coordination with Others

It's easy for a close-knit team to see themselves as the center of the universe, or the most important aspect of a project. They've been given, or have taken on, the responsibility for accomplishing some piece of work. In fact, dividing work into projects may reflect a concept of dividing some larger purpose into categories of similar types of work, each to be given to teams and individuals with the appropriate skill set. There are, of course, pros and cons to such a division. One of the consequences is that the different parts of the effort need to be coordinated and aligned to achieve the higher goals, the intended outcomes. That coordination and alignment requires some visibility into the progress and expected future progress of the various threads of work.

Parallel Development

Sometimes in the grand scheme of things, it takes more than one team to deliver all the software functionality you need to have the outcomes you seek. Small incremental improvements are safe, but often don't create the big breakthroughs in impact. Rather than have one team serially do everything that's required for a large idea, it's often preferable to have multiple teams working in parallel toward a common goal.

There are a number of ways this can play out. Perhaps you need to change multiple subsystems of a large system in multiple ways. Some of these might be system enhancements and some brand new. You might have different teams working on different subsystems or they may be working on different functional slices. In order to have it all come together, you need to integrate the various systems. And, as with all integration efforts, you don't want to risk leaving integration to the end, but instead integrate over time as the systems evolve. Not matter how you've worked to decouple the various pieces, you'll need a lot of collaboration touch points along the way.

It's best if these touch points are "just-in-time." If I've finished my system and gone on to something else, it's inconvenient if I need to come back later to make an adjustment when another system tries to integrate with the functionality I created and finds it wanting. It's both inefficient and ineffective. A jump back to previous work rarely catches the depth of awareness that previously existed, and such rework may not be of the same quality as the original.

When will a dependency be ready for collaboration, and what valuable work can we fit into the time before then? This is one of the questions that estimation may help to answer.

Other Systems

Often a desired change in functionality affects more than one system. A change in one system may depend on changing a backend service to provide the data or functionality it needs. From the perspective of that backend service, there's no point in making the change if there's no code that's using it.

You can, of course, serialize the development of the two systems. You can develop the backend service first, and then start working on the system that uses it. This, of course, lengthens the total time of development to the sum of the time of developing each piece, and the delay between the two. Surely you'd prefer to develop these in parallel.

You could start developing both systems at the same time, mocking the behavior of the other system during development. This is a good strategy, but it has some pitfalls. The mocked behavior may not match exactly, leading to the need for rework when the systems are integrated. If the development team of the system that needs rework has "finished" and gone on to other things, then they'll either have to drop what they are doing to come back to this, or the integration will be delayed until the other work is done. This sort of dynamic happens more frequently than you'd think, even in the completely serialized case mentioned above.

You'd prefer to have both systems ready for integration at the same time, and this synchronization requires estimating when each system will hit that point. And if you're trying to minimize integration risk, you'll want to have several synchronization points. You'll want some basic synchronization early, to ensure that the systems are basically compatible, and get progressive detail in the integration as the work proceeds. You probably won't be able to perfectly synchronize all of these integration milestones, but it's worth the effort to try to come close. Integration points are a major source of errors in combined systems. Juggling the needs of two flows of work to do rework on one is a major effectiveness drain, and also a common source of mistakes.

Deployment and Operations

In most situations, the development team is not handling all aspects of the developed system. Even in organizations practicing DevOps, there's a limit to how much a team can do. In most organizations, there are specialized groups for many activities, and handoffs to others' care.

In organizations that have not embraced a DevOps model, there may be a separate team that deploys to production. Sometimes this strategy is chosen for security reasons, to reduce the access to production servers. If the server hardware is shared among various applications, having a separate team can make sense for preventing accidental disruptions to applications unfamiliar to the deploying development team. There are cases where the application is not hosted on a central server, and perhaps there is no facility for pushing the application from a central location to many runtime environments. Rarely are the development programmers charged with traveling to dispersed machines for deployments. All of this needs to be scheduled and coordinated.

In a self-hosted DevOps model, shared resources such as storage subsystems might be managed by an infrastructure team rather than have every development team stirring the common pot for their own needs. In such a case, this team will need advance notice of needs so they can ensure sufficient storage capacity for the new application, without interfering with existing ones. Increasing the capacity may require the purchase and installation of new hardware, and that may take a while. This suggests that it's prudent to estimate and communicate these needs far enough in advance that this won't delay the deployment. A separate infrastructure team will also have responsibility for keeping the software running that keeps infrastructure up-to-date and patched for security issues. These duties need to be coordinated with new deployments.

System Users

One handoff that's pretty universal is the one to the system user. It can be helpful for users to know when a system will be available so they can prepare to use it in their work. Think how it would feel to have your work suddenly interrupted with an announcement that you had to immediately switch to an unfamiliar way of working. They may have logistical issues regarding changes in their workflow that are enabled or required by the new functionality. Can you tell them what changes they can expect, and when they can expect them?

Trainers

Consider the need for training the users of your system. Before we put new IT software on the desktops throughout the organization, we may need to train people on the new system. There will be differences in the operation of the new system from whatever they're doing today. If there's a wide user base, this usually means a significant training effort, visiting the locations of the users and training them on the differences and benefits of the new system.

That needs to be completed prior to releasing the system, but not so far in advance that they forget what they were taught.

Prior to that, someone needs to design that training. This needs to be late enough to provide the training team with accurate information about the system behavior. That's a milestone that should be estimated, so they can know when they can begin. Is there enough time between then and release for designing and delivering the training? They'll need to estimate that timespan.

It's likely they'll need pixel-perfect screenshots prior to delivering the training. How late in their training design can they wait for those? When can you provide them? These milestones need to be coordinated so that release and actual use of the system won't be delayed.

Help Desk

When new software, or a new version of existing software, is deployed, it is likely that users will have questions or problems using it. They may call the help desk for assistance. "How do I do this thing I used to do this way?" "Where did my shortcut go?" I've talked with help desk personnel who found out about a new deployment when the calls started coming in. It's so much easier for them to help the users if they know something about the software ahead of time. When do they need to be notified so they can prepare?

The Customer Who Requested the System

People who have requested new functionality, who may not be the direct users of it, did so because of the benefit it provides to their organization's work. The purpose of this work is likely not about software at all. They would like to know when their request will be fulfilled, and what other changes will happen at the same time.

If the system won't be available in time for some of their needs, the users or the people requesting it on the users' behalf may have to figure out an alternative plan. That may require some preparation, so knowing this in advance is helpful. Can you keep them informed appropriately?

Marketing

If it's software for sale to outside customers, then we want to start a marketing campaign early to build up the buzz. We want to pique peak interest at release date. Customers love to be first in line for a new exciting thing. If interest peaks late, we miss a market window. If it peaks early, it may cannibalize current sales. Customers quit buying the current offering to wait for the exciting new one. This has become known as the Osborne Effect after the bankruptcy of Osborne Computer Corporation who announced a new computer model, killing sales of the Osborne 1 and the cash flow needed to continue development. What's the earliest point they can start pushing the new system? How sure are you?

Packaging

Some software-based products still get packaged into physical boxes. If we start this project today, when will we likely need to start production of the associated physical components that have their own lead times, such as boxes, brochures, and servers?

Others

Organizations, especially larger ones, are complex systems. The actions in one place ripple through and affect the situation in other places. Often those at the place of action are unaware of the effects on others, and vice versa. Left unchecked, these unintended effects of local actions can encourage responsive action that, itself, creates further ripples. Visibility, both across the organization and into the future, can help. Who needs to know what, and when? How can you be aware of those needs and how can you provide the needed infor in a timely fashion?

Each of these coordination points is a milestone that needs to be communicated to others. It's generally OK if they change, as long as you can give enough advance notice. The point is that you need to keep people informed, giving them sufficient notice from the start, and when the picture changes.

Evaluating and Changing Plans

As discussed in Chapter 1, Starting Something New, on page 1, a primary reason to estimate prior to starting a project is to provide those with the fiduciary responsibilities with enough information to make responsible choices and plans. This need changes after the project starts, but doesn't go away. There are some who would try to freeze the decisions and plans and expect the project management to conform to those plans no matter what happens. This seems silly to me.

As time goes on, conditions change. We learn new information that gives us different insights on the data we had. The world does not stop for us. As you learn new things, you'll likely want to reconsider your plans in the light of what you now know.

Reporting Progress to Stakeholders

We've already looked at Chapter 4, Checking Progress, on page 75 for steering our project, but you might want a less detailed view when reporting progress to other stakeholders. They need to know how things are going so they can make plans and decisions at a macro level, but you don't want to invite micromanagement of work within the project. Give them the honest information they need.

If they need more detail, or the data worries them, then you can share a more detailed view with them. Most of the time, that more detailed data requires some tacit knowledge of the project to understand it. They probably don't have the time to stay up-to-date on the tacit knowledge of the project–hence the recommendation to give them a useful summary. If they need a more detailed understanding, it will probably be best to go over your signs of progress with them, helping them to understand the context within the project as they help you to understand the context surrounding it. Don't just give them numbers; tell them the story.

Telling the Story

Rory, the CEO of Empire Enterprises, stopped Marion in the hallway. "Last month I heard you were releasing the new call center software at the end of this month. Today I heard that it's not going to be complete. When will it be done?"

Marion replied, "Both of those things are true. We are releasing this month for use by the Applied Magnetics division. They have the lightest needs, and we can put the system into production there while we continue to extend it for other divisions. It will likely be suitable for the Paints and Pigments division three or four months after that. In fact, there are several divisions that will come online about the same time, once we demonstrate our confidence."

Rory looked puzzled. "Last time we rolled it out enterprise-wide, all at once."

"Last time we had much lower expectations for the system. It has evolved over time since then, and it's been customized for different divisions in different ways. This time we're planning for these customizations from the beginning, but not holding up those who need less customization. We're also allowing for changing priorities and unanticipated future discoveries. Would you like to see the current plan?"

Capacity for Other Work

When we finish this project, what will we do next? Do we just wander off into the sunset, leaving the organization to attend to whatever is their primary focus? Or does the organization have other development work they want us to do?

Most modern organizations run on software. And most of them have an inexhaustible appetite for new functionality or improvements to what they have. When you finish this current project, they likely have a few items already in mind for your next one. As you work on the current project, they may be wondering when would be a good time to start on these new items. Is there a good pausing point coming up on the current work so that something new can be done with minimal disruption?

"When will our current development capacity be available for these new ideas?" What will you tell them? Will you be stuck finishing all the work that was started, or can you offer reasonable cutoff points where value has been achieved, and further work can be deferred? No one wants to be stuck in a long-term plan that no longer fits current priorities.

Whether the stopping point is at the end of the originally planned project, or somewhere short of that, the business will want to know what options are available. Setting intermediate waypoints that are releasable offers them more options.

Trimming Expectations

Sometimes the success of a project is judged less by what value it brings, than by whether it meets expectations. We see this behavior frequently in the stock market. If a profitable company reports strong earnings, but it's slightly below their earnings forecast, then its stock is likely to take a hit in the market. When eBay Inc. missed the analysts' consensus earnings forecast by a penny a share in January 2005, its stock price fell 19%.[1] People don't like negative surprises. To avoid this reaction, companies often offer guidance ahead of time to soften the blow.

In similar fashion, it's prudent to keep stakeholders informed of significant risk to expectations. That's not to say you want to relay every tidbit of bad news to them. You do want to keep them abreast of the trends, however. And new information may trigger a reevaluation of their plans. They may have different priorities when facing the fact they might not get all they wanted.

Everyday Milestones

You may remember that I decided to run some errands on the way to the train station. (Casual Sense of Progress, on page 76) This made the trip to the train station somewhat different from ones in the past. Let's check in and see how this is going.

"OK, *that* took a bit longer than I expected. Let me look ahead. I should be able to get through the next three items by 10:00, and the last three by 11:00 if I skip the other ones on the list. Then I can drive to the café by 11:30 for lunch, and have plenty of time to make my train."

Sometimes the last items on the list aren't the lowest priority, but things you want to do last because they depend on the others. Or maybe they're things

---

1. http://articles.latimes.com/2005/jan/21/business/fi-ebay21

that are most sensitive to potential changes in the context around the project, so you want to delay them to the last possible moment to be able to account for the maximum amount of change. Do you remember avoiding spending the night on the side of the road in Benefit of Headlights, on page xi? Whatever the reason, it's possible that ticking off items in the planned order is not the preferred approach.

Canceling the Project

One of the biggest and perhaps best outcomes of changed estimation of a project is that you cancel the project. If it looks like you won't achieve your objectives within the time and cost budgets you've set out, canceling early is preferable to continuing to the bitter end. Step back and reconsider your objectives. Perhaps you can reach the same outcomes with an entirely different approach. Perhaps you should look to make an impact with different outcomes. In any event, continuing down a path that leads to a dead end is not what you want. Better to cut your losses early. (See Sunk Cost Fallacy in Cognitive Biases, on page 72.)

Even if you are on track for meeting your original objectives, it's possible that new options have been discovered that are a better investment today than continuing this project. It could be worthwhile to switch to that new option now, rather than delay it.

Stepping Back for a Broader View

We've looked at some of the ways that, even in the absence of artificial deadlines, real reasons exist for getting things done by a particular time. In those cases, you are likely better off reducing what you get done than missing the date. In most cases, however, what's late just gets left behind. The reduction in scope is a natural consequence, and it's up to you to make the best outcome you can of the situation.

When you're not bound to a hard date, then you can shift the focus to asking which scope brings you value. In general, realizing a small amount of value earlier is better than delaying it until you can realize a large amount of value all at once. Not only do you start accumulating value earlier, defraying some of the development cost, but you may learn something important. You might need to change your plans.

There are many coordination and collaboration reasons to look ahead. If no man is an island, rarely is a software development team, either. Others may be dependent on your work and deserve to be kept apprised of when you might be ready for them. You may be dependent on others' work, and want to keep them aware of when you'll need it. In both cases, you're trying to smooth the flow of work that weaves through multiple hands. These coordination points may be the most expensive parts of the whole operation, as they're where the most delays arise.

There are a lot of aspects to changing plans. Sometimes you're changing other plans to accommodate the reality of your current progress. Sometimes you're changing the expectations of others for the same reason. Sometimes you're altering the plans of your current work to bring it to a meaningful conclusion at an earlier date. And sometimes you're deciding to abandon the work you're doing, as it's not looking promising that it will provide the expected cost-benefit ratio. In all of these scenarios, it makes more sense to respond to the reality you see than to close your eyes and forge ahead with plans made on obsolete information.

For all these various reasons, you'll find yourself estimating different subsets of the work, for different audiences, and with different needs for accuracy, precision, and direction of error. That's hard work, and you're bound to get some of them wrong. What do you do when that happens? We'll explore that in the next chapter, Chapter 7, When Estimates and Actuals Differ, on page 149.

Now It's Your Turn

Consider your current or recent project.

1. What "deadlines" did others impose or imagine for that project? What were the consequences if those "deadlines" were not met? Think of the consequences to the organization's goals, to departmental goals, and to individual people.

2. On that project, what opportunities were there for early release of a subset of the functionality? Was there any appetite within the organization for doing so?

3. When, on that project, did you know that things were not progressing according to plan? Did others, either closer or further from the work, learn this at a different time? What observations led to the conclusion that things were not proceeding according to plan, and what steps were taken when it was realized?

4. Who else needed advance knowledge of project milestones to plan their own work? How far in advance did they receive that information? Did they receive updates on that information as things changed? What were the consequences if the dates were missed?

CHAPTER 7

When Estimates and Actuals Differ

When you make an estimate, you can be almost assured that it is not a perfect prediction of how reality will unfold. It's hardly helpful to you to label inaccurate estimates as "wrong" if that label will apply to 100% of them. You could consider "wrong estimate" to be a redundant phrase in that case.

Look at what goes on around you, though. I'd bet you'll notice people talking about "wrong estimates" all the time. Once you've reduced your analysis to a number, it's temptingly easy to start to trusting it more than you should. You might consider your estimates to be data rather than opinions.

Once you consider the estimate as your primary reference point, then all sorts of things start looking pretty shady. You can blame people for not meeting the estimate. You can blame the estimate for leading you astray. You can point a lot of fingers without solving any problems.

Or you can let reality teach you what was wrong with the estimate. Each time this happens, there is something to be learned. Steve McConnell, in *Software Estimation: Demystifying the Black Art [McC06]*, suggests comparing estimates to actuals "so that you can refine your personal estimating abilities." That will certainly help you in the future. In the meantime, I suggest making such a comparison in order to calibrate the estimates you have on your *current* project.

If you do that early enough and often enough, the things you learn can help you steer the project to success. Or, if it can't be steered to a satisfactory conclusion, you can quit before spending all your money.

Adapting to Reality
...continued from Everyday Milestones, on page 145

Hmmm, I've got the first three errands done, but it's 10:30 already. Missed that milestone! I think I'll cut the last couple of errands from the list. They can wait. I'd really like to get a good lunch, though. I think by cutting those errands, I'll have time to stop at my favorite lunch café. I'll need to do that by 11:30 to have time to eat and get to the station…

From the café, it's still about a half hour to the catch the train. I had planned to be there by 11:30 to have an early lunch, but that's not going to happen. Some errands took longer than expected. Traffic was slower than expected. There was a wreck and I had to detour. It's 11:45 now, and I'm probably 15 to 20 minutes away from the café. I could swing through a fast-food drive-through and eat while I'm driving. Or, if I can get to the café before noon, I could get some better food to go and eat on the train. If I'm later than that, I'm not sure I can afford the time to stand in line and wait for my order to be fixed. In that case, I think I'll drive past and continue straight to the train station. I can get a late lunch on the train. I really don't want to miss that train.

Driving Up Costs

A *USA Today* article about highway projects in New York had the subhead, "Design errors, planning lapses drove up costs more than 14%."[1] Among the things listed that "drove up costs" were:

- more asphalt than projected due to a math error

- more temporary concrete dividers than planned, as plans called for only half what was needed

- unanticipated excavation costs

It's true that no one likes for costs to exceed estimates, but exceeding estimates is a very different thing from driving up costs. Math errors can happen. You could quit paving when you spent the asphalt budget, but would that give you what you want? What determined the number of dividers needed? Was the number of needed dividers inherent in the length of highway being built? Perhaps it was related to the length of highway under both use and construction at any given time? There is often a trade-off between the duration of the project and the cost. It usually costs more to go faster. We might do the work in bigger batches to try to achieve a higher efficiency of scale, but this might require more equipment, such as dividers. Perhaps the organization of the work changed the number of dividers needed, after the estimate was made. When excavating, you never know what you'll find below the surface. Did they find boulders or incompatible soil? I know of a building project where, after construction began, a construction engineer discovered the soil type was too unstable to hold the weight of the planned building. It took weeks to truck out that soil and truck in replacement dirt at great expense.

Despite the unhappiness with the outcomes, those actual costs were accurate. It was the estimates that did not agree with later reality. Two of these items

---

1.   http://www.usatoday.com/news/nation/story/2011-12-11/construction-287-new-york-over-budget/51763184/1

seemed to be simple mistakes, but the third was apparently a bit of information that was not knowable when the estimate was made. Had these mistakes not been made and the excavation needs been known in advance, the resulting costs would have been the same. Only the estimates would have been different.

If the math error had gone the other way and less asphalt was needed, if plans had called for twice the dividers needed and they got by with fewer, and if excavation had gone more quickly than anticipated, would the headline say that design errors and planning lapses had saved money? In reality, contracting for more asphalt or concrete dividers than needed would likely have really driven up costs, though perhaps still come in under the estimate. Would that be preferable?

Once started down the path of blaming, it's easy for people to shift from blaming the estimate to blaming the estimator. "They should have known better." Perhaps they could have made a better estimate and perhaps not. And perhaps they made a perfectly good estimate for some other need than the one for which it was found wanting. In any event, there's little you can do now to improve a past estimate.

Worse is blaming the people whose work didn't meet the estimate. It's not a sure thing that they could have met the estimate. At worst, they may have failed to keep people properly informed. We'll look more deeply into that, later. (See Why Didn't We Know Earlier, on page 157.)

I've yet to see a situation where blaming made it better. We'll look more closely at that in Chapter 9, When People Clash, on page 177, but for now, let's examine what to do when we discover our estimate is wrong.

Salvaging the Situation

When you've missed some milestone, it's natural for people to want a new estimate for that milestone. How much longer *will* it take? When *will* it be done? Or, as a boss of mine once asked me, "How many more unforeseen problems are we going to have?"

Reestimating when we're in a hurry to make up for lost time is really frustrating. It's tempting to skip it. You'll meet that milestone when it happens, and you can't afford to waste time on estimation. Perhaps, though, you'd do better to skip the part about hurrying to make up for lost time. Hurrying has been known to be associated with making more errors, which creates more delays. Yes, it's true that you'll meet that milestone when it happens. That, however, doesn't change the needs of people who want to know when it will happen.

Obsolete Estimates

People talk about estimates being "wrong" when reality fails to match them. I find it more useful to think of them as obsolete. You now have more information and can see the situation more clearly. The estimate you made was rooted in the past and based on the assumptions and knowledge you had at that time.

Estimates don't become obsolete suddenly at the arrival of the estimated date or the accomplishment of the estimated work, however. They become a bit more obsolete every time you learn new information, or you correct an assumption. Long-term estimates age a little bit every day.

Tiny bits of information erode our estimate like dripping water on a soft stone. It happens so slowly you often miss it, especially if you're not specifically looking for it. You would do well to observe this slow degradation, and do something when you notice it. When the final reality proves our estimate "wrong," the most wrong thing is that you never updated it along the way. (See If Estimating Is Hard, Estimate More Often, on page 165.)

Replanning

When estimates and actuals don't match, trust the actuals. The actuals are data. It may be noisy data. It may be data that says things you don't want. But it's data. The estimates are opinion. Therefore it's prudent to adjust your plans to take that data into account. Recalibrating is the same process as Calibrating to Unknown Context, on page 44, but you have more information about the variability in the rate of progress.

What's past can't be changed, so delays you've experienced are going to add to the current plan. Don't expect that you'll go faster to make up the lost time. Denial and optimism do not make a healthy plan. Even if you identify some time-saving changes to make in your development process, it will take time to integrate those changes effectively. Don't count your chickens before they're hatched.

Should you adjust the estimates of future work? Yes, it's likely that there are lessons from the current delay that apply to this future work. (See What Didn't We Know Earlier, on page 154.) If you learn these lessons, and adjust your plan accordingly, you may avoid some repeated disappointment. Don't expect that you've solved your problems until you see it in the data, though. If you have eliminated the conditions that made progress slower than you expected, then you'll get a happy surprise in the future.

After replanning based on the reality you observe, you can attend to fitting that plan into your constraints. If progress is too slow to fit everything you want into your budgeted time or cost, consider trimming the scope of the work. This can be done by eliminating features or by slimming features down into easier-to-develop, though less capable, versions. You may have to make some difficult decisions about priority.

Observe where your delays and bottlenecks are. What makes the actual speed as slow as it is? If it seems that things "should be faster," then it's possible they would be, except for an accumulation of difficulties that impede progress. Perhaps there are some quick wins in outdated procedures that can be eliminated and thus speed up progress. Perhaps the internal quality of the code has been ignored to the point that everything is hard to change. It will take time to improve that quality, but it will eventually pay off in faster development speeds.

- Are there handoffs between one person to another or one team to another? Such handoffs always seem to create delays in matching schedules and in relearning the same lessons. Is there some way both people and/or teams can work together collaboratively to avoid a handoff?

- Are there times when some stream of work is waiting with no one actively working on it? Delays, like handoffs, decrease the efficiency of the work being done. Often such delays are due to work waiting on a bottleneck constraint. You may find it more effective on the whole if others help reduce that constraint, even if they're not as efficient about it as those already doing that work.

- Are there internal documents, reports, or work products that no one is using? Eliminating these may speed up the work. If these are being used to communicate across handoffs, then collaborating in parallel may eliminate the need.

- Do people have multiple work items in progress at the same time? Multitasking reduces efficiency and increases mistakes.

- Are people trying to accomplish work faster than their capacity to do the work? If you stretch people too thin, then the work takes longer to do, and more mistakes are made.

Learning from the Situation

Estimates can be used for more than simple prediction and tracking of progress. It's so discouraging when people treat estimates as a one-time chance to guess the future. The odds of winning that game are very low, indeed. Using estimates as your current best idea of that future is more helpful. And using them as a stake in the ground to detect changes in what you think you know is even more so.

There's little to be learned by the *fact* that estimates are wrong, but they can help you notice when things are not as they should be or, at least, not as you thought they should be. "Incorrect estimates" are not very useful when considered as failures, but are a goldmine of potential information and insight. It's instructive to examine in what ways they are wrong and how they came to be wrong. When actuals differ significantly from the estimate, it indicates that the assumptions of the estimate have not been borne out in fact. Why not? What was different from what was expected? What other estimates deserve another look based on this new knowledge?

As you adjust your view of the future, it should come more and more in line with reality. You can start with really rough, low-precision estimates. Over time you'll gain the information to make them more precise, if that seems worthwhile. Your estimates should converge with the final reality over time as you learn and as you address the risks and get closer to your goals.

What Didn't We Know Earlier

When we estimate, we are always working with incomplete knowledge of the situation. If we had complete understanding, we would calculate instead of estimate. We fill in the gaps of our knowledge with assumptions, both explicit and tacit. As is to be expected, those assumptions sometimes turn out to be unwarranted.

When events do not match the estimate, it's tempting to jump to single, proximate causes. "If it hadn't taken so long to figure out that legacy code we were modifying, we wouldn't be so late." This assumes that this or other legacy code won't be a problem in the future. That's similar to the assumption we made in our original estimate, that the existing code wouldn't slow us down.

What other assumptions are built into the estimate?

Let's reconsider all that might be suspect, given what we've learned from this failed prediction. It's easy to find reasons why things didn't go as planned, but these are not generally special cases. There are similar things you will not foresee in the future. Allow for them.

If it seems like you're slipping the schedule on a recurring basis, then there's something you're not learning. You must be injecting some unwarranted optimism. Perhaps you think too many things are one-time, special variations that won't be repeated, but the stream of one-time variations is endlessly ever changing. Whatever it is, you need to dig until you root it out. Adjusting expectations is a good thing, but people would like an increasing sense of trust in those expectations over time.

Revisiting Assumptions

When we first built our estimate, we did so in comparison to past history. This is, of course, an imperfect process. We tried to think of all the aspects where the proposed system might differ from the reference systems. (See Aspects to Compare, on page 34.) We can revisit those aspects and decide if we misjudged any of them.

The Code Isn't What We Imagined

We saw an example of things not being what they seemed in Misdiagnosis, on page 12. We can misdiagnose the situation in software development, too. It's certainly happened to me.

Someone asked me to change the way the system functions, and I thought it was going to be easy. "Sure, I'll have that done by close of business tomorrow." Then I started looking at the code and thought, "Oops, this code isn't at all what I expected."

The code for this functionality was spread over a number of source files, and architectural levels. Worse, it was commingled with other functionality and that interacted with each other. When I change this, I break that. Somebody must have been in a big hurry when they hacked in the last change. Perhaps they were trying to get it done within the time they had estimated.

I could try to do the same, that is, hack up the code until it looks like it might be working. As tangled as I found the code to be, though, it was unlikely that I'd get everything right for all cases. There were cases that would be affected that had nothing to do with the change I was making.

Or, rather, they should have had nothing to do with it. With that much coupling in the code, it would take me more than two days to figure out all the things that might be affected. Testing those things would take even longer. Ignoring this risk would likely cause some problems in the future. If I broke something I didn't know about, it might take a while before it's noticed.

When errors accidentally affecting other functionality aren't noticed right away, it hides the fact that the work I'm doing can't really be done in the expected amount of time. Ultimately, it adds to the time it will actually take.

I might make it look like I met the estimate, but I won't have done all the work that was expected to be included. It's expected that I add the new functionality and that I don't break anything else. I may meet the deadline, but invisibly miss the implicit expectation from my estimate.

Or I could do the job "properly." I clearly won't meet the expectation of "close of business tomorrow" that I gave when I was given the task. In other words, I will visibly miss the explicit expectation from my estimate.

Either way, my estimate was wrong. I wouldn't have the change done by close of business tomorrow.

Looking at it another way, my estimate wasn't really wrong. It was made in good faith based on the information available at the time. Now I have more information that makes the estimate obsolete. My updated estimate is that it would take me several days to two weeks to accomplish this, depending on the problems I had disentangling the code and how far I went in cleaning it up.

My best course of action was to talk with the person who asked me to make the change. I didn't want to leave them with the false impression created by my original estimate.

The Team Isn't What We Expected

Does your estimate depend on who is working on the project? A friend told me about carefully planning a project with someone who had deep experience in the domain, competence at the work, and also brought out the best in teammates. Shortly after submitting the plan, this key person was reassigned to another project. It was a crushing blow to the project and completely undermined the estimated plan.

The loss of crucial personnel can also happen in the middle of a project. This not only removes the knowledge and skill on which the estimate was predicated, but disrupts the rhythm of teamwork that had been developed.

I once consulted with a manager tasked to estimate a project where the personnel weren't yet known. He thought that the company would probably choose one of a few overseas contracting companies they'd used before, but he didn't know which one. And once they chose, there was no telling who they would assign to the project. They might be people recently hired just for the contract.

Even when working with known players, a team is more than the sum of its individuals. When a team jells, they cover for each other's momentary or permanent deficiencies in a way that makes them unnoticeable. They collaborate seemingly effortlessly in a just-in-time way that keeps the work flowing. There is a big difference between such a team and a work group that doesn't jell. Does your estimate assume that they will jell or not?

Blown Sprint

It happens sometimes that a development team "blows a Sprint" and doesn't deliver much in the way of functionality for an entire iteration. How does your organization respond to that?

If you're "working to plan," this throws a monkey wrench into the plan, and many organizations jump to blaming the development team for not meeting commitments. This, of course, damages the trust and communication between the development team and the part of the organization doing the blaming. In turn, it becomes less likely that the development team will notify the blamers, much less reach out for help, when similar situations come up in the future. Underlying problems get swept under the rug and ignored, making future disappointing situations even more likely. And things spiral downhill.

Rather than push hard to "catch up" with the schedule, recognize that this was one of the unforeseen situations for which you should have contingency planning in place. Stop and spend the time to examine the situation more deeply. My father, when he was an organic chemistry professor, would tell flunking students to stick it out and "earn their F." They had nothing to lose and an opportunity to learn. It would make their next attempt easier and more likely to succeed.

Perhaps it's worth taking a whole day for a retrospective. You might even want to have a multipart retrospective, with the development team examining their part of the situation, and the managers and other stakeholders examining theirs. Then, get all the parties together for a combined retrospective with each affinity group having taken a deep dive into their own experiences and failures. What can you learn from this?

You might not catch up with your preferred schedule, but that's water under the bridge. The goal now is to make the best choices for the future, and a temporary reset is a great way of doing that. And who knows, this might be just the impetus for a breakthrough that leads to a better conclusion than the original plan.

Why Didn't We Know Earlier

There are two common situations where we wouldn't know earlier that a milestone would be missed. One is that someone knew, or had a pretty good idea, but didn't tell anyone else. The other is that no one was paying attention to the things that would have let us know. In between, there are some variations, such as telling someone who wasn't paying attention, but rarely is there no warning at all.

Late Surprises

Picture this: The scene is a conference room at the Empire Enterprises IT department. Various IT and project managers sit around the conference table. Other project managers and tech leads sit in a second row of chairs around the walls, and yet more are attending by video conference. The current topic is reviewing the status of near-term milestones. Reviewing risks is scheduled next on the agenda.

The CIO is unhappy. "It's not unreasonable to say 'Hey, these dates don't make sense anymore.' It is unreasonable to say at the 11th hour, 'We're not going to meet that date.' It should be a dialog. Is this milestone on the critical path for something, or is it a stake in the sand? If you know you can't meet a date, don't kill yourself trying to do so. Think about the risk. Having a conversation is a really good thing to do." Everyone in the room takes a deep breath, and then the meeting continues.

In my experience, executives don't usually get upset when work is going to take longer than planned. Very few milestones are deadlines on inflexible schedules that can't be missed. What does upset executives is not knowing that things will take longer than planned. They depend on people to report reality so they can make the right decisions. You'll hear them say this at every status meeting where they get late notification of a problem.

Unfinished Kitty

...continued from TinyToyCo and the Robotic Cat, on page 18

"It looks like we won't be able to sell Fluphy Kitty™ for Christmas this year. If the retailers can't order it next month, it's missed the train."

"Yeah," Chris replied, "I got too carried away trying to get the prototype to jump, I guess. I wasn't watching the lead time for the big retailers. What are we going to do? We can't afford to keep developing at this burn rate for next year's season, and without Christmas, all our revenue projections are trash."

"Let's deal with the near-term problems, first," Pat replied. "What do we need to do to get a desirable, salable toy that can be sold?"

"Obviously we need to drop jumping, for now. I suspect that we could make the meowing more interesting to make up for that. Perhaps throw some recognizable words into the meows, even."

"Second, how can we sell this at Christmas? We won't be able to get it into physical stores, but perhaps we can do well with large online retailers. We'll need to investigate the timeline for that —and also think of how to do some viral marketing to create demand. I was counting on people buying on impulse when they saw Fluphy Kitty™ in action at the stores. I think we can replace that with online videos that are easy to share."

"That sounds good. Parallel to that, though, we need to take action so that this doesn't happen to us again. Let's estimate backward from hard deadlines. When do we need to deliver to online retailers to make this happen? How long will it take to manufacture and package prior to that delivery? How long to design the packaging after we know the final feature set, or close enough to know what to print on the box?"

"Good point. We're in this pickle because we didn't estimate when our last responsible moment for a working design really was. I'll spend the rest of today making phone calls for information, and tomorrow let's work out the known and unknown aspects of that timeline."

When things don't go as expected, you not only need to correct the problem, but correct your process so you don't repeat the same problem. Setting a milestone as a guard condition can let you know when to reassess your current plan while you still have time to do something different. See Danger Bearings, on page 167 for more on this concept.

Giving the Bad News

Imagine that you're in *that* meeting. And imagine, while your project's next milestone is further off than is currently being discussed, that there are things that worry you. Have you articulated these worries on the risk register, to be discussed next? Are you comfortable with bringing up your worries in this meeting? Unless the risk can be laid to dependencies outside the company, that's a very hard thing to do. No one wants to look bad in front of a lot of important managers and peers.

Yet those same people are depending on you to give them accurate enough information to make good decisions, and to give it early enough that there is still time for the best alternative options.

Hiding the schedule problems means that something less visible than time is sacrificed. Even with the best of intentions, time pressure causes people to rush and make mistakes. Time pressure affects their judgment of how much they need to think about the design, about the abnormal conditions the system might face, or about the understandability of the code. "We don't have time to sharpen the saw; we're in a hurry to cut down this tree."

You want to do the right thing, but how much courage do you have?

Asking for the Bad News

Now imagine that you're the CIO. You *really do* want people to give you the bad news as well as the good. Do you ask for bad news when none is evident? Perhaps you'd prefer that there be no bad news to give. How do you react when people give you bad news? Do you thank them for it? Or do you take charge of the situation by asking them questions and giving them advice?

Perhaps you have some other default reaction. Do you know what that reaction is? Are you aware of how your reaction in such difficult times is perceived by those witnessing it? Will your reaction make it easier or harder for people to report unhappy news in the future?

If you want people to tell you bad news, you need to do more than accept it when they do. You need to invite it, repeatedly, and you need to make people feel good when they provide it. They don't have to feel good about the news, itself, but they do need to feel good that they shared it. How can you reward people for highlighting when things aren't going to plan? How can you make it likely that people will investigate the potential consequences of new knowledge?

Stepping Back for a Broader View

As much as it pains you, working with the reality in front of you is more productive than working with your hopes and wishes. That means you've got to face the reality of your situation and deal with it. Blaming the estimates, estimator, or implementor for not meeting your plan is a destructive form of crying over spilled milk.

When things aren't coming together as you planned, it's time to change the plan. Nothing else is likely to work. Let's hope that you make the decision to replan early enough to accomplish the things that matter to you. There are some ways to detect problem earlier, which gives you more flexibility in your replanning.

The foremost way to get early warning is to welcome bad news. Celebrate when you receive it. Almost always there is someone who knows things are headed for a train wreck long before that wreck happens.

Another way to spot problems early is to integrate systems early. The most pernicious problems in system development are disagreeing assumptions between components. Don't leave that until last. Connect your systems first and then make them work correctly together.

Work in a fashion where progress is unambiguous. See things working to indicate progress. Estimating completion percentages is a great way to hide missed assumptions. Use functional slices, and measure them in a Boolean fashion; they're either done or not.

For safety, reestimate portions of the system from time to time. Are the new estimates in line with the old? Or have you learned something that changes your assumptions?

When the actuals don't match your plans, you've surely found something that violates your original assumptions. Dig in and figure out what it is. Don't be too easily satisfied, as there are likely multiple assumptions that need rethinking.

The questions you might ask yourself include:

- When we made this estimate, what did we assume that turned out to not be true?
- What has changed since we made this estimate?
- Have we seen similar issues with prior missed estimates?
- When could we have noticed this if we'd been checking our estimates periodically?
- If we account for these changes in estimates of future work, how does that change our plans?
- Does our new plan have enough safety margin for severe risks?

Do all of these things, and you can improve your future prospects. That's something to celebrate, isn't it? Does that make it easier for you to welcome bad news? It's a blessing in disguise.

In the next chapter, we'll look at ways to test our assumptions even earlier and more deliberately.

Now It's Your Turn

1. When the actuals prove your estimates were optimistic, what is your first reaction? What action do you take? What would you *like* your reaction and action to be?

2. When you suspect that your estimates were optimistic, who do you tell about that? How do you feel about telling them?

3. On your project or in your organization, do schedule slippages seem to recur on a regular basis? How far in advance of the scheduled date does the slippage become generally known?

4. How often do you ask your peers or those who report to you about what they've learned? What use do you make of that information?

CHAPTER 8

Planning for Incorrect Predictions

Sponsoring executives use estimates made prior to starting a project to determine if it will fit into their investment criteria. Project managers use estimates at the beginning of a project to build their plans of how to conduct the project in a way that meets the budget and time targets that have been set. These estimates, done when you know the least, are hard to do well and become less valuable over time. Yet we often try to manage the work using these stale estimates as a guide.

Since we know that estimates are not perfect predictions of the future, it seems foolish to do them once and then trust them. In fact, you can use them to get early warnings of your mistaken assumptions. This makes your "wrong estimates" valuable—valuable enough that you might want to create additional estimates specifically as *hypotheses to test your assumptions.*

When a milestone is missed, it's an easy reminder to revisit your assumptions. Wouldn't it be nice to notice before a public milestone is missed? What do you do when things seem to be going smoothly?

You can, of course, wait until there's a problem. If there's nothing critical relying on your milestones, that might be the most reasonable approach. Of course, if that's the case then you might not have needed the estimate at all. Be careful, however, that you're not overlooking someone else's important needs.

Most of the time there are consequences for missing a milestone. Those consequences might be minor, such as disappointing a stakeholder or delaying another team, or they might be major, such as missing a market window or incurring legal penalties. The nature of those consequences affects how much effort a development team or project manager may want to invest in prudence.

Seeking Out Information

Whenever new information comes to light, you can check your assumptions. Do they still seem valid? Which estimates depend on an assumption that no longer seems valid?

What sort of new information might affect the validity of your estimates? Almost anything, really.

- When someone leaves the team: What effect will that have on productivity?

- When someone joins the team: That's likely to slow things down for a while. Will it speed up again later?

- When a library, tool, or operating system releases a new version: What effects will that have?

- When there's a physical rearrangement of the workspace: What affordances are changed? How will it affect communication?

- When you find out that the codebase on which you're building this project was never deployed to production: What hidden incomplete work lies within it?

This is just a small start. It's really hard, of course, to evaluate all new information you receive and correctly determine *if* it meaningfully changes your assumptions, *which* assumptions, and in *what* ways. We make assumptions to simplify how we think about things and get some of the details out of our heads. There are too many details to document them all, so you won't have a comprehensive list to check. Trying to evaluate all information as it comes in sounds helpful, but it's too large and error-prone a task to rely on solely.

Rather than wait for information to come to you, you might want to seek it out. Be proactive, and specifically look for ways to avoid fooling yourself with a complacent trust in your estimates and assumptions. It's a lot easier to notice that information has changed when you're actively looking for it (than when it happens while you're doing other things).

If you're going to continually steer based on priority and projections, then you've got to keep those estimates up-to-date. Keep looking for where your assumptions may have changed. Have others challenge your estimates and assumptions. What do they notice that you have not? What do they not see that you've come to think is essential?

If Estimating Is Hard, Estimate More Often

Edgar R. Fiedler, former U.S. Assistant Secretary of the Treasury for Economic Policy, is quoted as saying, "If you have to forecast, forecast often." (*The Three Rs of Economic Forecasting-Irrational, Irrelevant and Irreverent [Fie77]*) In the Extreme Programming community circa 2000, there was a saying that "if something is hard, do it more often." When you do something more often, it becomes a smaller and easier job to do. It also becomes more effective. This is true of testing, code integration, delivering working software, and it's also true of estimation.

It would seem too expensive to reestimate everything from scratch on a frequent basis, but not if you use a lower-precision estimation process. You're looking for significant differences from your previous estimates, not minor ones. For long-term projects, you should likely be reestimating annually, if not quarterly. Things can get really out of hand in a year's time. Much more frequently, you should reestimate the near-term milestones. These should be relatively easy to check. If you find major discrepancies between your new estimates and your old ones, then you'll want to consider where those arise and what else is similarly affected.

Spot Reestimation

You may not wish to reestimate everything, but it would be prudent to reestimate those items where you notice that assumptions have changed. Perhaps more has changed than you've noticed. Look for potential problems, not confirmation.

Periodically perform spot reestimations in other areas, too. To guard against unnoticed changes in assumptions, take a small cross section of items and look at them anew. Try to focus on items that depend on different assumptions. Choose different items at different times to reduce your inattentional blindness. That's when you're so focused on one thing, you miss something else that should be completely obvious. It's not unreasonable to reestimate one or two parts of the project each month to give yourself a good shot at noticing changes. You can never remain aware of all the assumptions you made, so making them again might turn up something different. If the estimate has significantly changed, think about why. Are there other estimates you should revisit based on that reasoning?

How often should you do this? That's hard for me to say without knowing your context, but here are some clues to help you decide for yourself.

How much risk are you incurring if the estimate is wrong?

In some situations there may be very little risk. When an estimate turns out to be wrong, you learn from it at that time, adjust, and move on. In other cases, there's a lot riding on getting something particular done by a certain time, or in meeting your promises to someone else. In these cases, you'd want to spot-estimate more often.

How confident are you on the accuracy of your estimate?

If you're pretty confident that your estimate is "in the ballpark," then inaccuracies may be small enough that you can easily correct for them. If you're less certain of your estimates, then adjusting to new information may be a major undertaking. You'll want lots of time for a safety margin to make that adjustment, especially if the consequences are high. In that case, spot-check more often, and work to gain more confidence in the riskiest parts of the project.

Comparison to Plan

There's an old project management adage, "Plan the work and work the plan." This can work, but only if the initial plan is close enough to reality. Often it's not (see Driving Up Costs, on page 150), and if this maxim leads you to believe that the plan was the reality, then what will actually happen is a nightmare. Instead, you can learn from the variance to plan (see Learning from the Situation, on page 153).

Eisenhower made famous the old advice that "plans are worthless, but planning is everything." (*Remarks at the National Defense Executive Reserve Conference, November 14, 1957 [Eis58]*)[1] When the unexpected happens, it's better to change our plans. So instead of conforming to your plan, I invite you to compare to your plan.

Notice what has changed since the plan was made. What has not gone according to plan? What things needed doing that weren't in the plan? Were there also things in the plan that, with the fuller knowledge that came in time, maybe didn't need to be done?

Notice what changes repeatedly, for these are unstable areas of your plan. Do you *really* think they won't change again? Back up from the details of these changes and think about what's causing them to change.

---

1. http://quoteinvestigator.com/2017/11/18/planning/.

Vary your view. Look at things from multiple scales of granularity whenever possible. After focusing on your natural focus for the circumstances, take a look at the underlying details. Then back up and look at the big picture.

You can also vary your view by looking from different vantage points. Get opinions from people with different roles, backgrounds, or ways of thinking. Or, if you can't get their viewpoints, imagine you can. If you could ask them, and they could tell you their honest opinion, what would they say?

Setting Traps for Information

In addition to searching for new information and trying to judge its significance, you can also set traps to capture significant information that bears examination.

Danger Bearings

You can use estimates and measures based on estimates as guidelines to warn you when you're tending toward disaster. You want to plot your progress in a way that assures you're in a safe zone, or warns you if you're getting close to being outside.

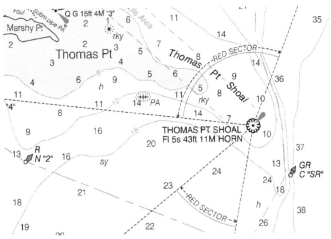

When navigating a boat, such a guideline is called a danger bearing. You plot a line on the chart from some visible point to some hidden danger. As long as you stay outside of that line, you're OK. You may think that by knowing your starting point and knowing the direction you're traveling, you would also know you're on a safe course. It's not that simple, though. As in software development projects, unseen currents can carry you off that course, even though you're still headed in the direction you planned. To make sure you're not drifting into danger, you can check whether you're outside of that line by checking the bearing to that visible point. Some permanent navigational marks have designs to keep you on the safe side of some hazard. The danger bearing is built into a lighthouse by a red filter in front of the light. If you see red light, you've crossed the line and are heading into danger.

One way to notice obsolete estimates is to record guard conditions—perhaps something similar to "if we haven't achieved this outcome by May, then this estimate is suspect." That lets you know that the estimate is obsolete. You can revisit it, and the larger estimates that include it, and decide what to do.

More generally, stay out of danger by using a BurnUp Chart. (See BurnUp Charts, on page 111.) Estimate the minimal amount that will be a valuable release, for whomever you need to please. Since you're looking for safety, make sure your estimate errs on the high side of what that minimum valuable amount might be. Express that in measurable terms, so you can tell when you reach it. Split it into smaller, but still measurable, increments of progress. As things move forward, look to see if the current trend line meets this bare minimum success criteria before a hard deadline, preferably well before. Of course, you'd rather deliver more than the bare minimum. But concentrate on reaching that level of success first, and then add enhancements as long as there is time to do so.

Hypothesis

It's helpful to position your estimates as hypotheses rather than predictions. You can test your prior hypotheses against what you actually achieve. This allows you to measure how far off your assumptions are, and to notice things you didn't know.

Experimentation is a powerful learning tool, and the scientific method rests on the performance of experiments to confirm or deny a proposed hypothesis. When I was young, I performed "scientific experiments" by mixing chemicals together to see what they would do. I learned that most random concoctions from my chemistry set would make a brown liquid that was often hard to clean out of a test tube and that sometimes they would create very smelly brown liquids. These were not really experiments, however. These were activities, and because I had no hypothesis to prove, I didn't really learn anything useful. Unless you can propose a hypothesis in advance, you cannot design an experiment to test it. Until you test the hypothesis, you haven't really learned anything.

"In general, we look for a new law by the following process: First we guess it; then we compute the consequences of the guess to see what would be implied if this law that we guessed is right; then we compare the result of the computation to nature, with experiment or experience, compare it directly with observation, to see if it works. If it disagrees with experiment, it is wrong. In that simple statement is the key to science. It does not make any difference how beautiful your guess is, it does not make any difference how smart you are, who made the guess, or what his name is – if it disagrees with experiment, it is wrong." – Richard Feynman, *The Character of Physical Law* [Fey67]

When you estimate how long it will take, or how much it will cost, to implement a desired amount of software functionality, you create a hypothesis that you can test. Your hypothesis may not be of enduring and universal value as a hypothesis that predicts physical laws, but it may still be extremely valuable to you in your situation. You can test your hypothesis, with all of its explicit and tacit assumptions, against the hard truth of reality. When your hypothesis is found wanting, you can consider which of its supporting assumptions is incorrect, or if there are necessary assumptions which are missing.

So, set up a few intermediate points that are on the way to your first milestone. Estimate these. That's your first hypotheses.

How early can you test the correlation between the estimates in your plan and the actual rate of progress? When work is performed in large blocks and integrated at the end, it's far too late for effective replanning when the difference is noticed. How can you validate your plan earlier?

I recommend setting your first hypothesis as within a couple weeks to a couple months, preferably less than 10% of the way to your first milestone of importance outside the project. While you need to inform others when the situation changes (see Evaluating and Changing Plans, on page 143), you first want to inform yourself. Perhaps you can correct the trajectory of the project before it becomes imperative to report it up the chain. Failing that, you'll have more time to develop a realistic plan to suggest.

Working in small increments and continuously integrating can help, but you also need to verify those small increments are actually done. Using estimates of "the database layer is 90% done" won't help, as you're back to depending on unverifiable estimates. Rather than creating small increments based on the building blocks of your project, try using small increments of functionality. These functional slices will touch numerous building blocks, but can be tested unambiguously as to whether or not they work as desired. Even better is if they can be put into production use and tested by real work. This roots out the unexpected undoneness that can throw your projections off so much. See Reliably Measuring Functionality, on page 82 for more discussion on measuring progress by testing the functionality of integrated code.

That's a lot of prescriptive description about how to start your project using estimates as hypotheses. Let's look at how this might play out in concrete circumstances. As you read this story, imagine yourself in the position of Jesse, and think about how you would normally handle the situation. Also think about how it would feel to handle it the way Jesse is handling it.

Planning a New Project at Riffle & Sort

World Of Friends has been a payroll customer of Riffle & Sort since they opened their doors. It is a small but busy nonprofit that would rather focus on their mission of helping arrange student and cultural exchange programs to further world understanding and peace, than deal with the humdrum bookkeeping.

They're finding that the world is getting more complicated, and there is more and more humdrum paperwork involved in making a successful exchange program work. Rather than increasing staff to handle the workload, they've come to Riffle & Sort for help.

While the project may be about automating the current paperwork processing, the goal is a higher-level ambition, "furthering world understanding and peace." A computer system cannot do that, but it can help people do that.

Eliciting the Requirements

Jesse, the project manager and onsite proxy for the customer, had interviewed several people at World Of Friends to get an idea of what they needed. The world had indeed made things more difficult for cultural exchanges. The process was something like this:

1. Students wanting to participate would fill out an application form, writing several essays about who they were and why they wanted to participate.

2. This form would be reviewed by World Of Friends to select those most likely to do well in the cultural exchange program. Since the students would be hosted in private houses, it was important to choose people who would leave a good impression with the hosts.

3. Those students selected as applicants by World Of Friends would be sent a letter outlining next steps. Accompanying the letter would be various government documents that would need to be filed to get permission to come and live for an extended time in another country. The visas, in particular, would need official government background checks. These would require fingerprints. Since the rules were complicated and frequently changing, these documents were to be sent back to World Of Friends for submission to the appropriate authorities.

4. In parallel to the official background checks and visa processing, World Of Friends would conduct their own background check in the applicant's home country. This was intended to turn up any red flags for behavior that would affect the host family.

5. Only after both of these investigative paths had been completed, a World Of Friends adjudicator would then make a final decision on the applicant. Part of this procedure was making

sure that all the proper documentation had been supplied, all questions had been satisfactorily answered, and necessary government permissions had been given.

6. Once the final acceptance was made, World Of Friends would match up each applicant with a prospective host family based on the stated preferences from both. A letter of introduction would be sent to the prospective host family, describing the applicant and providing the essays they had written on the original application. The host family might refuse for any reason. They might have seen something in the description or essays that gave them a bad feeling. Or they might have had a change of heart about being a host family for completely unrelated reasons. It really doesn't matter what the reason; another prospective host would be chosen and the same letter of introduction sent to them. This could happen multiple times until either a host family accepted or World Of Friends ran out of prospective hosts in the designated location.

7. Finally, a letter of acceptance introducing the host family would be sent back to the applicant. This letter would contain information on dates to arrive and how to make travel arrangements.

These are Jesse's notes on World Of Friends current work process. It's true that the people Jesse interviewed asked for these activities to be automated as much as possible. With a project manager less savvy than Jesse, Riffle & Sort might have been tempted to try to fulfill this request as stated. Jesse knew, however, that what people ask may not accurately reflect what they desire. Also, not everything that people mention has equal importance. Keeping the goal in mind, Jesse started analyzing the request with a view toward simplicity, feasibility, risk, potential value, and opportunity.

Assessing the Constraints

Jesse thought about the best ways to ensure that World Of Friends was happy with the result and stay within their budget. While they wanted to automate the process as much as possible, they realized they wanted to keep some human control at appropriate points. In any event, they needed to have the system ready to go in early January for the coming year's cycle of applications. The deadline for applications was mid-March, so things would be in high-volume mode by then.

It was currently early April, and World Of Friends was recovering from the big bulk of work handling this year's applications. But there was plenty more work to be done, and it would pick up again when the background checks started coming in from the government agencies and the applicants' home countries. Right now would be a great time to work closely with World Of Friends, but the development team was putting the finishing touches on another project. They wouldn't be able to turn their attention to this one until the beginning of May. That gave them eight months, more or less, to have a working version. It had to be especially ready for the entry and initial triage of applications. There would be time to enhance later operations, such as the matching with host families.

Most projects need to fit into some sized box defined by time and money. All projects need to fit the constraints of feasibility within the capabilities that can be brought to bear on them. If you cannot satisfy these requirements, then people will be unhappy no matter what you do well. This implies that a less-capable system that meets these rudimentary constraints will be better received than something fancier that doesn't.

Analysis and Planning

What's the simplest system that could work? Using the computer to be a filing system for scanned paper forms was definitely the simplest, Jesse thought. They could test this with forms from previous years, blacking out a bit of personal data to meet privacy standards. This would let the team concentrate on the workflow and decision points. Online entry of the original application was an obvious time-saver. This was the highest-volume processing to be done.

Submitting the government forms was the riskiest part of the operation. Jesse felt sure that the government would be the most stringent on what they would and would not accept. And it was likely there would be unexpected communication delays and incomplete descriptions of why a submission was not accepted. This should go early in the plan to mitigate the risk of unknowns outside Riffle & Sort's control.

World Of Friends would be matching applicants with host families this summer; it would be good to work on that aspect while they were doing it, to capture the little details that people forget about after they get past them.

Jesse considers simplicity, risk, and variability between different deadlines in developing an initial plan. This plan is, so far, without a schedule.

A Tentative Schedule

Jesse started making lists of the inputs the system would have to accept, the outputs it would send, and the decision points. For each of these, someone would have to work out the details, but it was enough to list them for the moment. With that list, they could document the flow and check its accuracy with World Of Friends. They could also estimate each of these processing points independently, assuming they would build the basic flow first. That basic flow could fake the inputs, stub out the output, and turn the decision points into simple buttons. That should be possible in the first two weeks, Jesse thought. Then everything else can be bolted onto this rudimentary flow as it's fleshed out. If that simplistic flow isn't finished in four weeks, it's a sign of major problems.

Not having any better data, Jesse counted the inputs, outputs, and decision points and divided the eight months by that. "Oh, better figure the government inputs and outputs as double the others," Jesse thought, and recalculated. "That's about two weeks each. Sounds barely doable, but since we can push out some of the later details after a January initial-release deadline, we should be in good shape. And some outputs, like sending letters, should be easy after the first one is done. I'll check if anyone in the development team can help me sanity check these estimates next week."

Notice how Jesse set an initial danger bearing of four weeks to get a rudimentary flow working. That includes the expected two weeks of development work, and any other "getting started" delays that might arise. In addition, Jesse already has in place a series of hypotheses that each input, output, or decision point can be done with two-weeks work (except for the interfaces with government systems). That's a good setup for alerting if things are going astray.

Some of the alternate flows, such as rematching with host families, are expected to be included in these estimates. Others that are less likely, such as an applicant having to drop out, may not be. If there's time, the system can be enhanced to include them. If not, they will be low-volume enough to be handled with manual work-arounds.

Avoid Traps for the Unwary

Remember that the point of a hypothesis is that you're trying to *disprove* it, not confirm it. Be wary about fooling yourself. It's so easy to do.

Measurement Errors

When events are matching the estimate or perhaps doing a little better, don't relax and celebrate. Look for ways that the measurement of actuals could be fooling you. Do these actual measurements include everything assumed in the estimate?

- The work is going fine, but it's all on different code branches? There's surely hidden integration work.

- The code is written, but it's not tested? I'll bet you dollars to doughnuts that there's rework to do.

- You've integrated and tested on the development machine, but not on a system that resembles production? What environmental differences have you overlooked?

- You've got 100% branch coverage with your automated tests? But are those tests checking all the things that are supposed to work? Exercising code isn't the goal.

In order to count something as done, it should really be functionally solid. It's OK if the done slice has limited functionality as long as that's what was estimated. What's built, though, shouldn't have parts that don't work right. Bugs in the functionality represent work that was counted as done, but isn't. Measurement errors like this will blind you to discrepancies in your hypotheses.

Unsustainable Work

Another way in which the work you've measured might not be representative of the longer-term goals is if the development team has been working in an unsustainable fashion. If they've been working overtime or otherwise working beyond their natural capacity in an attempt to meet the hypothesis milestone, then they've also been wearing down their reserve energy. The pace they demonstrate while burning themselves out is not indicative of the pace they'll achieve afterward.

Besides wearing down the people, an unsustainable pace is likely eating away the integrity of the codebase. When in a hurry, people cut corners. They postpone "clean up" work until later, when they think they'll have more time. The code gets harder to read, harder to understand, and harder to change without introducing errors; it becomes harder to isolate the errors that are noticed. This slows the work down more and more until, sometimes, it comes to a complete halt. Do you remember when Netscape started a complete rewrite of their browser because they had hacked in so many features, they couldn't make progress anymore? It killed the company.

You might start to notice this when more and more estimates turn out to be optimistic. An obvious thing to look for is people routinely working long hours. There are indicators you can see in the moment, also. Personal hygiene may not be maintained. Posture may become worse, triggering back, neck and shoulder pains. You may notice people making phone calls about personal business at work because they have little opportunity otherwise. Smiles and laughter are nearly absent. Enthusiasm lags. Tempers flare. These behaviors are the canary in the coal mine, giving you early warning that the environment is not healthy.

It's clear, when you see these things, that people are trying to maintain a plan that's out of step with reality. Step back and take another look. Have you, or they, been believing past estimates over current reality? Reestimate, replan, and get back on a feasible track to success. If you can't redefine success as something that's achievable, perhaps it's a good time to pull the plug on the project before wasting more effort.

Have Appropriate Safety Margins

When the final outcomes are critical, plan in a safety margin for risk avoidance. Set up a danger bearing to alert when your critical needs are potentially in trouble. If your danger bearing alerts you of trouble, you need time to adjust. You won't be able to increase speed appreciably, so do this with scope adjustment. In order to be able to make sufficient adjustment, prioritize the work carefully. Get the essential things done first, and leave the "nice to haves" undone if time runs out. This may mean interleaving work on different features, as you get the essential parts of each essential feature done before embellishing them with bells and whistles. Some less essential features might, in severe cases, be completely dropped or deferred to another milestone. If they can't be deferred, then they must be more essential than you thought.

Stepping Back for a Broader View

It's highly unlikely that your primary goal is to meet your estimate. Meeting the estimate is a tactic toward achieving some higher goal, such as business prosperity or making the client happy so they bring you in for future project management jobs. Therefore, it makes sense to look at estimates in terms of how they can help you meet your goal.

Since we're talking about estimates rather than measurements or calculations, we know that they're not precisely accurate except by chance. If we want them to be valuable, we should treat them as the assumptions they are. Then, when they show themselves, we can learn what we mistook that caused us to make an inaccurate estimate.

If we know how to analyze our missed estimates to discover mistaken assumptions, then we can *intentionally* add estimates for milestones that have no external need, but would be convenient points to notice upcoming problems in time to take corrective action. This can help us steer our project to success, or at least notify people so they're not caught off guard.

Not everyone is content using estimates to guide their plans. Sometimes they fall into the trap of using estimates *as their plans*. When they do that, they may want to alter reality to fit the estimates. This will naturally create friction between people. The reason that people get so upset about estimation is the "bad blood" between those asking for estimates, those providing estimates, and those doing estimated work. In the next chapter we'll look more deeply into these human dimensions.

Now It's Your Turn

1. What information could you seek out to disprove or question your past estimates? Do you evaluate changes in the situation by examining how they might affect the current plan?

2. What ways of reestimating your project might be practical in terms of time and effort, but give you a reasonable chance to notice when your assumptions have changed?

3. What milestones could you estimate as early indicators when reality was not following your plan?

4. In what ways might your reevaluation or reestimation be fooling you? How are you working to avoid Confirmation Bias? (See Cognitive Biases, on page 72.)

CHAPTER 9

When People Clash

We've looked at reasons for needing estimates, and what kinds of estimates meet the needs behind those reasons. We've explored different approaches to estimating. We've discovered how to wring value out of estimates, especially when they prove wrong. And thanks to our example stories, using estimates effectively to help us achieve the goals we want sounds easy, doesn't it?

I can imagine what you're thinking. If you could talk to me through this book, you'd probably say, "But the stories you tell aren't believable. The people get along so well, even when they disagree. That's not how it happens in the *real world*! People fight and argue. People don't believe each other. People take advantage of each other."

Yet it *is* easy to use estimates in effective ways. What's hard is giving up counterproductive behavior, especially when that behavior is part of a mutually reinforcing cycle of behavior in an organization. The relationships between people in an organization are not always healthy. Sometimes one part of the organization seems to treat another part as if it's the enemy rather than a collaborator for achieving business success. Managers can get isolated from the organizational purpose and diverted to power plays within the organization. When they do, they surely isolate the development teams from the organizational purpose, too. Teams can feel they are the bottom rung and all the bad stuff rains down on their back.

Most of the estimation problems I hear complaints about are not about the estimation, but about the behavior surrounding estimation. While I don't want to focus the book on bad behavior, I would be remiss if I didn't acknowledge it and offer some ideas on making it better.

It Starts So Innocently

People don't intend to make things difficult. It just seems to happen.

How Much Work Would It Be...?

"How much work would it be to add auto-scheduling to the appointment calendar?"

"You mean to have the calendar automatically select the next open slot big enough for the appointment?"

"Yeah, that would work."

"Let's see, I'd have to create a preliminary appointment and then walk through the calendar in chronological order, looking for conflicts with existing appointments. I could do that in a day or two."

"Great, I'll let my boss know."

And just that simply we have an estimate of how much work it will take to implement this new functionality.

But what is left out of that estimate? There's nothing in there about controlling the new feature, either through configuration or by the user. There's probably nothing related to integrating with the existing GUI. It certainly doesn't account for new discoveries made in the codebase while developing it, or new enhancements that will be desired with it. Nor is there anything for technical dead ends reached while implementing. Or delays due to meetings, other commitments, or lack of availability of the person who can answer questions. It's just an estimate of the known development work.

Why Isn't It Done Yet?

Are you done with the appointment auto-scheduling feature?"

"No, the UX designer had some ideas that I hadn't considered. And the appointment code wasn't designed to be extendable. It should be done in another week."

"Another week? But you said it would take two days!"

And just like that, a simple estimate got turned into an involuntary commitment.

A single sentence of disappointment from a person with higher positional power in the organization will make that developer think twice before giving an estimate the next time. What might they do in the future?

One possible response is to pad the estimate as a contingency for the unknown. Contingency buffers really belong in the plans, not the estimate. If the estimate is taken as a plan, though, what's a poor programmer to do?

Padding the Estimate

"How long would it take to add automatically recurring appointments?"

"Hmmm...I could do that in three weeks?

"Three weeks!? My toddler could do it in less time."

A larger than expected estimate often raises fears of sandbagging—that the developer is intentionally estimating pessimistically for their own advantage. And, in this case, it might be quite reasonable for the developer to sandbag the estimate to be sure to meet the expected commitment. Sandbagging doesn't work so well, though, if it's not convincing.

Sandbagging is often greeted with negotiation. As soon as there is a counteroffer, you know you're negotiating rather than estimating.

Negotiating the Estimate

"How about you do it in one week?"

"I'll try to get it done in two, but I don't know what problems will pop up."

Some managers will negotiate estimates as a matter of course, thinking that by putting pressure on the development team they will produce faster. This starts down a very deep rabbit hole of reduced quality, increased defects, burned out development teams, and lack of trust.

How It Goes Wrong

From such an innocent start, we see it takes very little to spiral downward. The actions we took in the past cause others to alter their behavior to compensate. That change causes us to alter our behavior. Our behavior causes others to change theirs. When we reach the point that our behavior, through a loop of such effects, reinforces itself, then the behavior becomes deeply entrenched. It doesn't take much of a negative influence to turn into really pernicious behavior.

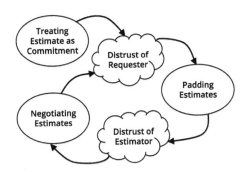

Treating an estimate as a commitment increases distrust in the requester, which increases padding, which increases distrust in the estimator, which increases negotiations, which increases distrust in the requester... Around and around it goes, forming a feedback loop that maintains the behavior.

Ordering Enough Parts

Years back, I was on a project designing a custom integrated circuit as part of a product. We had breadboarded a solution that proved the functionality but had uncovered some potential timing issues in the design. We redesigned some aspects of the circuit, and were ready to breadboard a second version to verify the redesign before committing to custom-fabricated silicon. This meant that we needed to order a sizable number of parts to breadboard the new design.

We drew the schematic and tallied up the parts needed. To cover for parts that might not work, or might be accidentally destroyed while building or testing the circuit, we added another 10% to the totals. That would surely be enough to build the prototype circuit without delays.

"Wait a minute! Every time we order parts, the boss thinks we're being profligate and cuts the order in half. If he does that, it will delay the entire project, and several upcoming products are dependent on this chip."

"You're right. I'll double the numbers for the purchase requisition. He'll likely cut the numbers in half even without looking at it."

This true-life story illustrates how poor communication and distrust around estimates leads to others altering their behavior to compensate. No doubt this boss had run into people doubling their parts orders before, and that triggered his habit of halving them. Lack of trust begets secrecy and subterfuge. These, in turn, engender loss of trust. The cycle is self-reinforcing unless someone takes extraordinary action to break the loop.

Sad Footnote

This story has a sadly amusing footnote. When we gave the boss the purchase requisition, he had just come from an executive meeting that emphasized how critical the project was. Without conferring with us, he doubled the quantities to ensure that lack of parts would not delay us. When we discovered that, we couldn't say anything. Doing so would reveal that we'd previously doubled the order.

On top of that, a few weeks later and before the parts started arriving, a new commercially available chip was announced that could perform the function we were designing a custom integrated circuit to do. The chip design project was canceled, but too late to cancel the quadruple order for parts to breadboard it.

This story describes estimating the need for physical things, but similar behavior happens around estimating work and time.

A manager asking for an estimate doesn't even need to behave badly to become involved in the reinforcing loop. Once it gets started, it takes on a life of its own. The programmer may be so used to managers treating estimates as commitments that they expect that from all managers, whether they've behaved that way toward them or not. The manager may be so used to programmers padding their estimates that they expect that from all programmers.

When someone is responding to "them, there, then" rather than "us, here, now," it takes special effort to break out of the situation. Benign behavior is not enough. The memory of past situations is strong, and people will usually choose to act the way they have in the past.

In stories like How Much Work Would It Be...?, on page 178 and Padding the Estimate, on page 179, the developer is facing a dilemma. Should they pad the estimate or give the optimistic "programming only" estimate that is most familiar to them? Which they choose has more to do with their past experience and past choices than it does with current circumstances.

Likewise, the requester of the estimate has a dilemma between accepting the estimate given or challenging it. Both players are caught between seemingly opposite choices.

This is a common stopping point. You've got two polar opposite responses. If you reject one, then you have to select the other, right? "I have to pad my estimate or else I'm going to get blamed for not meeting it." Or, at least, you lean toward one end of the spectrum or the other.

Or do you? Human behavior does not fit neatly on a linear scale between polar opposites. What's a third way to respond?

Rule of Three

Virginia Satir said that

> One option is a trap. Two options is a dilemma. Three options is a choice.

Jerry Weinberg often phrased this as

> If you haven't thought of a third option, you haven't thought enough, yet.

I use the Rule of Three to get myself out of dilemmas all the time. I find myself in a position where I've got a favored option and another that makes it look good by comparison. I've trained myself, when I notice I'm stuck at this point, to consciously look for a third option. When I find it, I often notice that by breaking the binary straitjacket of choosing one option or the other, I suddenly can think of options four, five, six, and many more.

What might be a third option when asked for an estimate?

If the requester doesn't frame the request in a way that helps you collaborate with them, perhaps you can open a dialog to help do that. "I want to provide you with an estimate that is most useful for you. Can you help me understand what decision depends on this estimate?"

Does that seem possible in your situation? It might be hard, especially in strongly hierarchical organizations, where the assumption is that commands move down the chain and answers move up. It's good advice, even if you don't know how to put it into action. More importantly, it helps you see that there are options outside the range from "bare minimum" to "a safe bet." You might want to answer, "there are some unknowns that make it too risky to give any number, yet."

If you can't talk with the requester to reframe the situation, perhaps you can reframe it in your reply. "If a budget is being formulated, then perhaps you want this conservative estimate with these caveats. On the other hand, if this is a rough order of magnitude for prioritization, then you might want this estimate of a likely value, taking into account these other caveats."

This is a start. With more detailed knowledge of the specific circumstances, you can probably think of a number of other options. The options are not necessarily mutually exclusive, either. You might be able to try some of them in parallel.

And what might be a third option when receiving an estimate you've requested?

Rather than accept or challenge it, you might inquire about the assumptions being made in it. What things are included? What things are left out? What things are risky and therefore enlarged to cover that risk?

People are generally antsy around the topic of estimation. They know that their estimates, whether made or received, are wrong. They just don't know by how much. They'd like to take them as truth, because they aren't very good at dealing with vague probabilities. But they can't treat them as fact without getting into some trouble or another. This uncomfortable uncertainty puts people on the defensive.

Most books and articles on estimation are focused on estimating more accurately and precisely so that you stay out of trouble when you give an estimate to someone. When the topic of estimation comes up, though, people don't tend to talk about how to estimate better. They talk about the bad behavior that typically accompanies estimation, both before and after, in most organizational environments. When running workshops, that same bad behavior comes out in simulations using fictitious situations. Clearly there is a problem.

Also clearly, the problem is not estimation itself. If people are behaving badly, better estimates won't help. How can we alter our behavior so that we can work effectively in spite of the fact that our estimates will never be as accurate and precise as some people will sometimes want?

Understanding Human Behavior

Since better estimates won't fix the relationships between people, let's look at some models of these relationships from the fields of psychology and social work. This will give you some background understanding to help you identify and address the issues.

Congruence

Congruence is a term that psychologist Carl Rogers borrowed from geometry to describe the alignment of different aspects of a person, including what they think and feel, the affect they present, and how they behave with others. This is often expressed as a person's image of who they are today being aligned with their image of their ideal self, even if not fully realized.

Building on this idea, Virginia Satir, a social worker and family therapist who also worked with Jerry Weinberg to apply her ideas to business situations, described achieving congruence as balancing the needs of yourself, the other with whom you're interacting, and the context of the situation.

This balance of concerns allows us to be genuine, and have our outward affect match our inner self. When we are concerned about possible risk, our actions show this concern rather than a false appearance of devil-may-care. When we are happy at achieving some goal, it shows on our face and in our posture. You might think that this is a risky thing to do, tipping your hand to others and making yourself vulnerable in the situation. If you were only reflecting your own thoughts, emotions, and needs, then you might be right. When you're considering theirs and yours, plus the situation at hand, then this transparency becomes a benefit to the situation and current interaction.

Congruence, as described by Virginia Satir, goes further than "the inside matches the outside." It also includes attuning the inside with what's happening around you—not just the physical happenings, but what's happening with the people around you. Understanding that requires some empathy for those people.

Empathy

Empathy is the ability to see and feel the world as others do, from their point of view. This is different from sympathy, which allows you to have compassion for their situation as seen from your own point of view.

There is a cognitive aspect to empathy, which allows you to understand the other's worldview and goals. This aspect clues you into what makes sense to them, and why it does so. There is also an emotional aspect, which allows you to understand how their situation feels to them. Again, this is from their point of view, not how it would feel to you if you were in their position.

Together, these aspects help you understand the other person's rational and emotional needs, as they understand and feel them. Such understanding is important if you're to keep their needs in mind during an interaction. This does not obligate you to agree with them. Their thoughts, feelings, and viewpoint are, however, a fact. They exist. Ignoring them blinds you to a part of the world that is important to this particular interaction with them.

Some people worry that "too much empathy," especially the emotional aspect, will be overwhelming and lead to making poor decisions. Rather than a problem with the *amount* of concern, this indicates being out of balance, and paying insufficient attention to the needs of yourself. Likewise, the congruent attention to the needs of the context will balance out cognitive aspect of empathy. This avoids the situation where you give the other whatever they demand.

Let's take a look at the various directions that these concerns can get out of balance. That way you can recognize the lack of balance more readily, and more easily figure out where to restore the balance.

Coping Stances

When we're facing a difficult situation, we generally fall back on habitual patterns of coping. When we are born, we know nothing about how to survive in the confusing and scary world into which we have suddenly found ourselves. As we interact with our environment and the people around us, we start learning that some behaviors "seem to work," and we therefore tend to repeat them in other situations. As we learn and grow, we acquire more and more sophisticated responses to our world, but retain a base of the patterns we learned as babies and toddlers. So, when problems arise, such as:

- Needing to ask for an estimate from someone who doesn't trust you
- Being asked for an estimate by someone you don't trust
- Receiving an estimate that doesn't match your desires or expectations
- An estimate given for one set of assumptions that gets used for something else

how do you respond? If you're like most people, you respond in a fashion that's like the way you've responded before. You follow familiar patterns of dealing with an emotionally volatile problem. And the other person does likewise. This leads to the patterns of bad behavior that are so well-known in our industry.

As Virginia Satir often said, "The problem is not the problem. The problem is the coping with the problem." How we react to problems affects us more than the problem itself, and that's especially true in problems of human communication.

When we fail to balance the trio of needs, we fall into less effective coping stances. We each tend toward a certain off-balance stance. We habitually respond in particular ways when something goes wrong. Some of these habits we learned very early in life and have reinforced them ever since.

Let's take a quick look at the coping stances identified by Virginia Satir. You can find more detail on these in many of Satir's books, including *Making Contact* [Sat76], *Helping Families to Change* [SST76], *The New Peoplemaking* [Sat88], and *The Satir Model* [SGGB06], among others.

Blaming Stance

When something you're involved with goes badly, what is your reaction? One common reaction is to declare that it's not your fault. And if it's not your fault, the next assumption is that it's someone else's fault. If we point out the person whose fault it is, that surely clears us.

"The project missed the release deadline because the development team gave me an optimistic estimate."

This implies, "there's nothing *I* could do about it. *They* made the mistake." Blaming works by neglecting the needs of the "other" person. Doing so magnifies the attention to our own needs at the expense of theirs. "I am important and you are not." This leads to much of the unhappiness around estimation. Someone in the scene is blaming someone else.

If that person blames back, you may get a shouting match. You may have noticed this if you've seen someone respond to a request for an estimate with a refusal.

> "They shouldn't have believed the estimate. It was made when we knew the least about the project. In fact, they shouldn't ask us for estimates at all. You don't need an estimate to create software. It will get done when it gets done."

We all hate to get blamed for something, especially when we feel it's outside our control. It's common to duck blame by shifting it to someone else. You might be on the blaming side or the receiving side of this situation. The truth in difficult situations is that the result is due to a combination of influences, including the behavior of all of the people involved.

If you find yourself blaming others, take some time to explore their needs. You don't have to agree that their needs are more important. Just being aware of them will help you negotiate the conflict.

Placating Stance

When someone is blaming you, an obvious stance to quiet things down is to give in, no matter what.

> "I'd better give them exactly what they ask for, or else they'll blame me."

This is the placating stance—neglecting your own needs in deference to the other person's. It may be quieter but it's no better at solving your or the organization's problems. And it can leave you feeling like you've been blamed whether or not the other person has done so.

Some people are skilled at manipulating the empathetic people around them to get what they want. They play to the sense of empathy and compassion, heightening the emotional aspect of empathy to the point it obscures the sense of self. This, also, is a placating stance. It doesn't matter whether you're denying your own needs out of fear or compassion; if you neglect yourself, you will lose the balance of congruence.

The blaming and placating stances reinforce each other well. They're like bookends of dysfunction.

If you find yourself "giving in" frequently, and especially if you do so in anticipation of what hasn't happened yet, consider what needs of your own you might be neglecting. And think of how you can assert those needs in a neutral, nonconfrontational way.

Super-Reasonable Stance

Another coping stance is to focus just on the context, trying to take a cold, impersonal view. This ignores the people along with their needs and emotions. There is no a priori need for estimation, however. We estimate to meet the needs of people trying to make their business or other organization successful.

"The work is going to take exactly some amount of time. Our job is to calculate that precisely and accurately."

You would think that would take care of the organizational problems, but that's not the way that organizations composed of people work. This response ignores the human emotions of uncertainty. If you don't handle the needs of the people, the organization also doesn't work well. You cannot deal effectively with risk without acknowledging that uncertainty.

Also, it's my experience that the super-reasonable stance often isn't as neutral as it's made out to be.

"It's going to take however long it takes. Estimates don't change that."

This statement is tautologically true, but pointedly ignores the needs of the person wanting the estimate, while infringing little on the needs of the person on the hook for providing the estimate and the software. A different expression of the needs of the context might imply the opposite.

"It's going to ship on August 15. Difficulties in development don't change that."

This expression obviously ignores the needs and worries of the development team, but it also might bother the product manager who wants to ship on an announced date but also include promised functionality that works correctly and doesn't embarrass the company.

If you find yourself avoiding the personalities involved, then remember that humans run on emotions as well as thought. Spend some time learning how to get in touch with your feelings and recognize the feelings of others.

Irrelevant Stance

The irrelevant coping stance ignores all the needs. You may recognize this stance by remembering the class clown in school. It has made a resurgence in software development as a meme that is sometimes phrased as "no cares given."

When adopting the irrelevant stance, a person gives up on the situation altogether. They quit trying to meet the needs of any person or the organization. They build a shell to protect themselves, and present that shell to the world instead of their needs and feelings. This serves as a distraction from the uncomfortable situation. As you can guess, this doesn't help solve the problems, either.

If you find yourself playing the role of joker in tense situations, consider how you can more often address the issues *and* feelings at hand, rather than obscuring them.

You've probably noticed the three sets of needs, which may be acknowledged or ignored, results in 2^3 or eight possible combinations. Of these possibilities, blaming, placating, super-reasonable, and irrelevant are the four most common coping stances, not just of software development organizations, but of people. They're called incongruent because the externally visible affect doesn't match the internal feelings, beliefs, expectations, and yearnings. This dissonance between the internal self and the external self is uncomfortable, though people may hang tightly to it because they're familiar with it. The incongruence between internal and external reliably gets in the way of solving the actual problems. It leaves us fighting battles that no one wins.

Congruent Stance

To do our best work, we'd like to maintain a congruent stance: one where our internal feelings match our outward actions; one where we balance our attention on our needs, the needs of others, and the needs of the context in which we're operating.

This allows us to make the best decisions we are capable of making, given our skills and knowledge. Balancing these three viewpoints, we come closest to a rational view of the situation. We can see the conflicts between needs and make informed trade-offs based on our core values. Our external actions truly harmonize with our internal thoughts, feelings, and values.

This is not an easy balance to maintain. In fact, it's impossible for mere mortals to stay in perfect balance, respecting the needs of our self, the other, and the context, all the time. Events and emotions push us around and knock us off-balance. It's a dynamic balance; it's not something we can do once and then relax. We may be thrown off our balance, but with practice we can notice this and return to that balance point.

While we can learn to control our own behavior, we cannot control the behavior of those around us. If someone is blaming us, we cannot *make* them stop. What can we do?

If you can cope congruently, it will immediately help. When you realize that the blaming behavior of the other person is a result of their incongruent coping, then it takes some of the sting out of it. Even if you did something that, in retrospect, you would do differently if you had it to do over, attending to your own needs includes realizing that you, like all people, make mistakes. Admitting this without defensiveness, and also attending to the needs of the blamer and the situation, will go a long way toward a better resolution.

Paying attention to the needs of others, both the ones related to your common context and those they personally perceive, will give you clues that may help. With this starting point, look back to the Rule of Three, on page 181 and explore potential ways to improve the situation.

What would that better situation look like? Let's explore some possibilities together.

Imagine a Better Situation

Picture in your mind's eye the scene where someone asks someone else for an estimate. What do you see?

You probably envision two people facing each other, looking in opposite directions. This sets a scene ripe for confrontation. Or perhaps they don't make the request in person, so the estimator is receiving a disembodied request. How impersonal and how easy it is to respond without considering the person at the other end.

Now let's zoom out to the larger picture surrounding estimation. There is a need to make a decision, and an estimate might help inform that decision. Therefore, someone may ask someone else to perform an estimate. That person comes up with an estimate and reports it back. The first person responds in some way to the estimate and presumably makes the decision that required it. This is the basic workflow of estimating for someone else's needs.

Now let's imagine this workflow taking place in a way that respects who each person is, what they know and know how to do, and the needs they have. Given the Agile Manifesto's value, "Customer collaboration over contract negotiation," it seems natural that organizations adopting agile software development would collaborate with their development teams as peers having different skill sets. Certainly, agile teams will respect the needs of the business paying them to program. Even when those needs are more perceived than real, collaboration asks us to approach others where they are.

Look Together at the Work

What would it take to structure the scene to one with two people side by side, looking in the same direction at the work to be done and the goals to be achieved? When you think of the scene that way, does it change the way you might phrase the request, or phrase the response?

If they're communicating virtually rather than in person, how can they make contact, person to person, before launching into the request or response? How can they focus the request on a shared goal rather than the estimate itself?

I've often noticed that people working on the same project think that what they see is obvious to everyone else on the project. When people on a project start sharing what they've seen and heard with each other, they're usually surprised to learn that someone didn't know, or didn't notice, some of the things they did. They may be shocked to learn that they've overlooked some things that are obvious to others.

If you don't have agreement on the basic facts, it's little wonder that you don't agree on how to interpret those facts and what significance they may have.

Understanding Others' Needs

Imagine the situation of a junior executive in a large organization. You've got business goals to accomplish, and several large programs in flight toward meeting those goals. You might also be considering a new program, or perhaps starting a pilot project. The work to accomplish these programs and projects is delegated to people who report to people who report to you. How do you know what's going on? How do you spot potential problems that deserve closer attention? Does it make you nervous that your success or failure is in the hands of scores of people?

Now imagine the position of a technical lead of a project just starting up. You're considering various technical approaches to the work. You're wondering who will be available to work on the project. Who can you get with enough experience to fill a couple critical roles? What if the best choice in technology doesn't match the skills of the development team? How much will the requirements change over the project? What if other teams, on whom you're dependent, don't deliver when you need them? And now you're being asked to give an end date to the project when all you have are questions!

Wherever you work in whatever organization, can you have empathy for these two hypothetical people? Can you sense what the situation looks and feels like to them? Can you do the same for the real people in *your* organization?

Congruent estimation requires understanding the needs of the other person in order to balance their needs with yours and those of the context.

Communicating Your Needs

Congruent estimation also requires understanding your own needs, and making them accessible to others. You're not helping yourself or your project if you don't work to make it clear what you need from the situation.

As people, we have a hard time articulating clearly what we mean. We have a picture in our minds but have not thought clearly enough to put it into words. We use words that are not precise and could be taken to mean several different things. We use relative pronouns with unclear antecedents. We soften our words to sound more polite than the words that we're thinking. We make assumptions that are not apparent to our audience, but we assume they understand. We use words that are commonly understood by some people, but perhaps not the same way by our audience.

> I know that you believe that you understand what you think I said but I am not sure you realize that what you heard is not what I meant. –Anonymous

We have just as much trouble as listeners. Sometimes we don't hear clearly and hear words other than what was said. Sometimes we assign meaning to the words that are not what was intended. And those meanings tickle our emotions and make us feel things, sometimes strongly. They may remind us of other situations in the past that made us feel that way, and that baggage gets piled onto what we're hearing. And then we respond based on those feelings, perhaps aggressively, perhaps defensively, perhaps deflecting. It's a quick and complicated process that has been studied as the Satir Interaction Model. It's a wonder we ever succeed on a "hot topic" like estimation.

Often, though, the crux of the problem is that we haven't made the needs behind the request for estimates clear. If we need a rough order of magnitude for planning purposes, but our request is heard as a request for detailed precision predicting the delivery date of a project we barely understand, then there will be frustration, and we're unlikely to be satisfied with the estimate we receive. If we want to publicize our go-live date of a new service, but ask for a rough guess of when things will be done, there will be public embarrassment when we miss that date. In either case, what we thought we requested and what the hearer thought we requested could easily be different things.

Retraining Ourselves

With that vision in mind, you can change the way you approach estimation to make it your reality. Perhaps not perfectly, and certainly not immediately, but you can train yourself to operate in more effective ways.

When Asking for an Estimate

Let's start from the point of view of the person requesting an estimate.

When you ask for an estimate, what information do you give? Do you explain how the estimate will be used and what decisions depend on it? Do you discuss the accuracy and precision needed, and the desired direction of error? As we discussed in When You're Asked to Estimate Something New, on page 3, these are things that the estimator needs to know to produce an estimate appropriate for the need.

Or do you assume that the estimator already knows this? Perhaps they've been told once. Or it's "common knowledge" how we do this, here.

Do you even *know* how the estimate will be used? Are you, perhaps, stuck in the middle, relaying someone else's request for an estimate? This is a tough position to be in, sharing the difficulties of both sides of a request for an estimate. Your job becomes one of facilitating the flow of information and understanding. If you can get the person needing the estimate in direct communication with those providing the estimate, you'll save a lot of missed connections. You'll still need to facilitate the conversation and help ensure that both sides get what they need. That's easier, though, than being the conduit of information and trying to help each other understand the other's needs without direct connection.

Verify a Common Understanding

First, make contact with the other person. What do I mean by that? I mean connect with them as a person, and invite them to connect with you as a person. At that level, we are all peers. How you start the conversation has a great impact on how the conversation goes. Offer them the safety to respond in a genuine fashion.

Making a request, and even describing the need behind the request, is insufficient for effective communication. Has the other person fully understood the request and the need behind it? How do you know?

When you simply make a request, you can't be sure it was even received. If the request is acknowledged, you have an indication that it got there, at least in part. If the request is repeated back to you, then you can tell whether the words were heard. At this point you're still not sure if the meaning has been conveyed. Human communication can be ambiguous, and the message may be taken to mean something other than what you intended.

When communications are going well, humans can share an understanding so intimately that complete sentences are unnecessary to convey the message with all of its subtle shadings. Until you reach that point, a dialog is a great tool for completing the communication. Note that in *dialog*, the emphasis is on understanding the other, and in *discussion*, ideas are set against each other to determine which is best. There is room for both, but if you're trying to get alignment, then dialog is more suitable. Explore the terrain of the estimation request, including the background needs and the feasibility of understanding what is needed to complete the estimate.

Failing that, at least ask the question of what the other person understood from the request. Close the communication feedback loop.

Communicate the Need

Describe how the estimate will be used. With that use in mind, discuss the minimum accuracy and precision that will be helpful, and the desired direction of error.

If there may be multiple uses, talk about all of them. You may need multiple estimates. In fact, it's highly likely you will.

Think of the Outcomes

All of this seems like a lot of work. Can't you make a simple request and get an estimate? Perhaps you can, but perhaps not. Read on, and we'll discuss some of the difficulties that can arise. More than that, think about what outcomes you'd like. What would you like to have happen?

Getting an estimate is not the outcome on which you should focus. The estimate is only a tool to answer some question or make some decision. That question or decision is in service to some larger goal. Focus on that larger goal. Shortcuts may be expedient in the moment, but are foolhardy if they undermine your larger goal.

When Asked for an Estimate

When you are asked for an estimate, how well do you understand the intent of the request? Do you feel you have a common understanding with the requester? Do you feel in a position to counter with other ideas, or even to ask for clarification on the needs or the planned use for the estimate? In other words, do *you* feel that you and the requestor are side by side, looking in the same direction at the work to be done and the goals to be achieved?

Often I notice that those who are asked for an estimate would answer "no" to all of those questions. That's a strong indication that something has already gone wrong in the situation.

Make Contact

If the requester hasn't made a person to person connection, it's up to you to try to do so. That can be difficult if the requester is operating under the assumption of a strong power hierarchy. It's an essential part of success, though. Find some commonality between you and them, whether it's alignment on the business goals or a bit of humor. It may take multiple different probes to find that common ground if you don't know much about the other person, but keep trying.

Explore the Need

Happiness depends on developing an estimate that meets the need. It's important to understand that need. Get some idea of what decisions depend on the estimate. This will help you judge the accuracy, precision, and direction of error that will help make that decision possible. Explore the acceptable level of risk in the decision that depends on the estimate.

Deliver More Than a Number

Describe the unknowns and potential risks in the estimate. Discuss ways you can notice the level of risk passing the threshold of concern as the estimate ages. Make plans now to revisit the estimate based either on the simple passage of time or some indicator that you're tending toward danger.

When Responding to an Estimate

How you respond when you receive an estimate affects both the current estimate and all future requests. Immediately, a congruent response helps you receive the estimate in the way it was intended. If you misunderstand the estimate, it's the same thing as if the estimate was wrong. A congruent response gives you a better opportunity to discover and correct any misunderstanding.

Longer term, how you receive and use this estimate will affect your relationship with the estimator. Will you build trust or tear it down? At the same time, it will affect your reputation within a larger community. Word gets around, and you may gain or lose the trust of people you haven't yet met.

Accept Estimates with Appreciation

Everyone likes to be appreciated for their work. Appreciation goes beyond saying "thanks" or "good job." It includes a level of understanding of what went into the work and what value the work has. Without that, it's a hollow statement and comes across as insincere. This can have the opposite of the intended effect.

When people feel appreciated, it strengthens the bonds between them and increases trust. It also makes them more likely to help wholeheartedly in the future. Both of these results indicate an increased reciprocal appreciation.

Explore the Details

Go over the estimate with the person delivering it. How was the estimate derived? What parts of it are confident and what parts are conjecture? What expectations have been included in the estimate? What circumstances could affect the accuracy of the estimate?

Successful use of the estimate depends on understanding it well. An estimate that proclaims "this project won't be finished before July" is not saying "this project will be finished in July." There are many ways to delay completion, and no estimate can cover all of those.

Avoid Misuse

Use the estimate to inform your plans, but do not assume that it is one. A projected finish date is not a guarantee or a commitment. It's a stake in the sand, subject to revision as conditions change.

Remember that a good estimate is made with a particular use in mind. It hasn't considered the universe of assumptions to support all possible uses. Don't reuse an estimate without reexamining it and the assumptions behind it to see if it's appropriate for the new use. A rough order of magnitude estimate for budgeting purposes is not useful for writing a fixed-price contract. An estimate of feasibility is not useful for judging the productivity of the development team.

If you have multiple needs, all is not lost. The effort done to produce an estimate may likely be useful in producing another, different estimate on the same work. Keep your notes, but redo the estimate. Let the previous notes inform the new estimate.

Tools for Better Understanding

There are many books on personal interaction and tough conversations. There's no way to fully cover this topic here. There are a few things I'd like to mention, though, as I've found them useful in these sorts of situations. Think of these topics as starting points.

What about When the Other Person Is Being Unreasonable?

You cannot change another person. You can only choose your own behavior; that's hard enough. So what can you do when faced with someone who is acting badly toward you?

Realize, first of all, that you do not have to stay. I don't say this lightly. There may be many advantages to staying in that organization or situation, and many disadvantages to leaving. It may be very costly to give up that job and very difficult to find another. These trade-offs vary with the situation and the person. I'm not recommending that you leave, but I am recommending that you realize that's a possibility. You are not a prisoner, even if it might feel like it. You *can* find a way to go somewhere better if you put your mind to it. Knowing that can help you cope with staying.

And while you cannot change another person's behavior, you *can* choose how you cope with it. A congruent coping stance will help minimize the damage to yourself, and provide the most options for how you choose to behave. When you're balanced, you can better recognize the unmet needs that the other person cannot articulate, especially the personal needs. When you're balanced, you're prepared to respond in many directions, without giving up your self-esteem.

What about When You React out of Habit?

As I said, incongruent coping stances are often longstanding habits first formed in early childhood. You *will* revert to them from time to time. When you do, try to figure out what triggered you to take that stance. In my experience, it's usually a conversation gone wrong.

There's a lot that goes on in a conversation, and most of it isn't visible from the outside. We process what we hear through a lot of filters before we give our response. Much of that processing is based on past experience more than current events. There are many places and ways that it can go astray. And it all takes place in the blink of an eye, or perhaps faster than that, for every part of the conversation.

Ingredients of an Interaction

All of this activity is described in another of Virginia Satir's models of human behavior. This one is called the Ingredients of an Interaction. Let's walk through an example to see how it works.

We start with actual data. Light enters our eyes and is focused on our retinas. Oscillating air molecules beat on our eardrums and get transmitted to our inner ear. Chemicals in the air find receptors in our nose. All of these things generate nerve signals that go to our brain. This sensory input is as close to raw data as we can get.

> Roy and Kelly are having a conversation at the whiteboard. They don't notice as Lou walks up to them and holds out some papers to Roy. Roy stops in mid-sentence as Lou says, "Could you estimate this feature for the September release?" As Roy is reaching for the papers, a whole lot of things are already going on.

Intake

As part of the sensory intake, Roy heard "Would you estimate this feature for September release?" Note that this isn't quite what Lou said, but it's pretty close. Roy had been preoccupied with his conversation with Kelly, and wasn't primed for careful listening. Still, he got the gist of it.

He also saw that the sheaf of papers was fairly thick, and stapled together. As he took the papers, he looked up and noticed that Lou was looking down at the papers and wasn't looking him in the eye.

There are other things that Roy could have noticed, such as the fact that Lou was wearing a blue-striped, button-down shirt, and there was a slight aroma of cigarette smoke in the air. These facts were filtered out before Roy was aware of them, common enough to be unremarkable.

Roy also didn't notice that Lou had paused for a moment before saying anything. During that time Lou was looking directly at Roy, but that went unobserved. Roy didn't notice that Lou was there until he started to speak.

Intake depends not just on what is happening, but how we focus our attention. There's a lot of stuff we don't notice because we're focused on something else, or because it seems unremarkable. Even when we're paying attention to something, we might not be completely focused and might not get it right. Our eyes and ears can get fooled.

We've already lumped some basic meaning into the intake description. We've converted sounds into words, and light waves into recognizable objects. That's the level of data that is convenient to describe, but there could be errors in that interpretation. We saw an example of that when Lou said "could" and Roy heard "would."

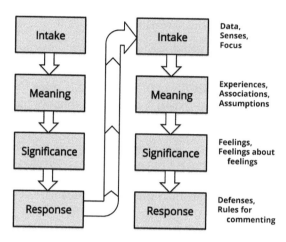

Meaning

Making meaning of the data goes much deeper than this, though. Roy looked at the sheaf of paper and presumed that, since they'd written down the description of what they wanted in the feature, he was not going to get to interact with the business people asking for it. Therefore, he was not going to be able to negotiate the scope.

We make meaning of what we sense based on our past history and experience. Who does this person remind me of? When has this, some part of this, or something like some part of this happened in the past? The association may be a minor part of the sensory intake. What has happened in similar situations in the past?

That scope wasn't negotiable was an assumption based on past experience, but the truth is that he'd never tried to negotiate the scope of written requirements since coming to work for Riffle & Sort. He'd tried it once when he worked at Empire Enterprises and it hadn't worked out well. Not only did it waste a lot of his time, but the business people weren't interested in negotiating and told his boss that he wasn't a team player. He hadn't tried again since that happened.

With that assumption, Roy further assumed that he was being directed to find a way to fit everything in the requirements document into the software by September. He didn't stop to consider other possibilities. It could be that...

- Lou wanted to know if it might be possible to do it all by September,
- Lou wanted to know what might be possible to do by September, or
- Lou wanted confirmation that the request was not feasible.

I'm sure you can think of other possibilities. Roy's mind, however, raced on. "Since Lou wouldn't look at me, it's surely going to be a death march." Since Roy hadn't noticed Lou earlier, he hadn't seen Lou looking at him directly. Without that data, to him, it hadn't happened. Roy attributed it to Lou's feeling about the project and their relationship rather than to the moment in time when Roy noticed Lou's presence.

While we, at our leisurely pace, can notice some likely and possible discrepancies in meaning, Roy's brain is still charging ahead at full speed. It grabs the first meaning it makes of the data and plows full speed ahead into the significance of that meaning.

Significance

At first, Roy felt annoyed at being interrupted in his conversation with Kelly. As he comprehended the meaning of the interruption—as he interpreted it—he felt a dread of getting into trouble, one way or another. It might be for not estimating accurately, for not getting the work done, for misinterpreting the requirements, or for myriad other things that could happen. He felt stuck in a bad position.

He didn't like feeling stuck. It made him angry to feel this way, *yet again.* His heart beat faster and he felt a bit jittery. His blood vessels dilated and his face turned red. He could feel the heat radiating from his face.

From our uninvolved viewpoint, we can notice that the significance of an event, from a personal point of view, is related to how it makes us feel—and to how that feeling makes us feel. In the software development field, many people value rationality over emotion, or may even want to deny the existence of emotion. This doesn't make emotions go away. In fact, it illustrates the emotional aspects of the human animal. We operate by both emotions and rationality, but if one is primary, it's surely the emotions.

From Roy's point of view, this is likely the first point in the process where he becomes aware of his reaction. Everything has happened so fast that it's hardly noticeable. The physiological changes from an emotional change got his attention. His response is likely more about his feeling of the significance than it is about the trigger.

Response

When we respond, we go through a couple more filters. One is the ego defense, which helps us maintain our sense of self. In this story, Roy thinks "Lou doesn't like me." In reality, this is probably a projection of Roy's anger and dislike onto Lou. Rather than being Lou's actual emotions, Roy assigns them to Lou.

But Lou is obviously above Roy in the power hierarchy of the organization. Roy doesn't feel comfortable speaking freely and openly to him, especially when he's upset with Lou. Effectively, Roy has a commenting rule that says "I can't express negative feelings to my boss."

Finally, we reach an observable outcome. Roy says, "Sure thing, boss." These words were spoken in a flat tone with tight lips and accompanied by steely narrowed eyes. And, of course, there is the flushed face. The visible signs are not congruent with the words, and this mismatch may also be noticed.

These observable responses, if noticed, become part of the intake for Lou. Lou will also interpret his sensory perceptions through the lens of his past experience and history, will attach significance based on feelings and the secondary feelings about the primary feelings, and then respond according to his defenses and rules for commenting. Back and forth it goes following the same complicated but very fast processing by each participant.

Most of the time, we are not aware of all the steps we go through. If we remain unaware, we cannot choose our behavior. Our patterns choose it for us, and we usually get similar results. Awareness is the key to opening up conscious choices in how we respond.

Changing for the Better

Changing our behavior is hard and, especially at first, feels uncomfortable and disorienting. That makes us want to retreat to the familiarity of how we've been. If we stick to it, we reach an "aha" moment where it starts to make sense. From there, it's mostly a matter of practice to assimilate the change in our "new normal."

Not changing leaves you stuck in the place where you've been. Picture that "better situation" surrounding estimation again. See yourself shoulder to shoulder with your counterpart, looking out for the needs of the organization. Imagine them paying attention to your needs and working to understand you.

That won't happen without your doing the same with them. Notice them hearing your concerns and what you have to say. That starts with your listening to their concerns.

Stepping Back for a Broader View

Sometimes it seems that the hardest thing in the world is for people to understand and get along with each other. There is no technical solution to relationship problems. It's a problem that requires empathy and honesty, both with others and with yourself.

You can, however, pay attention to your communication problems. By doing so, you can identify places where the communication became scrambled and try to unscramble it. With a bit more work, you can understand how it got scrambled, and try to avoid similar problems in the future.

Change takes time and effort. Old habits don't just disappear when you choose. Instead you must work to build new habits that crowd out the old ones. This is hard when the habits involve only yourself, and even harder when they involve interpersonal relationships. Take heart! Incremental progress is possible. Sharing the journey with others will make it easier. And when you fail, realize that you, too, are human. Apologize to those you may have hurt or offended and resolve to do better in the future.

The results are worth the effort. The practices that support better relationships will help in all parts of your life. You don't have to be perfect at them to notice the improvement, not only in your own behavior toward others, but their reciprocal behavior toward you.

Now It's Your Turn

1. In your experience with estimation, what dilemma do you find yourself facing repeatedly? Which option do you generally favor and which seems like an also-ran that can't compete? What's a third possibility that you haven't considered?

2. Think of the last time you were involved in estimation, either requesting it or providing it. In that situation, what needs did the person on the other side of that request boundary have? How could you have probed for needs you didn't know about?

3. Reimagine the "better situation" from earlier in this chapter. What is one small step you could take to help your organization move from the status quo toward that vision?

Conclusion

Looking back over these chapters, you'll notice that there are many suggestions but no recipes for success. No project is an average project. Each has its own unique challenges and circumstances. Learning how to recognize the variance between expectations and reality, and adjust for them, is a key part of success.

There are many suggestions and warnings here based on my experience and preferences. These are intended as a starting point. There is no destination called "perfect estimation." Feel free to go beyond my suggestions. You are likely to discover things I haven't yet. (And please let me know what you discover!) Feel free to do things that seem appropriate for your circumstances, even if I've warned against them. Just do them with eyes wide open, aware of the potential problems. You'll likely find other means to keep those problems in check.

Start with examining what needs you are trying to fill. As in software development, if you don't know what you're trying to achieve, you're unlikely to do so. Also, as in software development, realize that you're unlikely to know all the needs at the start. Keep your eyes open for needs that you overlooked or that have arisen since the start.

Take a deep breath and look around. See the options you have. Note the alternatives to "what you've always done" and to "the way we do things around here."

Start with understanding what you want. No, not the first thing that comes to mind. If you had what you wanted, what would it do for you?

The real need is never the estimate. Usually it's some decision that needs to be made. Sometimes it's reassurance that things are generally OK, or a warning if they are not.

Sometimes it's not your need that needs to be addressed. Your need might be that someone else is satisfied. This complicates things as it requires understanding their need.

There may be multiple competing needs. These needs might not be satisfied with the same approach to estimation. They may have different needs for accuracy, for precision, for distribution of error, or other considerations. You may need to estimate in more than one way.

If you do need an estimate that is both precise and accurate, realize that this is a high art that requires skill and practice. And it requires accurate and appropriate historical data. Even then it's always possible that something you didn't, and possibly couldn't, anticipate can make your estimate completely wrong.

Most of the time you need little precision and not even very much accuracy. Most of the time you need situational awareness so that you can prepare for the future and notice when conditions change. This requires attention more than correctness. It requires some smaller, nearer estimates to sense the problems in the larger, more distant ones.

The differences between your estimates and reality give you clues as to what assumptions you've made that aren't holding true. Estimates are not the same thing as plans. Estimates inform plans, but as the situation changes, or your understanding of the situation changes, plans generally need to change as well.

The information power of incorrect estimates is so powerful that it's beneficial to quit thinking of estimates as predictions and instead think of them as hypotheses. An estimate, properly framed, is an experiment. If the results don't come out as expected, you've learned something. This feature of estimates may be powerful enough to convince you that you want more estimates, rather than fewer.

This reframing should also defuse a lot of the angst and blame surrounding estimation. Where it doesn't, yet, realize that change is a process, not an event. As Esther Derby suggests in *7 Rules for Positive, Productive Change [Der19]*, ask yourself "why might reasonable intelligent people act this way?" Others may be viewing the situation differently from you. Where can you find common ground? Where can you have dialog to understand each other's point of view?

Estimates with value still take thought and effort. I hope that this book will help guide your thought and reduce effort that doesn't contribute to meeting your needs. I would like it if you would let me know how it has helped, and even where it has not helped. In the latter case, perhaps I can offer something I neglected to include.

For now, go forward and estimate with all the confidence you can. Use those estimates for your greatest benefit. Prosper to the best of your ability.

Bibliography

[Coc04]   Alistair Cockburn. *Crystal Clear: A Human-Powered Methodology for Small Teams*. Addison-Wesley, Boston, MA, 1st Edition, 2004.

[Coh05]   Mike Cohn. *Agile Estimating and Planning*. Prentice Hall, Englewood Cliffs, NJ, 2005.

[DeM09]   Tom DeMarco. Software Engineering: An Idea Whose Time Has Come and Gone?. *IEEE Software*. 26[4]:96-95, 2009, July.

[Der19]   Esther Derby. *7 Rules for Positive, Productive Change*. Berrett-Koehler, San Francisco, CA, 2019.

[Eis58]   Dwight D. Eisenhower. Remarks at the National Defense Executive Reserve Conference, November 14, 1957. *Public Papers of the Presidents of the United States*. 1958.

[Fey67]   Richard Feynman. *The Character of Physical Law*. MIT Press, Cambridge, MA, 1967.

[Fie77]   Edgar R. Fiedler. The Three Rs of Economic Forecasting-Irrational, Irrelevant and Irreverent. *Across The Board*. June 1977.

[Jon07]   Capers Jones. *Estimating Software Costs*. McGraw-Hill, Emeryville, CA, 2nd Edition, 2007.

[JS06]   Magne Jørgensen and Dag Sjøberg. Expert Estimation of Software Development Work: Learning through Feedback. *Software Evolution and Feedback: Theory and Practice*. 2006.

[Mag11]   Troy Magennis. *Forecasting and Simulating Software Development Projects: Effective Modeling of Kanban Scrum Projects using Monte-carlo Simulation*. Create Space, Scotts Valley, CA, 2011.

[Mag15]   Troy Magennis. The Economic Impact of Software Development Process Choice – Cycle-Time Analysis and Monte Carlo Simulation Results. *2015 48th Hawaii International Conference on System Sciences*. 2015.

[Mal68]   Albert Paul Malvino. *Transistor Circuit Approximations*. McGraw-Hill, Emeryville, CA, 1968.

[McC06]   Steve McConnell. *Software Estimation: Demystifying the Black Art*. Microsoft Press, Redmond, WA, 2006.

[Sat76]   Virginia Satir. *Making Contact*. Celestial Arts, Berkeley, CA, 1976.

[Sat88]   Virginia Satir. *The New Peoplemaking*. Science and Behavior Books, Palo Alto, CA, 1988.

[SGGB06]   Virginia Satir, Maria Gomori, Jane Gerber, and John Banmen. *The Satir Model*. Science and Behavior Books, Palo Alto, CA, 2006.

[SST76]   Virginia Satir, James Stachowiak, and Harvey Taschman. *Helping Families to Change*. Jason Aronson, Inc., New York, 1976.

Index

DIGITS

50% level estimates, 9

7 Rules for Positive, Productive Change, 203

90% level estimates, 9

A

accessibility, 38

accuracy
  comparison-based estimation, 29, 47
  decomposition, 51–52, 57
  defined, 6
  judging need for, 202
  of memory, 33
  of recorded data, 33, 123
  in RFPs, 10
  spot reestimating and, 166

actuals
  comparing estimates to, 109, 131, 149–161
  comparing large and small items, 64
  comparing model-based estimation to, 109, 131
  costs of errors in estimating, 150
  exercises, 161
  learning from estimation errors, 149, 153–160, 166
  reestimating after estimating errors, 151–153
  trusting, 152

additive adjustments, comparison-based estimation, 30–32

affinity estimation, 58–60, 63, 126–130

Agile Estimating and Planning, xiii, 57

Agile Manifesto, 190

anchoring bias, 71–72

Andersonville, 134

appreciation, 195

approximations, xvii

assumed precision, 7

assumptions
  in asking for estimates, 192
  confidence and, 8
  estimates as hypotheses and, 168
  intuitive projects, 23
  isolating values from costs, 2
  learning from estimation errors, 154–157, 203
  looking at together, 190
  progress priorities, 100
  spot reestimating and, 165
  testing, 163–164

attention and intake, 197

B

Beck, Kent, 57

behavior
  congruence, approach with, 189–201
  congruence, understanding, 183–189
  coping stances, 184–189, 196

difficulty of changing, 200

mis-communication, 178–183

relationship clashes and, 177–201

unreasonable, 196

biases
  anchoring bias, 71–72
  avoiding, 42, 72
  confirmation bias, 72
  numeracy bias, 57, 72, 108
  precision bias, 57, 72
  in sizing errors, 65
  subjectivity in model-based estimation, 107–109
  Sunk Cost Fallacy, 68, 71–72, 146

blame
  blaming stance, 185, 188
  coping with congruent stance, 189
  disadvantages of, 149, 151, 157

blink estimation, 42

bloat, 38

blown Sprints, 157

bottlenecks, 91, 94, 118, 153

break-even, 16–18, 136

broken windows, 99

budgeting
  new project considerations, 10, 19, 23
  prototypes, 46
  spikes, 45

bugs, as sign of undoneness, 83, 94, 173
BurnDown Charts, 116
burnout, 88, 96, 173–174
BurnUp Charts
    comparison-model hybrid, 127–130
    Cumulative Flow Diagrams, 118–119
    early releases, 137
    Earned Value, 86
    model-based estimation, 111–119
    moving goal line, 115–117
    projections with, 113–119, 127–130
    reading, 83
    using multiple milestones in, 117
    warnings from, 168

C

C3 (Chrysler Comprehensive Compensation), xii–xiii, 57
calibrating
    approximations and, xvii
    with industry data, 44
    model-based estimation, 108, 123
    need for, 65
    recalibrating, 152
    Story Points, xiii, 44
    to unknown context, 44
capacity
    comparison-based estimation, 41
    as criteria for new projects, 14
    increasing, 15
    managing, 91
    for other work, 144
    questions on, 15
    storage capacity, 141
    unsustainable work pace, 173
Captain Ron, 77
cashflow
    as criteria for new projects, 16–18
    Osborne Effect, 142
CD3 (Cost of Delay Divided by Duration), 22
CFD, see Cumulative Flow Diagrams

change
    difficulty of, 200
    as process, 203
charge codes, 34
charts, see BurnUp Charts
checkpoints, large fixed-price bids, 11
Chrysler Comprehensive Compensation (C3), xii–xiii, 57
Coastline Paradox, 69
Cockburn, Alistair, 61
code, assumptions about, 155
cognitive bias, see biases
Cohn, Mike, xiii, 57
communication
    blame and, 157
    delays, 153
    dialog, 193
    errors in estimating, 159
    exercises, 201
    gathering information for new projects, 4
    mis-communication, 178–183
    needs, 191, 193–194
    progress, 75, 84–90, 144
    reporting milestones, 144
    rule of three, 181, 189
    strategies for, 192–196
    team changes and, 94
    trimming expectations, 145
    trust and, 157
comparison-based estimation, 27–47, see also decomposition
    additive adjustments, 30–32
    aspects of, 34–42
    combining with model-based estimation, 125–130
    comparing large and small items, 63
    defined, 27
    development context, 39–41
    everyday estimation, 27, 76, 145, 149
    exercises, 47
    expert judgment, 28, 32
    gestalt estimation, 42
    memory and, 33
    model-based estimation as form of, 108

    with multi-level decomposition, 63
    multiplicative adjustments, 30
    questions for, 28–30, 35–41, 46
    recording data for future estimate, 32–34
    system aspects, 35–38
    of unknowns, 43–46
confidence
    in parametric model-based estimation, 123
    requirements for new projects, 8–9
    spot reestimating and, 166
confirmation bias, 72
congruence
    congruent coping stance, 188, 196
    defined, 183
    strategies for, 189–201
    understanding, 183–189
conjecture, xiv
Connextra format, 54
constraints, system, 36
context, in congruence, 183–189
contingency planning, 157
continuous integration, 82
conventions, xix
coping stances, 184–189, 196
Cost of Delay, 21, 80
Cost of Delay Divided by Duration (CD3), 22
costs
    capacity and, 15
    choosing between projects, 21
    Cost of Delay, 21, 80
    Cost of Delay Divided by Duration (CD3), 22
    errors in estimating, 150
    isolating from value, 2, 14
    Return on Investment, 4, 13
    speed and, 150
    Sunk Cost Fallacy, 68, 71–72, 146
coupling, unexpected, 155
Crystal Clear, 61
Cumulative Flow Diagrams, 94, 118–119

customers
    collaboration with, 190
    coordinating milestones, 142
    delays and, 41
    developing fixed-price bids, 10–12
    relationships and development context, 39–41
    system context and, 38
cycle time vs. velocity, 106

D

danger bearings, 167, 172, 174
data
    accuracy of, 33, 123
    actuals as, 152
    industry data, 17, 44
    for large fixed-price bids, 11
    from milestones, 143–146
    quality of, 123
    recording for future estimates, 32–34
    subjectivity of, 108
    uncollected, 34
deadlines
    aspirational, 134
    confidence and, 8
    fixed vs. target dates, 135
    imperative, 134
    in linear model-based estimation, 112
    as milestones, 134–136
    missing and effect on releases, 136
    term, 134–135
decisions
    choosing between projects, 10, 20–22
    determining if project is worth starting, 10, 13–18
    in gathering information for new projects, 5
    progress priorities, 98–100
    time pressures and, 159
decomposition, 49–73
    about, 43, 49
    affinity estimation, 58–60, 63, 126–130
    approaches to, 49–56
    by functionality, 52–58, 63, 84, 111, 126
    by implementation, 51, 70

by phase, 50
Coastline Paradox, 69
comparing large and small items, 63
errors, 64–71
exercises, 73
as implementation plan, 70
with Large Number of Small Parts, xiii, 57
level of detail, 69, 71
losing focus, 69
mismatch with design, 70
in model-based estimation, 104, 107, 110
multi-level, 62–64, 110, 126–130
number of parts, 56–58, 63, 66–69, 71
ordering, 60–62, 126
questions for, 72
reusing estimates, 50
with Small Number of Large Parts, 58, 62–64, 110, 126
testing, 51
with unmanageable number of pieces, 66–69, 71
with User Stories, 53–58, 61, 67–69, 71, 104, 107
visualizing progress and, 84
delays
    comparison-based estimation, 31, 41
    comparison-model hybrid, 126
    Cost of Delay, 21, 80
    Cost of Delay Divided by Duration (CD3), 22
    customer relations and, 41
    in feedback, 95
    foreseeable, 31
    large fixed-price bids, 11
    last responsible moment, 126
    model-based estimation, 124
    observing, 153
    replanning and, 152
    smaller fixed-price bids, 12
delight, measuring, 78
delivery, measuring progress with, 83

DeMarco, Tom, 78
deployment, 140
depth sounders, 97
Derby, Esther, 203
design
    mismatch with decomposition, 70
    redesign, 71
development context, 39–41
DevOps, coordinating milestones, 140
dialog, 193
disappointment, 178
diversity, 42
documentation, 153
doneness
    bugs as sign of undoneness, 83, 94, 173
    customer relations and, 40
    decomposition, 51–52
    hypothesis approach, 169, 173
    measuring output and, 81
duplication, speed and, 88, 94

E

eBay Inc., 145
Earned Value, 80, 86
Earned Value Management (EVM), 86
The Economic Impact of Software Development Process Choice, 125
efficiency
    multitasking and, 153
    progress and, 87
effort, measuring, 80
ego defense, 200
Eisenhower, Dwight D., 166
empathy, 184, 186
Empire Enterprises example
    about, xx
    budgeting considerations, 20
    checking progress, 76, 80, 84
    choosing between projects, 20
    comparison-based estimation, 31, 34

comparison-model hybrid, 127–130
decomposition, 50, 56, 58, 62
milestones, 137, 144
mismatch between estimate and actuals, 158
negotiation in, 198
origins, 2–4
progress, 81
project models, 24
Return on Investment, 13
encapsulation, 70
endpoints, 3
errors in estimating, 149–161
  capturing information, 167–174
  communicating, 159
  costs, 150
  decomposition, 64–71
  direction of, 7, 65
  hypothesis approach, 168–173, 203
  learning from, 149, 153–160, 166, 203
  measurement errors, 173
  misdiagnosis, 12, 155
  as obsolete estimates, 152, 156
  planning for, 163–175
  random errors, 64
  reestimating after, 151–153
estimating, *see also* actuals; comparison-based estimation; decomposition; errors in estimating; milestones; model-based estimation; new projects; progress
  adjusting estimates for future work, 152
  advantages of, xi–xii
  affinity estimation, 58–60, 63, 126–130
  as approximations, xvii
  blink estimation, 42
  challenges of, xi
  congruent approach, 189–201
  conventions, xix
  defined, xiv
  disadvantages of using single estimate, 6
  as fractal, 69
  frequency of, 165
  gestalt estimation, 42
  vs. guessing, xiv

hypothesis approach, 168–173, 203
judging when needed, 3
misuses, 4, 195
padding estimates, 178–181
relative estimates, 22
responding to estimates, 194
reusing estimates, 50, 195
terms for, xiv
as tool to achieve goals, xvi, 175, 193
treating estimates as commitments, 178, 180
uses, xv–xvi, 163, 175
using estimates as plan, 175, 195, 203
Estimating Software Costs, xvi, 33, 104
estimation tools, 44, 123
everyday estimation
  checking progress, 76
  comparison-based estimation as, 27
  trimming expectations, 145, 149
EVM (Earned Value Management), 86
exercises
  about, xx
  actuals, 161
  checking progress, 101
  communication, 201
  comparison-based estimation, 47
  decomposition, 73
  milestones, 147
  model-based estimation, 132
  new projects, 25
  relationships, 201
experimentation, 168
Expert Estimation of Software Development Work, 28
expert judgment, 28, 32
extension, in linear model-based estimation, 112–113
Extreme Programming, xii, 57, 109, 165

F

fear, 100
feature parity, avoiding in rewrites, 40

feedback
  delayed, 95
  early releases and, 138
Feynman, Richard, 168
Fiedler, Edgar R., 165
fixed-price bid needs, 10–12
Fluphy Kitty, *see* TinyToyCo example
focus
  intake and, 197
  losing during decomposition, 69
  speed and, 89
forecasting
  defined, xiv
  vs. estimating, 107
  with stochastic model-based estimation, 124–125
  subjectivity in, 107
Forecasting and Simulating Software Development Projects, 125
Function Points, 104, 122, 125
functionality
  comparing large and small items, 63
  decomposition by, 52–58, 63, 84, 111, 126
  differences in slicing, 61
  hypothesis approach, 169
  measuring progress by, 81–83, 107
  number of slices in decomposition, 56–58
  testing, 169

G

gestalt estimation, 42
Goodhart, Charles, 89
Goodhart's Law, 89
governance, 85
Grenning, James, xiii
guard conditions, 159, 168
guessing, xiv
Gummi Bears of Complexity, *see* Story Points

H

handoffs
  coordinating milestones, 140
  delays from, 153
  large fixed-price bids, 11

headlights, benefits of, xi

help desk, coordinating milestones, 142

Helping Families to Change, 185

Hendrickson, Chet, xiii

highest paid person's opinion (HiPPO), 23

hypotheses, estimates as, 168–173, 203

I

IFPUG (International Function Point Users Group), 104

impact, measuring, 78

implementation, decomposition by, 51, 70

implicit expectations, 36–38

imposed projects, 23

income
    as criteria for new projects, 16–18
    early releases, 136–139
    Osborne Effect, 142

information
    adjusting assumptions to new information, 164
    in asking for estimates, 192
    budgeting, 20
    capturing, 167–174
    datasets for large fixed-price bids, 11
    gathering for new projects, 4–9, 20
    industry data, 17, 44
    learning from estimation errors, 154–160, 203
    middleman for, 192
    from milestones, 143–146
    obsolete estimates, 152, 156
    surprises, 157
    unknown information, 151

Ingredients of an Interaction, 197–200

intake, 197, 200

integration points, 140

Interaction, Ingredients of an, 197–200

International Function Point Users Group (IFPUG), 104

internationalization, 38

interpersonal aspects, *see* relationships

intuitive projects, 23–24

irrelevant stance, 188

isolation, between cost and value, 2, 14

J

Jeffries, Ron, 82

Jones, Capers, xvi, 10, 33, 104–105, 122

Jørgensen, Magne, 28

K

Kanban simulations, 125

L

landmarks, 133, *see also* milestones

Large Number of Small Parts, xiii, 57

lawsuits, 11

learning
    from estimation errors, 149, 153–160, 166, 203
    speed and, 96
    tax, 39

legacy systems
    number of User Stories, 68
    Walking Skeletons, 62

linear model-based estimation, 109–119, 126–130

listening, 191

low-hanging fruit, 99

lump variance, 28

M

Magennis, Troy, 11, 125

Making Contact, 185

Malvino, Albert Paul, xvii

management
    about, xv
    capacity for other work, 144
    capacity, work to, 91
    communicating errors in estimating, 159
    communicating progress, 75, 84–90, 144
    communication strategies for, 192–196
    intuitive projects and, 23

mis-communication, 178–183
    optimization and, 90–93
    push for speed, 87
    surprises and, 157

marketing, coordinating milestones, 142

math in model-based estimation, 28, 110

McConnell, Steve, xvi, 10, 32, 149

meaning in Ingredients of an Interaction, 198

measuring
    delight, 78
    effort, 80
    errors in measurement, 173
    Goodhart's Law, 89
    impact, 78
    output, 81
    progress, 75, 78–83, 107

memory, 33

mental models
    comparison-based estimation, 28
    new projects, 22–24

milestones, 133–147
    arbitrary, 133
    as warnings, 159, 163
    coordinating, 139–143
    deadlines as, 134–136
    early releases, 136–139
    evaluating and changing plans, 143–146
    exercises, 147
    financial, 17
    frequency of estimating and, 165
    learning from estimation errors, 158
    in linear model-based estimation, 112, 114, 117
    multiple milestones in BurnUp Charts, 117
    multiple releases, 138
    reestimating after estimating errors, 151–153
    reporting progress, 144
    trimming expectations, 145

mis-communication, 178–183

misdiagnosis, 12, 155

model-based estimation, 103–132
    advantages, 130
    calibrating, 108, 123

combining with comparison-based estimation, 125–130
datasets for large fixed-price bids, 11
exercises, 132
as form of comparison-based estimation, 108
linear approach, 109–119, 126–130
math for, 110
modeling randomness, 124
parametric approach, 119–123
prevalence of, 28
rate, modeling, 103, 106
size, modeling, 103–106, 110
stochastic approach, 124–125
subjectivity in, 107–109
Monte-Carlo simulation, 125
multi-level decomposition, 62–64, 110, 126–130
multiplicative factors and adjustments, 27, 30
multitasking, 32, 41, 153

N
Nebulous Units of Time (NUTS), *see* Story Points
needs
communicating, 191, 193–194
competing, 202
estimates as not the same as needs, 202
understanding others', 190
negotiation
after inaccurate or ambiguous requirements, 7
vs. estimating, 179–181
in Ingredients of an Interaction example, 198
The New Peoplemaking, 185
new projects, 1–25
budgeting considerations, 10, 19, 23
choosing between, 10, 20–22
confidence required, 8–9
determining if doable, 10, 18

determining if worth starting, 10, 13–18
exercises, 25
fixed-price bid needs, 10–12
information for, 4–9, 20
mental models, 22–24
originator of project, 4, 23
rate uncertainty, 130
starting, 1
understanding reason for, 4
when to use estimates, 3
North, Dan, 42, 69
numeracy bias, 57, 72, 108

O
Ohno, Taiichi, 85
optimism
learning from estimation errors, 154
linear model-based estimation, 113–119
optimization, 90–93
order
comparison-model hybrid, 126
decomposition, 60–62, 126
trimming expectations and, 145
User Stories, 55
orders of magnitude, 30
Osborne Computer Corporation, 142
Osborne Effect, 142
other, in congruence, 183–189
output
Function Points, 104, 122
linear model-based estimation, 109
measuring, 81
overcorrections, 95
overestimating, decomposition errors and, 66, *see also* errors in estimating
overhead
decomposition errors, 65
model-based estimation, 105
slowed progress and, 95
uncollected data, 34
overtime, 34, 173

P
packaging, coordinating milestones, 143
padding estimates, 178–181
parallel development, 139, 153
parametric model-based estimation, 119–123
Parkinson's Law, 87
Payne, Bob, xiii
peak performance, 96
personnel, *see also* capacity; management
appreciation, 195
burnout, 88, 96, 173–174
changes in, 32, 107, 119, 156, 164
clashes, 177–201
communication strategies for, 192–196
comparing plan from a variety of viewpoints, 167
coordination of milestones, 139–143
mis-communication, 178–183
originator of project, 4, 23
overtime, 34, 173
parallel development, 139, 153
productivity and numbers of people, 20
rate of work, 130
role in checking progress, 76
unreasonable, 196
unsustainable work pace, 173
pessimism, linear model-based estimation, 113–119
phases, decomposition by, 50
placating stance, 186, 188
planning
capturing information, 167–174
comparison to plan, 166
contingency planning, 157
for estimation errors, 163–175
long-range planning with User Stories, 68
for reestimating, 194

replanning, 152
using estimates as plans,
175, 195, 203
Planning Poker, xii–xiii, 42,
55
precision
assumed, 7
decomposition, 57–58
defined, 6
frequency of estimating
and, 165
judging need for, 202
linear model-based esti-
mation, 114–115
precision bias, 57, 72
in RFPs, 10
prediction, *see also* forecasting
defined, xiv
planning for errors, 163–
175
prioritizing
comparison-model hy-
brid, 126
decomposition, 126
expectations of system
context, 38
governance and, 85
progress and, 98–100
updating estimates and,
164
User Stories, 55
privacy requirements, 37
probability
probability distribution,
124
zone of probability, 114
products vs. projects, 3
progress, 75–101
bugs as sign of undone-
ness, 83, 94, 173
calibrating to unknown
context, 44
communicating, 75, 84–
90, 144
defining goals, 78
detecting, 75, 77
efficiency and, 87
everyday estimation, 76
exercises, 101
going fast enough, 93
measuring, 75, 78–83,
107
moving goal line, 115–
117
need to check on, 75–77
optimizing, 90–93

oscillating, 95
overall vs. peak perfor-
mance, 96
priorities in, 98–100
project manager role, 76
questions on, 90
situational awareness,
90, 97–100, 118
slowing down, 94
speed of, 75, 87–97
speeding up, 95
trimming expectations,
145
visualizing, 75, 83, 94,
111–119
warnings, 77, 99
project managers, role, 76
projections
with comparison-model
hybrid, 127–130
defined, xiv
with model-based estima-
tion, 113–119
subjectivity in, 107
updating estimates and,
164
projects, *see also* new
projects
canceling, 146
evaluating milestones
and changing plans,
143–146
imposed, 23
intuitive, 23–24
vs. products, 3
sensing, 23
terminating, 19, 146
prototypes, 46

Q

qualitative aspects, 35
quality
speed and, 88, 94
system aspects, 36–37
system context, 37
unsustainable work pace,
174
quantitative aspects, 35
questions
capacity, 15
comparison-based estima-
tion, 28–30, 35–41, 46
customer relations, 39–
40
decomposition, 72
determining if project is
doable, 18

development context, 39–
41
financial milestones, 17
hypothesis approach, 173
for mismatch between
estimates and actuals,
161
for new information, 164
progress, 90
reestimating, 175
responding to estimates,
195
security, 37
spikes, 45
system aspects, 35–38
what questions, 5
when asked for esti-
mates, 194
when asking for esti-
mates, 192
why questions, 4–5

R

randomness, modeling, 124
rate
averaging, 129
modeling in comparison-
model hybrid, 129
modeling in model-based
estimation, 103, 106
uncertainty, 130
recalibrating, 152
recording
accurate data, 33, 123
data for future estimates,
32–34
User Stories, 67
redesign, 71
reestimating
after estimating errors,
151–153
capturing information,
167–174
decomposition errors, 71
estimates as hypotheses,
168–173
frequency of, 165
planning for, 194
questions, 175
spot, 165
traps, 173–174
Reinertsen, Don, 21
relationships
clashes, 177–201
congruence, approach
with, 189–201

congruence, understanding, 183–189
coping stances, 184–189, 196
customer relations in comparison-based estimation, 39–41
deadlines and, 134
difficulty of changing behavior, 200
exercises, 201
Ingredients of an Interaction, 197–200
making contact, 194
miscommunication, 178–183
rule of three, 181, 189
tools for, 196
relative estimates, 22
releases
cashflow and, 16, 142
early releases as milestones, 136–139
missing deadlines and, 136
multiple releases, 138
successive releases in model-based estimation, 117
reliability, 37
replanning, 152
request for proposal (RFP), 10–12
requirements, *see also* User Stories
aspects in comparison-based estimation, 35–41
prioritizing, 38
rewrites, 40
response in Ingredients of an Interaction, 200
retrospectives, 157
Return on Investment (ROI), 4, 13
reusing estimates, 50, 195
rewrites, feature parity and, 40
RFP (request for proposal), 10–12
Riffle & Sort example
about, xx
capacity, 14
hypothesis approach, 170–174

Ingredients of an Interaction, 197–200
parametric model-based estimation, 120–122
stochastic model-based estimation, 124
risks
communicating, 194
decomposition, 51–52, 61
safety margins, 174
speed and, 89, 92
spot reestimating and, 166
Rogers, Carl, 183
ROI (Return on Investment), 4, 13
rounding in estimates, 57
rule of three, 181, 189
Running Tested Features (RTF) metric, 82

S

safety, *see also* warning signs
comparison-based estimation, 37
danger bearings, 167, 172, 174
margins, 174
speed and, 89
sailing examples, 97, 135, 167
sandbagging, 87, 179
Satir Interaction Model, 191
The Satir Model, 185
Satir, Virginia, 181, 183, 185
scalability, 37
schedules, *see also* delays; milestones; progress
Cost of Delay and, 21
decomposition and, 73
handoffs and, 153
increasing capacity and, 15
release, 99
using estimates for, 4
Weighted Shortest Job First (WSJF), 22
scope
in comparison-based estimation, 35, 39
decomposition, 53
imposed projects, 23
in Ingredients of an Interaction example, 198
intuitive projects, 23

in linear model-based estimation, 112, 114–118
reducing, 14
sensing projects, 23
trimming after mismatch with actuals, 153
uncertainty in, 114–115
screens
modeling rate in model-based estimation, 106
modeling size in model-based estimation, 104
Scrum simulations, 125
SEC example, 8
Section 508, 38
security
comparison-based estimation, 37
coordinating milestones, 141
deployment, 141
self
congruence, 183–189
ego defense, 200
self-deception, 89
sensing projects, 23
sensory intake, 197, 200
service-level agreements, 37
significance in Ingredients of an Interaction, 199–200
situational awareness, 90, 97–100, 118
size
comparing large and small items, 63
in comparison-based estimation, 29
decomposition, 43, 63
difficulty of judging, 30
errors in estimating, 65
factors of, 127
of functional slices, 63, 84
modeling in model-based estimation, 103–106, 110
orders of magnitude, 30
of User Stories, 67, 111, 125, 127
Small Number of Large Parts, 58, 62–64, 110, 126
Software Estimation, xvi, 32, 149
spaces, overlooking, 65

speed
    balancing with risk, 92
    costs and, 150
    going fast enough, 93
    oscillating, 95
    overall vs. peak perfor-
        mance, 96
    progress, 75, 87–97
    replanning and, 153
    side effects of, 88
    slowing down, 94
    speeding up, 95
    velocity vs. cycle time,
        106
spikes, 45
spot reestimating, 165
Sprints, blown, 157, *see al-
    so* Story Points
stochastic model-based esti-
    mation, 124–125
storage capacity, 141
Story Points
    in comparison-model hy-
        brid, 125
    decomposition, 55
    development of, xii
    measuring progress with,
        80, 107
    in model-based estima-
        tion, 105, 109
    unknown contexts and,
        44
    using as few as possible,
        44
    velocity and, 106
subjectivity, in model-based
    estimation, 107–109
Sunk Cost Fallacy, 68, 71–
    72, 146
super-reasonable stance, 187
sympathy, 184
synchronization points, 140
system
    aspects in comparison-
        based estimation, 35–
        38
    context, 36–38, 44
    coordination of mile-
        stones, 140–143
    implicit expectations, 36–
        38
    legacy systems, 62, 68

T
Tardiff, Michael J., 78
teams
    about, xv
    burnout, 88, 96, 173–174
    changes in, 32, 94, 107,
        119, 156, 164
    clashes, 177–201
    comparing plan from a
        variety of viewpoints,
        167
    coordination of mile-
        stones, 139–143
    increasing capacity and,
        15
    keeping effective teams
        together, 32
    mis-communication,
        178–183
    parallel development,
        139, 153
    rate of work, 130
    speeding up progress, 95
    unsustainable work pace,
        173
technical debt, 94
testing
    assumptions, 163–164
    decomposition by phase,
        51
    estimates as hypotheses,
        169
    functionality, 82, 107,
        169
    User Stories completion,
        56
throughput, 37
time, *see also* rate
    cycle time, 106
    in linear model-based es-
        timation, 112
    pressures and decision-
        making, 159
TinyToyCo example
    about, xx
    cashflow and break-even,
        16–18
    determining if project is
        doable, 18
    origins, 1, 3
touch points, 139
trainers, coordinating mile-
    stones, 141
*Transistor Circuit Approxima-
    tions*, xvii
trust
    in actuals, 152

blame and, 157
coping stances and, 185
responding to estimates,
    194
treating estimates as
    commitments, 180

U
underbids, 8
underestimating, *see also* er-
    rors in estimating
    decomposition errors, 65–
        66
    overlooking spaces, 65
    sizing errors, 65
unknowns, comparison-based
    estimation, 43–46
unreasonableness, 196
usability requirements/expec-
    tations, 38
Use Cases, 54
User Stories
    in comparison-model hy-
        brid, 125
    counting, xiii, 55, 104,
        107, 109–111
    decomposition by func-
        tionality, 53–58, 61,
        67–69, 71, 104, 107
    defined, 53
    deleting, 68
    development of, xii
    encapsulation, 70
    format, 54
    linear model-based esti-
        mation, 109
    long-range planning with,
        68
    measuring progress by
        functionality, 82
    in model-based estima-
        tion, 104, 107, 109
    modeling rate in model-
        based estimation, 106
    numbers of, xiii, 55, 57–
        58, 67–68
    order of, 55
    pairing scaffolding with,
        61
    sizing, 67, 111, 125, 127
    splitting large, 54
users, coordinating mile-
    stones, 141

V

value
  choosing between projects, 21
  communicating progress, 84–90
  Cost of Delay and, 21
  early releases, 136–139
  Earned Value, 80, 86
  isolating from costs, 2, 14
  Return on Investment, 4, 13
variance, 28, 105, 124
velocity vs. cycle time, 106
visualizations, *see also* BurnUp Charts
  BurnDown Charts, 116
  Cumulative Flow Diagrams, 94, 118–119
  linear model-based estimation, 111–119
  progress, 75, 83, 94, 111–119
  work flow, 94, 118–119

W

Walking Skeletons, 61–62, 73
warnings
  checking progress and, 77, 99
  danger bearings, 167, 172, 174
  milestones as, 159, 163
  safety margins, 174
waterfall development, decomposition in, 50
WBS (Work Breakdown Structure), 69, 86
Weibull Distribution, 125
Weighted Shortest Job First (WSJF), 22
Weinberg, Jerry, 181
what questions, 5
why questions, 4–5
Wirz, Henry, 135
Work Breakdown Structure (WBS), 69, 86
work flow
  Cumulative Flow Diagrams, 118–119
  strategies for congruence, 189–201
  visualizations, 94
work in progress, in Cumulative Flow Diagrams, 118
working to plan, 157
WSJF (Weighted Shortest Job First), 22

Y

Yesterday's Weather, 44, 109, *see also* linear model-based estimation

Z

zone of probability, 114

Thank you!

How did you enjoy this book? Please let us know. Take a moment and email us at support@pragprog.com with your feedback. Tell us your story and you could win free ebooks. Please use the subject line "Book Feedback."

Ready for your next great Pragmatic Bookshelf book? Come on over to https://pragprog.com and use the coupon code BUYANOTHER2020 to save 30% on your next ebook.

Void where prohibited, restricted, or otherwise unwelcome. Do not use ebooks near water. If rash persists, see a doctor. Doesn't apply to *The Pragmatic Programmer* ebook because it's older than the Pragmatic Bookshelf itself. Side effects may include increased knowledge and skill, increased marketability, and deep satisfaction. Increase dosage regularly.

And thank you for your continued support,

Andy Hunt, Publisher

Pragmatic Bookshelf

SAVE 30%!
Use coupon code
BUYANOTHER2020

Designing Elixir Systems with OTP

You know how to code in Elixir; now learn to think in it. Learn to design libraries with intelligent layers that shape the right data structures, flow from one function into the next, and present the right APIs. Embrace the same OTP that's kept our telephone systems reliable and fast for over 30 years. Move beyond understanding the OTP functions to knowing what's happening under the hood, and why that matters. Using that knowledge, instinctively know how to design systems that deliver fast and resilient services to your users, all with an Elixir focus.

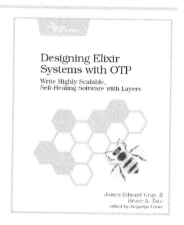

James Edward Gray, II and Bruce A. Tate
(246 pages) ISBN: 9781680506617. $41.95
https://pragprog.com/book/jgotp

Modern Systems Programming with Scala Native

Access the power of bare-metal systems programming with Scala Native, an ahead-of-time Scala compiler. Without the baggage of legacy frameworks and virtual machines, Scala Native lets you re-imagine how your programs interact with your operating system. Compile Scala code down to native machine instructions; seamlessly invoke operating system APIs for low-level networking and IO; control pointers, arrays, and other memory management techniques for extreme performance; and enjoy instant start-up times. Skip the JVM and improve your code performance by getting close to the metal.

Richard Whaling
(230 pages) ISBN: 9781680506228. $45.95
https://pragprog.com/book/rwscala

Programming Phoenix 1.4

Don't accept the compromise between fast and beautiful: you can have it all. Phoenix creator Chris McCord, Elixir creator José Valim, and award-winning author Bruce Tate walk you through building an application that's fast and reliable. At every step, you'll learn from the Phoenix creators not just what to do, but why. Packed with insider insights and completely updated for Phoenix 1.4, this definitive guide will be your constant companion in your journey from Phoenix novice to expert as you build the next generation of web applications.

Chris McCord, Bruce Tate and José Valim
(356 pages) ISBN: 9781680502268. $45.95
https://pragprog.com/book/phoenix14

Programming Kotlin

Programmers don't just use Kotlin, they love it. Even Google has adopted it as a first-class language for Android development. With Kotlin, you can intermix imperative, functional, and object-oriented styles of programming and benefit from the approach that's most suitable for the problem at hand. Learn to use the many features of this highly concise, fluent, elegant, and expressive statically typed language with easy-to-understand examples. Learn to write maintainable, high-performing JVM and Android applications, create DSLs, program asynchronously, and much more.

Venkat Subramaniam
(460 pages) ISBN: 9781680506358. $51.95
https://pragprog.com/book/vskotlin

Programming Elm

Elm brings the safety and stability of functional pro-
graming to front-end development, making it one of
the most popular new languages. Elm's functional nature and static typing means that runtime errors are
nearly impossible, and it compiles to JavaScript for
easy web deployment. This book helps you take advantage of this new language in your web site development.
Learn how the Elm Architecture will help you create
fast applications. Discover how to integrate Elm with
JavaScript so you can update legacy applications. See
how Elm tooling makes deployment quicker and easier.

Jeremy Fairbank
(308 pages) ISBN: 9781680502855. $40.95
https://pragprog.com/book/jfelm

Technical Blogging, Second Edition

Successful technical blogging is not easy but it's also
not magic. Use these techniques to attract and keep
an audience of loyal, regular readers. Leverage this
popularity to reach your goals and amplify your influence in your field. Get more users for your startup or
open source project, or simply find an outlet to share
your expertise. This book is your blueprint, with step-
by-step instructions that leave no stone unturned.
Plan, create, maintain, and promote a successful blog
that will have remarkable effects on your career or
business.

Antonio Cangiano
(336 pages) ISBN: 9781680506471. $47.95
https://pragprog.com/book/actb2

Build Chatbot Interactions

The next step in the evolution of user interfaces is here. Chatbots let your users interact with your service in their own natural language. Use free and open source tools along with Ruby to build creative, useful, and unexpected interactions for users. Take advantage of the Lita framework's step-by-step implementation strategy to simplify bot development and testing. From novices to experts, chatbots are an area in which everyone can participate. Exercise your creativity by creating chatbot skills for communicating, information, and fun.

Daniel Pritchett
(206 pages) ISBN: 9781680506327. $35.95
https://pragprog.com/book/dpchat

Test-Driven React

You work in a loop: write code, get feedback, iterate. The faster you get feedback, the faster you can learn and become a more effective developer. Test-Driven React helps you refine your React workflow to give you the feedback you need as quickly as possible. Write strong tests and run them continuously as you work, split complex code up into manageable pieces, and stay focused on what's important by automating away mundane, trivial tasks. Adopt these techniques and you'll be able to avoid productivity traps and start building React components at a stunning pace!

Trevor Burnham
(190 pages) ISBN: 9781680506464. $45.95
https://pragprog.com/book/tbreact

Small, Sharp Software Tools

The command-line interface is making a comeback.
That's because developers know that all the best features of your operating system are hidden behind a
user interface designed to help average people use the
computer. But you're not the average user, and the
CLI is the most efficient way to get work done fast.
Turn tedious chores into quick tasks: read and write
files, manage complex directory hierarchies, perform
network diagnostics, download files, work with APIs,
and combine individual programs to create your own
workflows. Put down that mouse, open the CLI, and
take control of your software development environment.

Brian P. Hogan
(326 pages) ISBN: 9781680502961. $38.95
https://pragprog.com/book/bhcldev

Programming Ecto

Languages may come and go, but the relational
database endures. Learn how to use Ecto, the premier
database library for Elixir, to connect your Elixir and
Phoenix apps to databases. Get a firm handle on Ecto
fundamentals with a module-by-module tour of the
critical parts of Ecto. Then move on to more advanced
topics and advice on best practices with a series of
recipes that provide clear, step-by-step instructions
on scenarios commonly encountered by app developers.
Co-authored by the creator of Ecto, this title provides
all the essentials you need to use Ecto effectively.

Darin Wilson and Eric Meadows-Jönsson
(242 pages) ISBN: 9781680502824. $45.95
https://pragprog.com/book/wmecto

Web Development with ReasonML

ReasonML is a new, type-safe, functional language that compiles to efficient, readable JavaScript. ReasonML interoperates with existing JavaScript libraries and works especially well with React, one of the most popular front-end frameworks. Learn how to take advantage of the power of a functional language while keeping the flexibility of the whole JavaScript ecosystem. Move beyond theory and get things done faster and more reliably with ReasonML today.

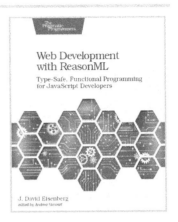

J. David Eisenberg
(208 pages) ISBN: 9781680506334. $45.95
https://pragprog.com/book/reasonml

Programming WebAssembly with Rust

WebAssembly fulfills the long-awaited promise of web technologies: fast code, type-safe at compile time, execution in the browser, on embedded devices, or anywhere else. Rust delivers the power of C in a language that strictly enforces type safety. Combine both languages and you can write for the web like never before! Learn how to integrate with JavaScript, run code on platforms other than the browser, and take a step into IoT. Discover the easy way to build cross-platform applications without sacrificing power, and change the way you write code for the web.

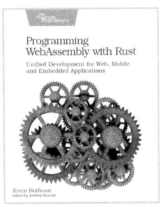

Kevin Hoffman
(238 pages) ISBN: 9781680506365. $45.95
https://pragprog.com/book/khrust

The Pragmatic Bookshelf

The Pragmatic Bookshelf features books written by developers for developers. The titles continue the well-known Pragmatic Programmer style and continue to garner awards and rave reviews. As development gets more and more difficult, the Pragmatic Programmers will be there with more titles and products to help you stay on top of your game.

Visit Us Online

This Book's Home Page
https://pragprog.com/book/gdestimate
Source code from this book, errata, and other resources. Come give us feedback, too!

Keep Up to Date
https://pragprog.com
Join our announcement mailing list (low volume) or follow us on twitter @pragprog for new titles, sales, coupons, hot tips, and more.

New and Noteworthy
https://pragprog.com/news
Check out the latest pragmatic developments, new titles and other offerings.

Save on the ebook

Save on the ebook versions of this title. Owning the paper version of this book entitles you to purchase the electronic versions at a terrific discount.

PDFs are great for carrying around on your laptop—they are hyperlinked, have color, and are fully searchable. Most titles are also available for the iPhone and iPod touch, Amazon Kindle, and other popular e-book readers.

Buy now at *https://pragprog.com/coupon*

Contact Us

Online Orders: *https://pragprog.com/catalog*
Customer Service: *support@pragprog.com*
International Rights: *translations@pragprog.com*
Academic Use: *academic@pragprog.com*
Write for Us: *http://write-for-us.pragprog.com*
Or Call: +1 800-699-7764

Milton Keynes UK
Ingram Content Group UK Ltd.
UKHW010942300724
446286UK00002B/4